ASTROLOGICAL MAGIC

Basic Rituals & Meditations

BENJAMIN N. DYKES, PhD

& JAYNE B. GIBSON

The Cazimi Press
Minneapolis, Minnesota
2012

Published and printed in the United States of America
by the Cazimi Press
621 5th Avenue SE #25, Minneapolis, MN 55414

© 2012 The Cazimi Press

ISBN-13: 978-1-934586-21-1

A NOTE ON DIVINE NAMES & CAPITALIZATION

In this book we have employed Qabalistic (i.e., Hebrew) Divine and Archangelic names, but for readers who prefer other pantheons we have included lists of some alternative names in Appendix 5.

We use the Qabalistic Divine Names partly because of our Golden Dawn tradition, but there is another reason. While the Qabalistic God Names may sound paternal in nature, *i.e.*, "God" and "Lord," they are in fact ultimately combinations of certain Hebrew letters, which when combined, form an idea or a concept that illustrates the nature of the Element, Planet or Sign. However, the scope of this book does not give us the opportunity to teach much about the nature of the Hebrew letters, or explain how their combinations work. If the reader is interested in this type of study, Greer 1996 is a good source.

Readers will also see that words like Temple, Element, Sign, and Planet are often capitalized. We have tried to follow a rule of capitalizing certain words when they are used in a specifically ritual context, especially with the idea of a Divine being operating through that planet. Thus we use "planet" when discussing astrological elections, but we "Planet" when speaking of the objects of a particular ritual.

ACKNOWLEDGEMENTS

We would like to thank the following friends and colleagues, in alphabetical order: Chic and S. Tabatha Cicero, Matt McDonough, and Ian Phanes. We would also like to recognize and thank other important teachers and influences on our work and how we think about ritual: Adam and Isidora Forrest, Melita Dennings and Osborne Philips, Dion Fortune, John Michael Greer, Donald Michael Kraig, Colonel Charles Seymour, and the founders of the original Order of the Golden Dawn.

Also available at www.bendykes.com:

Choices & Inceptions: Traditional Electional Astrology translates numerous classical texts from Latin sources: Sahl, al-Rijāl, al-'Imrānī, and others. It contains an extensive introduction and commentary on the theory of elections, including moral questions about undertaking them.

Designed for curious modern astrology students, *Traditional Astrology for Today* explains basic ideas in history, philosophy and counseling, dignities, chart interpretation, and predictive techniques. Non-technical and friendly for modern beginners.

Two classic introductions to astrology, by Abū Ma'shar and al-Qabīsī, are translated with commentary in this volume. *Introductions to Traditional Astrology* is an essential reference work for traditional students.

The classic medieval text by Guido Bonatti, the *Book of Astronomy* is now available in paperback reprints. This famous work is a complete guide to basic principles, horary, elections, mundane, and natal astrology.

The famous medieval horary compilation *The Book of the Nine Judges* is now available in translation for the first time! It is the largest traditional horary work available, and the third in the horary series.

The Search of the Heart is the first in the horary series, and focuses on the use of victors (special significators or *almutens*) and the practice of thought-interpretation: divining thoughts and predicting outcomes before the client speaks.

The Forty Chapters is a famous and influential horary work by al-Kindī, and is the second volume of the horary series. Beginning with a general introduction to astrology, al-Kindī covers topics such as war, wealth, travel, pregnancy, marriage, and more.

The first volume of the *Persian Nativities* series on natal astrology contains *The Book of Aristotle*, an advanced work on nativities and prediction by Māshā'allāh, and a beginner-level work by his student Abū 'Ali al-Khayyāt, *On the Judgments of Nativities*.

The second volume of *Persian Nativities* features a shorter, beginner-level work on nativities and prediction by 'Umar al-Tabarī, and a much longer book on nativities by his younger follower, Abū Bakr.

The third volume of *Persian Nativities* is a translation of Abū Ma'shar's work on solar revolutions, devoted solely to the Persian annual predictive system. Learn about profections, distributions, *firdārīyyāt*, transits, and more!

Expand your knowledge of traditional astrology, philosophy, and esoteric thought with the *Logos & Light* audio series: downloadable, college-level lectures on CD at a fraction of the university cost!

TABLE OF CONTENTS

TABLE OF FIGURES

INTRODUCTION

We are very happy to present *Astrological Magic: Basic Rituals & Meditations*, a book on astrological magic, meditations, and devotions for both beginners and experienced ritualists. We write as two long-time practitioners of ceremonial magic, astrology, and other disciplines, and while our special backgrounds are in Golden Dawn practices and traditional astrology, our goal is to make astrological magic and its techniques accessible, affordable, and spiritually enriching for all contemporary astrologers (whether modernists or traditional), ceremonialists, and pagans in the Western tradition. For example, the rites here utilize Tarot meditations, but if you do not have Tarot cards and have no interest in buying them, we offer alternative meditations. The rites can be worked more than once, so anyone who owns a Tarot deck can even work a ritual with them first, and then work them again using the alternative meditation. This is a brief example of how we have designed the book for a broad audience.

We are also excited about a set of forthcoming soundtracks specially composed for this and future volumes, by our friend and colleague MjDawn, a professional musician with years of ritual practice. Information on ordering these excellent soundtracks can be found at www.bendykes.com, and www.atmoworks.com. In these soundtracks, the ambient sounds have a progression and interrelated structure: thus the Elemental tracks are more primitive and raw, the Planetary ones have more personality and draw on themes in the Elemental tracks, and the Zodiacal tracks build upon the previous two. This type of musical construction goes along with the concept of "upward" movement which we describe in §2 below.

In this Introduction, we present a number of important topics for modern readers, such as: the nature and use of magic, some cosmological models for astrological magic and meditations, how to approach and perform ritual, and astrological elections for ritual. *It is very important for beginners to read these sections.* Following this, the book is divided into three Parts: (1) Elemental rituals, (2) rituals of the Planets, and (3) rituals of the zodiacal Signs. Each Part has its own introduction, and we have supplied culminating rituals which sum up the work of each Part.

We hope this book will be the first in a series of progressively more sophisticated works on ritual for individual or group practice, expanding beyond astrological topics to embrace much more, helping practitioners bring their astrological, devotional, and ritual interests together in an experience of Divine Love and Light.

§1: Why this book: our needs today

When we started planning a book of rituals several years ago, we had imagined something written in a more formally Golden Dawn style. But upon reflection, and after hearing from friends old and new, we were persuaded to write this book on astrological magic for a broader audience. In fact, one way to look at this book is in terms of healing. On the one hand, there is the healing involved in one's own personal growth, balancing, and spiritual beautification. The powers related to the Elements, Signs, and Planets, are good in such a project, and we will talk more about that below. But we also want to help heal a division between ritual practices and astrology which became more stark over a century ago. We feel the time is ripe for these two sides to engage with each other again, especially in light of the recent traditional revival in astrology.

Since antiquity, ritualists have included astrological concepts into their work and worldviews, often giving them a central place—even if they were not actually taking clients or reading charts. Likewise, although astrologers could easily take clients as their day job while experiencing spirituality only at church or the synagogue or mosque, an astrologer with the right books or connections could easily gain personal enrichment involving astrological magic, planetary angels, and so on. But things began to change during Copernican Revolution, when astrological reformers were often busy trying to make astrology more "scientific," and distinguishing themselves from ritual practitioners. Things got worse in the late 19th Century, in a divide that can be emblemized by the Golden Dawn and the Theosophy movement in London, where the Hermetic Order of the Golden Dawn represents ceremonialists, and the Theosophists more theoretical astrological types.[1]

In late 19th-Century London, membership in the Golden Dawn and the Theosophical Society overlapped, as part of the general excitement over spiritual and ritual experiences at that time. But the Golden Dawn was really interested in Qabalism, Hermeticism, Rosicrucianism, and ritual magic, not practical chart reading—and anyway, by that time many of the older medieval techniques had been forgotten or were no longer being practiced. The astro-

---

[1] See Cicero 2003, pp. 40-43.

logical component of the Golden Dawn was conceived more as part of the medieval and Renaissance Qabalistic cosmology they taught, and served as an access point to planetary and zodiacal angels, talismans, evocations, and so on. Some members were also influenced by a statement in the somewhat infamous *Sacred Magic of Abramelin the Mage*, to the effect that the work of the magician ultimately goes beyond normal astrological influences.[2] These factors led to a decline of interest in chart-reading, but astrologically-themed magic was kept very much alive.

The Theosophists were more interested in mysticism and Eastern thought, rather than ritual. And due in part to some surprising developments, a few influential Theosophists laid the groundwork for what we now recognize as mainstream modern astrology.[3] In a well-known case in England, a London astrologer named Alan Leo got into trouble with the law in 1914, when he was accused of practicing fortune-telling. As a result (and to make a long story short), Leo decided to repackage astrology as a system of personality description, with its predictive elements reduced to character potentials and tendencies. This change, in addition to his revolutionary promotion of Sun-sign astrology and automatized chart readings, not only saved him from further trouble[4] but changed mainstream astrology for the rest of the 20th Century. Astrology broke decisively from its already weak connection to ritual practice.

Although ceremonialists were pretty much divorced from chart reading and electional astrology, they were at something of an advantage: they were still using astrological concepts and images in their work, and in a central way. But mainstream astrologers really missed out, probably in part due to modern dissatisfactions with organized religion and its hostility to astrology. As a result, this divide left many modern astrologers without much of a concrete spiritual expression that spoke directly to their *astrological* interests. Instead, for many decades now, modern astrology has often had to adopt non-astrological approaches to spirituality, and graft them onto astrology: for example, Jungian psychology and generalized, eclectic, New Age paths. Many of these approaches are also more subjective and psychological. In fact, even people who have adopted the recent revival of traditional astrology as their

---

[2] See a short discussion of this in §5 below, on using astrological elections for rituals.

[3] The account here is based on Curry, pp. 145ff.

[4] At least, in principle: Leo decided not to appeal one conviction, but died shortly thereafter.

path often feel left without an astrologically relevant way to express their spiritual yearnings.

And so, we've written this book largely in response to requests from astrologers—both modern and traditional—who have asked for a more personal experience of, and spiritual connection with, what they study so diligently. After years of learning (sometimes decades), many students and practitioners have concluded that they need more. Some people recognize that an intellectual understanding of astrology does not necessarily convey its meaning in its entirety, and that in order to gain a further comprehension of our passion for astrology, we must experience it as well. Scholarship enhances the mind, but ritual and meditation enhance experience and feed the soul. We gain a far greater appreciation of an ancient ruin if we visit it in person, rather than just reading about it: in this case, the journey and experience happens through ritual engagement and the mind. Other astrologers feel as though concentration on psychology has led astrology into an equation of "spirituality" with "my personal psychology," and a crippling obsession with outer planet "deep personal transformations." They want to connect practically with something spiritual but objective, which pertains to their minds but is not limited to their own personal psychology.

So while we want to reconnect contemporary astrologers of all kinds with ceremonial and devotional practices and experiences, we also want to reconnect ceremonialists with some forgotten astrological lore, and principles of understanding a chart: for example, through understanding elections. And as we said above, this book is not written exclusively for astrologers and people already into formal ritual: many other Western spiritualists and pagans also want to connect astrology and ceremonial practice, especially in a way that is not expensive, imposing, or technical. After you have completed the rites in this book, you will be able to create your own rituals which will aid your spiritual growth: you will know how to invoke any Elemental, Planetary or Zodiacal occult power. Other topics left out of this book, such as the Sephiroth on the Qabalistic Tree of Life, will be addressed in further volumes.

Finally, we'd like to reassure some of our readers who are leery of a ritual approach being too "religious." You don't need to believe in any organized religion to do the rituals in this book, and you certainly don't need to believe in the image of an old, bearded, God so often used to control children and fearful adults. But we are indeed using religious imagery to do deal with something beyond our own personal minds. If you like, consider the view of the German philosopher Hegel: that art and beauty, religious imagery and actions, and philosophy, are the highest ways in which the Divine moves through us, and in which we can consciously participate in the conduct of the universe. Each uses a different type of thinking and approach, but each has an important role to play in our lives. In this book, we will coordinate color, sounds, emotions, the body, the intellect, *and* religious imagery, in order to have a more complete spiritual experience of astrology, orienting ourselves towards the cosmos and other beings in it, without promoting a particular religion.

§2: What is magic, and why do it?

In this section we'd like to offer some thoughts on what magic is and why we should do it. We don't claim to have the Absolute Truth on this, but we want to provide some possible answers that will help you approach ritual and devotion constructively, without crippling reservations and mental distractions. In what follows, we draw on thinkers like Plato and the Neoplatonists, Qabalists, and others.

Ritual magic is a broad subject. It can range from high-level angelic evocations, to creating talismans for practical results, or consecrating objects as sacred mandalas or as ritual equipment, the disciplined attainment of visions, ritual meditations, initiations, different forms of personal healing, and more. This makes it difficult to define magic succinctly, and we won't attempt that here. Instead, we'll emphasize one aspect of ritual: healing.

What we mean by healing is a kind of conscious balancing of the soul as a whole, leading to practical benefit in one's daily life, increased enlightenment and happiness, and generally recovering and enhancing our full human natures.

An astrological and magical cosmology

In many traditional ways of thought, humans have the potential to be happy and fulfilled, expressing our talents and realizing the Divine in our lives and the world around us—including, for many, building a connection with higher angelic beings which have a direct relationship to our embodied lives (sometimes called guardian angels, and the like). Now, the distinguishing feature of humans is that we are *microcosms*, which means that the various components of the human being each correlate to features of the cosmos. For example, corresponding to our own reason is a kind of cosmic Reason or Intelligence (including perhaps higher intelligent or intelligible beings), which we should be able to access via our higher faculties; corresponding to our soul (broadly conceived) is a kind of world-soul or broader principle of life throughout the universe; corresponding to our bodies is the entire material universe. There are other, more complicated ways to put this, but we think you get the idea: aspects of the human are miniature expressions of larger aspects of the cosmos.

So being a microcosm is distinctive, and suggests a kind of special fulfill-ment attainable by human beings. But this special nature is so complex that it provides reasons for things to go awry. For example, Plato teaches that simp-ly being embodied presents problems, because it distracts us from higher realities not visible to the senses: so, the more we take the merely physical world to be real, and the less we follow our reason (as opposed to sensations and desires), the worse off we will be—both individually and socially. Then again, since our internal chemistry can be disrupted in various ways, we fall prone to illnesses, emotional imbalance and so on. Ancient teachings are full of these sorts of warnings. So although we have reason and higher faculties, we often don't pay attention to them. Although we have bodies, they are often out of balance. These complications are what make happiness, fulfill-ment, and enlightenment, so precious, rare, and important.

Take a look at the following diagram, which is a very simplified ancient cosmology. The idea is that the universe has a tiered structure. At the "low-er" end of the spectrum is where we spend most of our lives: the sensible, changeable world, composed of the elements, in which we live as material beings and express the lower aspects of our souls: the senses, desires and passions, everyday values of pride, and so on. We might even say that a lot of society is implicitly based on many of these things: the rough and tumble world in which people's emotions and desires govern how we all get along. This aspect of the universe is one of relativity, change, time, and less stable unities.

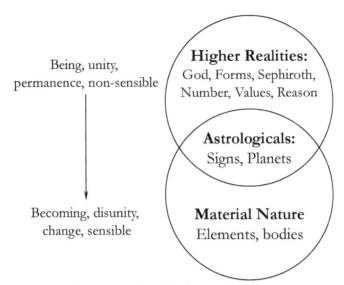

Figure 1: A simplified tiered cosmos

At the "upper" end of the spectrum are higher realities which have permanent being, more stable unities, and are non-sensible. It is an intelligible realm of reason, the Divine, other intelligent beings without sensible bodies (such as angels), and other kinds of structures which provide stability and function for the things at the lower end, in material nature: mathematical objects, values like Beauty, and, in the Qabalistic approach, the Sephiroth themselves. This realm corresponds to our reason and higher faculties, and when our reason is working at its best, we are able to understand the deeper principles of the universe, be in communion with higher beings, and channel the Divine more purely. Unfortunately, although in truth we yearn for this connection, life in the material world often leads us to concentrate instead on our lower functions and daily tasks.

In the middle are what we might call the "astrologicals": the planets and signs. In the type of cosmos we are constructing here, they occupy a special place and serve special functions. As for their place, on the one hand they exhibit mathematical relationships, intelligible regularity and periods, beauty—in other words, the kinds of structure which are associated with the higher realities in the realm of Being, Reason, the Divine. On the other, they exhibit motion and have sensible qualities which we find in the material world of becoming. So the astrologicals occupy an intermediate position between the realms of Being and Becoming.

But they also serve certain special functions, especially in Plato's cosmos, and we can think of this in terms of a double movement in the cosmos as a whole: one downwards, one upwards.[5] As for the movement downwards, the higher realities introduce organization, intelligibility, beauty, and goodness into what would otherwise be a disorderly material world. For the astrologicals, this means that they *reveal, through time and other categories, the content of the Divine world.* As for the movement upwards, this revelation of higher reality stimulates and inspires us to go beyond our normal way of life, engage with those eternal beings, and use the higher functions of our soul or mind. When both of these movements are coordinated in the right way, our insights and enrichment (upwards) can be used consciously to organize, enhance, and balance our values, behavior, and lives (downwards).

Now, it's important not to get confused by the fact it's a diagram. That is, since any diagram is spatial, it may seem that the Divine realm is simply "up there," separated from everything else. But that is a limitation of images and diagrams. For although things in the "higher" Divine realm have their own integrity and existence, they are in a sense all around us, working in and through us: they are *here, now.* For example, Mars is a visible planet, but "above" or "behind" Mars is a Divine principle which Mars reveals through his behavior and appearance, and this same principle is actively present in Martial things and activities in our sensible, material world. So these higher beings actively provide structure and organization throughout these levels, but our everyday inability to be conscious of, integrate, and apply these levels in life, is an important factor in our unhappiness and confusion, and can make them seem distinct and foreign. Astrological magic can be a vehicle for changing this situation, so let's turn to that now.

Astrological magic: a form of healing and development

On this view, what astrology reveals is the Divine project of bestowing order and goodness and intelligibility on the world, and it reveals this sensibly through the planets, signs, stars, and so on. It is not the only way to be led to higher realities, but it's an important one. And in particular, the birth chart can be seen as being a time-slice of planetary movement which de-

---

[5] In some spiritual philosophies, this movement can be understood in terms of the exhalation and inhalation of a Divine Spirit or Breath.

scribes how our own particular beings (which we *live out* in time) are present in the Divine Mind's own *timeless* comprehension and plan.

So astrology provides an inspiration and opportunity for us to recover a full sense of our humanity, our microcosmic dignity, and a happy life, if we can organize properly all of our internal parts and aspects of our lives. Ritualized actions and meditations may be seen as a practical technology for *consciously* doing this—not just at the time of ritual, but ideally throughout life (see below).

In order to understand this, let's look at how astrological categories can reveal different aspects of life, using the diagram above. (1) At the lower level, each of us has a certain physiology, exhibiting different temperaments related to the Elements;[6] certain types of diet and exercise are appropriate to all of us as humans, but especially based on the particular bodies and temperaments and physiologies we each have. Traditionally, some of this is seen through the lord of the Ascendant, the rising sign, and other types of chart calculations. (2) In the strictly astrological realm, the planets and signs suggest different, value-driven types of behavior and activities. We're sure that most of you are already familiar with these features of the signs, but you can consult Appendices 1 and 2 for traditional versions pertaining to the signs and planets. In the Hermetic work *The Divine Pymander*, the cosmic *Nous* or Reason tells the author that as our souls (or perhaps, only enlightened souls) rise up through the planetary spheres, they shed the vices associated with them: thus we shed the changeability of increase and decrease when passing beyond the Moon, evil schemes when passing beyond Mercury, and so on.[7] (3) In the higher realms, we might first of all identify angelic beings which are associated with the signs and planets. For example, Plato believes that each of us has a special planetary or zodiacal spirit associated with us in this incarnation, and in some traditions this might be called a Holy Guardian Angel, or at least an angel intermediate between us and our personal Angel.[8] We will not be dealing with that topic here, nor the various astrological methods of identifying this planet and being.[9]

---

[6] For a brief description of temperament types, see Appendix 1. Greenbaum (2005) is also an excellent resource.

[7] See Copenhaver, p. 6.

[8] See for example *Phaedrus* 247a-248a and *Timaeus* 41b-42e.

[9] Some methods can be found in Dykes 2011, *The Search of the Heart*.

But we must assume that astrological categories also describe how eternal beings and realities are in concrete *things* and *activities*, and not just as mental associations. This is especially important in ritual: when we use rose incense or oil in a Venus ritual, or utter a certain holy word, it is because we really are dealing with Venus and its eternal reality, through the incense, oil, and the formula of the word; and when we drink wine and eat bread and salt, it is because the Elemental qualities are really in and part of those things: they are not simply "in the mind."

Horizontal and vertical balance and healing

In order to make sense of this, let's speak in terms of *vertical* healing or balance, and *horizontal* healing or balance.

Vertical balance takes place microcosmically, when we gain a proportional balance between the levels of our being, insofar as they correspond to the macrocosm. That is, just as we have reason and higher faculties corresponding to the Divine world, and concrete emotions and values corresponding to the astrological world, and sensations and desires and bodies corresponding to the sensible world, so we have to balance each of those levels within ourselves. Traditionally this means that instead of being guided from the bottom up (focusing on matter and acting as material beings), we are guided from the top down, while giving each level its proper due. For example, many of us act as though most of our desires and needs and emotions are just brute givens, especially when we say things like, "all feelings are valid." But there is good reason to think that while some of these things belong more or less solely to the material world (such as hunger and thirst), many other emotions and values belong more to the higher realm of choice and thought. Thus it is at the level of our value systems that we feel anger, fear, joy, and so on: people get angry because of their notions of justice, rather than anger just being a mysterious feeling surging up from below. People feel joy and fear because of broader views of human benefit and harm, and their broader view of life, which cannot be reduced to sensations. Astrologically these things pertain more to the planets and signs: so, accessing, understanding, and expressing these value systems in that way allows us to internally reorganize our emotions and physical needs so as to serve higher values. Likewise, being guided by more abstract and eternal principles of Justice, Beauty, and the like, or even seeing human relationships in terms of astrological principles like trines and squares, gives us the critical distance to feel less immersed in our lower needs and emotions, so that we can even be guided by eternal principles corresponding to Forms or Sephiroth. We can gain critical distance from the sensible world, so as to focus on more eternal states of being, rather than the constant change and flux and relativity down here. Ritual magic combines all of these levels together, from color and scent, to music and words, to ritual motions imitating celestial movements, and meditations on symbols. Ideally, ritual becomes practice for *life itself*, and should make us feel more vertically balanced in whatever we do.

Please note that this does *not* mean escaping embodiment by denigrating it. It refers to a change and transformation of emphasis, in which we cooperate with the Divine project and Divine creativity, of which embodiment is still a key part.

Horizontal balance refers to the ability to express the different dimensions which exist *within* each level of reality. So in the sensible world, we gain facility in expressing all of the senses, or behavior patterns corresponding to the four temperaments (since these are related to the Elements). In the realm of the Planets and Signs, we are able to achieve a balance between the constructive expressions of planetary values: the pleasure of Venus, the generosity of Jupiter, the seriousness and concentration of Saturn, and the like. If we view the signs as representing something of the hero's journey (as we suggest in the zodiacal rituals here), this points to a horizontal balance among the signs. In the Divine realm, we can move easily among higher values like Justice and Beauty, informative mathematical relationships and symbols, and so on.

Ideally then, by aiming for these two types of balance, we can achieve a full flow of the downward and upward movements, which will enhance not only our personal lives but society, too: the enhancement of life through art and beauty, the forming of harmonious social relationships, a commitment to education and justice. Ritual work can be a key component in this organization of all levels of our being, recovering a full and conscious sense of our humanity: not just being *awake* (which is important enough), but being *actively* awake. A ritually-informed life tries to combine all levels of our being into one *active, consciously-driven experience*.

§3: How to approach ritual

There is a great deal to be said about ritual before you attempt to perform it. Many private schools first teach the rudiments and then the finer aspects of ritual, in order to assist students in this very endeavor. It can take years to become an accomplished ritualist, but that does not mean that effective ritual cannot be performed by people taking their first steps into the arena. Much of the effectiveness of ritual comes from earnest desire, and this desire will drive you to put as much of yourself as you can into this art form, and ritual is most definitely an art form.

Body, emotions, visualization

Before you begin to work the rites in this book, we will first need to talk about how to approach them. If you simply jump to ritual and read from the book as you go along, you will fail to experience much, and the rite will become an intellectual exercise, which you could have gotten if you had simply stuck to studying.

Ritual ideally encompasses the entire person performing it: body, mind, and emotions. Much in the same way that actors become who they portray while performing a role, the ritualist must emulate and therefore become what is being explored during a ritual. Now, we could go into a long explanation about how the ritualist is the medium of manifestation and how this works, but that is unnecessary here. Rather, we'll just say that unless you put every aspect of yourself into the rite being worked, your experience will tend toward the flat, unmoving, and boring. If you truly are seeking to have an *experience* of astrology and higher realities, to gain a finer understanding of the nature of it on an integral level, as well as magically manifest the power of the force with you are working, then you must do more than merely read as you go along.

Let us first stress the importance of correspondences (lists of which are in the Appendices). Astrology teaches that Elements, Planets and Signs have correspondences assigned to each of them. It is through these correspondences that one comes into contact with and gains a better appreciation of the different aspects of astrology. Correspondences are partly psychological devices which illustrate the concepts being explored, and also are a means of concentrating the focus of the conscious mind in ritual. If you know the colors, sounds, emotion, visualizations, and Divine Names associated with an

Element, Planet or Sign, you can use these correspondences to create an atmosphere conducive to working with it. But of course we have also suggested that these correspondences are not merely in the mind: they are objective relationships, too.

To illustrate this concept, we will focus on the Element of Fire and how the correspondences of Fire can be used in a ritual. Fire is, first and foremost, light and illumination (as illustrated by the Sun), but Fire also relates to the passions (sexual, emotional, physical and intellectual) and the fervent will to achieve (as illustrated by Mars). It is most definitely an Element of force and power. If you are working a ritual that is focused on an aspect of Fire, whether Elemental, Zodiacal or Planetary, you must think, move, speak and feel as an agent of Fire. Every thought, action and word must be fiery in its delivery.

So, let us break down each aspect of the performance of ritual, in order for you to know how you can have a positive experience of what you are exploring:

The Body. Ritual employs physical movements, and these movements must have a purpose which matches the working. Pentagrams and symbols are drawn in the air while being visualized, and the way these are drawn are indicative of their nature. Using Fire as the example, you might draw a Fire Pentagram forcefully and with determined movement. You would stand erect and straight with shoulders back, and would walk with resolute purpose. For Water, on the other hand, your physical movements would be much more fluid and soft. You would draw Water Pentagrams and symbols in a languid and flowing style, and would walk in a slow and dreamlike manner. For Air, you would make the Pentagrams and symbols quickly and lightly. Your physical steps and movements would also be quick and light. For Earth, your movements would be heavier, slower and more concrete.

The Mind. There is much visualization in ritual, which also must align with the nature of what is being explored. Visualization is key to working magic, because it directs the flow of magical energy towards the desired goal. Words, although very important, are not enough in themselves to direct magical energy. Images illustrate much more clearly the desired direction and goal of the working, and images are the language of the astral plane, playing a great role in both the conscious and unconscious mind. For although you do perform magic physically in your sacred space,[10] you are also operating on other planes of reality such as the mental plane and the astral plane, manipulating the spiritual forces of that realm before they manifest in the physical world.

Moreover, visualization affects not only the mind, but the physical brain: this in turn aids in ritual, and is part of the comprehensive ritual experience we have been emphasizing. Recent scientific studies of the brain underscore the close relationship which both visualization and actual perception have in neural responses. For example, electromyogram (EMG) studies have shown that the brain seems to differentiate little between the thought of an action and an action really performed;[11] likewise, it is very difficult to tell simply by looking at an electroencephalogram (EEG) output, whether a test subject is listening to or only imagining music.[12] In other words, if you close your eyes and imagine a hippopotamus, your visual cortex will become active very much as it would if you were actually looking at one. Just so, if we visualize ourselves as being in a Venusian realm during meditation, the physical brain reacts to a great extent as though we are actually there. From this we may conclude that visualization is a key means by which the energies we are interested in, are activated and organized on all levels of reality, through the medium of the magician. All that is manifest has its origins in the astral plane and in higher levels of reality, as we suggested in our cosmological model above.

The *manner* in which we visualize is also important. Again, in the case of Fire, the images should be very distinct and bright, and come into the imagination with force. For Water, they should be more ethereal, even dreamlike and enter into consciousness slowly, forming as if out of a mist. For Air, they might form quite quickly, and flit by in rapid succession before choosing one that is most appropriate. For Earth, an image should be very concrete and three-dimensional, as if you could walk around it and see it from all sides. Think about the nature of what you are working with, and proceed in accordance with that nature.

Finally, the visualization of color is key. Color affects the psyche, and not only illustrates the nature of the forces but is also a form of manifestation of

---

[10] We will refer to your personal ritual space as a "Temple" from now on.
[11] See McTaggart 2008.
[12] See Janata, 1997 and 2009. See also Hawkins and Blakeslee, 2004.

those very energies. The color of a force is in some sense the force itself. For more on color, see Appendix 4.

The Emotions. Unfortunately, we have often observed ritualists speaking in monotones while performing rites, not projecting any type of emotion. This negatively affects the outcome of the rite for both the person performing it, and for others who might be participating. If you truly want to experience the nature of an Element, Planet, or Sign, then you must align yourself emotionally with it. For Fire, the emotions should be powerful but controlled: that is, exhibiting a kind of confident leadership, excited but controlled even when provoked, not yelling or getting angry. For Water, they should be soft, loving and gentle. For Air, expressing thoughtfulness and mental alertness. For Earth, more determined, solid, and balanced. One of the nice things about working alone is that you will not feel awkward when expressing these emotions—no one is watching! Once you have become experienced in the art of ritual, this fear will subside when working with others, because you will all understand the effectiveness of the emotional component.

Preparation for ritual

Now that we have discussed how to act in ritual, let's look at how to prepare for the ritual itself. First and foremost, read the ritual before you perform it. This will give you a general feeling of what the rite is about, where you will be moving, what symbols you will be making, and what will be said. There is no need to memorize the ritual in advance. It is a common practice among ritualists to read from a script, but this does not detract from the working if they know generally what they will be doing, and where. It also is not uncommon for ritualists to physically walk through a ritual in a casual way before performing it formally.

Know your correspondences: we cannot stress this enough. Read about them in the Appendices, but also in other books.[13] As stated above, study enhances the mind. It gives you a treasure trove of images and ideas that will enrich your performance. While it is very simple to say that when working with a Fiery energy, you should act in a Fiery manner, it is actually a little more complicated than that when working with Planets and Signs. Mars is not the Sun, and vice versa. They are two distinctly different aspects of a

---

[13] We have used some correspondences from William Lilly's famous *Christian Astrology*.

Fiery energy, and we must adjust our Fiery attitude to match their attributes. The same holds true for the Signs. Virgo is a common Earth sign, ruled by Mercury, Taurus a fixed Earth sign ruled by Venus, and Capricorn a movable Earth sign ruled by Saturn: they are not the same expression of an Earthy energy. If you know the differences, then you can adjust how you would approach them.

For each ritual of this book, we have included instructions on how to set up the space you will be working in. Do this beforehand and make sure everything is in its place, whether you have a dedicated Temple space or are moving furniture aside in your living room. Focus is very important in ritual, and there is nothing more distracting than forgetting to have an item in its place and having to go and get it. This will break your concentration immediately, and it can be very difficult to get back into the right frame of mind. Shut off phones, tell the people you live with to leave you alone for an hour or so, close the drapes, and lock the doors. In other words, do everything in your power to make sure you will not be interrupted. When Jayne was first starting to perform ritual, she forgot to shut the door to the room. As she sat on the floor, with eyes closed and intently focused on what she was doing, her dog quietly walked into the room and licked her face. This not only startled her, but she had to get up, lead the dog out of the room and shut the door. When she tried to pick up where she had left off, the mood was broken, the atmosphere was gone, and the ritual was effectively over.

The physical Temple, tools, and alternatives

You do not need to have a room that is used exclusively for ritual, although that is the best scenario. A private space where you will not be interrupted is fine.

You also do not need to have elaborate ritual equipment. A small table will work as an Altar, and if you like to sit on the floor, you can place your ritual items on the floor in front of you. (Just be careful not to knock them over if you have to get up as part of the ritual.) Have a special place to put your ritual equipment, so that it will not be disturbed and handled by others.

Choose some special, clean, comfortable clothing for ritual, and wear it only when performing a rite. Over time, this will come to act as a signal to your consciousness that you are about to perform a ritual, and it will aid you when attempting to get into the proper state of mind.

Your lighting should be lowered, but bright enough that between it and the ritual candlelight you will still be able to read the rituals.

Play ambient music in the background while you perform the rituals. This not only blocks out extraneous noise, but helps you slip into ritual consciousness by the very nature of the music. Again, we recommend the forthcoming soundtracks by MjDawn, in development for this volume.

Buy the properly colored fabric for the Altar cloths from a store, about one square yard apiece. Cotton is cheap and easily cleaned. Cloth place mats for dinner tables or small hand towels also work well. Also purchase colored candles that correspond to the working. You will not burn an entire candle in one working, and it can be used repeatedly. However, if finances are tight, there are alternatives to colored Altar cloths and candles. If you cannot afford to buy colored cloth, you can print out the appropriate colors on paper, paint them on small plaques or canvas which can be purchased at any hobby store, or you can color them with crayons. If you cannot afford to buy colored candles, simply buy inexpensive votive candles and engrave the symbols onto the candle with a sharp object. Whatever you do, the color of the force you are working with must be present, because visualization of the proper color is an absolute necessity in ritual. People often tell us that they cannot visualize color, so we recommend staring at the color while visualizing a symbol.

Likewise, although we have designed these rituals for use with Pentagrams and Hexagrams, some people do not resonate well with them. If you find it difficult to work in this way, you may substitute the symbols of the Planets and Signs instead, and for the Elements you may use the Elemental triangles (these appear in the center of the Elemental Pentagrams in the ritual diagrams).

The ritualist is also influenced by incense, which modulates the physical and mental atmosphere of the ritual, and superimposes a frequency in keeping with the nature of the rite being worked. A correct atmosphere is of vital importance to any kind of magical action, and in setting up proper atmospheric conditions in a Temple. In Appendix 3 we suggest typical incenses for the rituals in this book, along with some hints for choosing them.

§4: Helpful hints

We've been doing ritual work for over twenty years, and can speak from experience about many things you won't often find elsewhere. In this section, we've organized a lot of advice for beginners (both hints and warnings), to help you make your experience as rich and effective as possible. In some cases, we feel strongly about our advice precisely because we've gone the other way and things don't work as well!

Attitude: love, expectation, joy. Many people have a certain image of ritual magic, in which adepts control spirits with a wand in a consecrated circle, pronouncing adjurations in a commanding voice. There's a certain amount of truth in this for certain rituals and traditions, but not very much. When we began more high-level and serious ceremonial magic, we expected to do a lot of that type of thing, but were rather surprised to find that some of the most important and transformative ritual experiences happen when one moves slowly, in the quiet, and especially when one can feel genuine yearning and love.

Ritual, properly performed, is a kind of meditation or prayer. Even when adopting a Martial attitude for a Mars working, try to feel a kind of love and trust in what you are doing: love for the Divine, trust in your heart. When you perform some meditation or ritual, you should have a sense of joyful welcoming, that you and your deeper Self are engaged with ultimate realities in a bond of gladness and peace. This will help you with another key attitude: not focusing on the ultimate goal or concrete results of your work. Concentrate with curiosity and cheer on what you are actually doing, be in the present, feeling the motions and visualizing the Light, without breaking off mentally to think about what it's going to be like when it's all over.

Do it well, rather than quickly. The most important thing in performing ritual magic is to impress and respect yourself by doing it *well and meaningfully*, rather than trying to impress others (or your image of them) by doing it quickly, mechanically, or merely theatrically without real inner feeling. So don't rush it: focus on how things feel, draw on your authentic yearning, and let the visualizations be strong before proceeding within a ritual.

Practice makes perfect. Sometimes a ritual might not feel right at first, or as though it hasn't "worked." In some cases, it has worked just fine (see below). But if you are inexperienced, you might try doing a test run of the ritual in street clothes and without any ceremonial voice, before doing it for real. It's better to feel comfortable with simpler rituals than to think only of the culmination ritual, rushing through the series so as to get to the "good stuff." At this point you are training your mind and soul to a new way of coordinating symbols and energy, and as you progress certain things will be automatic, easier, and more obvious.

Managing difficult emotions. Sometimes you may feel bored or anxious about your practice, especially hearing the "chatter" of your everyday mind saying things like "I have to cook dinner soon…what is this about?…Is this even working?…Am I doing it right?" If you let the chatter continue, you will find yourself frustrated and pessimistic. You might even get anxious before your next ritual, thinking, "What if it happens again?" Instead, take a calming breath, visualize the glow of Light in your aura, try to reconnect with your sense of love, turn off the chatter, and continue. It may take some experience for you to trust yourself and calm your mind. It's certainly a learning experience to see how little concentration we often have in our daily lives, and how much internal chatter there really is! But don't give up, it will be rewarding in the end.

The danger of shortcuts. Some people who work with this book will have experience in other traditions. And many will have heard of the old claim that since we are only working with symbols anyway, there's no need to follow these rituals to the letter. This attitude may be correct so far as it goes, but only for those who already know what they're doing, and know *when* to use shortcuts. We have met too many people who believe they should change the ritual before even understanding it, or who even use shortcuts as an excuse not to even do ritual, as though they can do high magic by sweeping the newspapers off their breakfast table, lighting a cigarette for a Fire Wand, and using a cup of coffee for a Water Chalice. The symbols, speeches, and movements in these rituals—and in any system—are there for a reason. *Learn a system first, then make changes once you are proficient and understand it.*

Two analogies might help here. First, just as it is hard to know how a composition will sound just by looking at the sheet music, so it can be difficult to imagine how a ritual will be and make you feel, just by reading the script. Once the symbols, movements, incense, music, mood, and speeches are combined, what looks arbitrary and easy to change on paper, comes alive and has its own integrity once you stick to the formula fully. Likewise, when learning a foreign language, it is usually best to learn the grammar rules thoroughly before learning all of the slang and casual shortcuts of everyday life.

For these reasons we recommend that you follow the rituals as they are written, and try to make them as special and precise as you can. This even goes for things like the six Hexagrams of the Sun: it may be tedious to do all of them at once, but you only have to do it a couple of times, and there are symbolic reasons for them. Even if you decide later that you want to substitute something else, do things the official way first before deciding to alter and change them.

Enhancing the performance of ritual. You'd be amazed at how a putting a little effort into finding the right incense or lighting can enrich your experience. Take advantage of the Appendices and other advice in this book, to make sure you have jasmine for rituals of the Moon, or the right music (such as our preferred music by MjDawn). If you want to create special lighting, buy a set of colored light bulbs to be used in different rituals. If you have recessed lighting or even track lighting, buy some colored cellophane at an art store, trim it to the size of your fixture, and tape it on: your whole room will be flooded with the color pertaining to your ritual. Performing a Mercury ritual with yellow lighting is wonderful!

If you find it hard to carry this book around during a ritual, then photocopy the relevant pages and use those instead. Make sure that you have special ritual clothing, or a special ring or other jewelry which you only wear for this purpose: it will help you feel sacred and put you in a special frame of mind. *Slow down,* and make even the Pentagrams and Hexagrams meaningful: imagine and feel the flickering heat of flame being traced in a Fire Pentagram, or the shimmering, cool, blue beauty of the Water Pentagram.

Respect and Temple etiquette. Respect for yourself and your sacred purpose, goes hand in hand with respect for your practice. This implies certain things about how you ought to behave during ritual time, and what your physical space should be like. This should be a time in which the mundane world recedes and you enter a sacred and beautiful time and space. If you don't have a separate Temple space devoted to ritual, then make one in your living room or bedroom. But be clean and neat (Venusian spiritual virtues): pick up your dirty clothes, vacuum the floor, wash your face and hands. The more seriously you take apparently simple things like this, the more the experience will change you. Make noisy kids leave for an hour. Do not smoke cigarettes or do drugs in Temple, though some people might have a small glass of wine to relax. If you work with others, speak softly, and do not swear or engage in idle gossip. Address each other respectfully, and preferably by calling each other "brother" or "sister" (Latin *frater, soror*) or by some special ritual name. Avoid doing ritual if you are very sick or distracted, because you will not get much out of it—but do not use stress or distraction as an excuse to avoid the work altogether!

Ongoing awareness and keeping records. The more you immerse yourself in these experiences and in your sacred journey, the more you will start to make connections between symbols in ritual, and their appearance in everyday life. You will also begin to track emotional and atmospheric changes during ritual itself. Pay attention to how you feel during a ritual. Do you feel light and airy at some point, or does a certain speech make everything "click" for you? Does the temperature suddenly raise or lower? These are often signs of a powerful connection with an astrological energy, as opposed to just going through a ritual mechanically. For instance, the temperature tends to rise and the atmosphere feel thick when the energy is present, but when it goes, it is usually accompanied by coolness and the room seeming more hollow or the air thin.

Immediately after your workings, write down your experiences, or any particularly interesting emotions or meditative images which appeared. Pay attention to your dreams. Keep these in a special ritual journal so you may look back on these experiences and find informative patterns. In your everyday life, begin to notice synchronicities with your ritual work, as a way of seeing how your mundane life and sacred journey intersect. Do you find that people want to be around you and socialize when you work with Venus? Or do you find yourself with more leadership qualities or associating with leaders after working with Mars or the Sun? Sometimes it may feel as though the ritual did not really work or you did not get properly engaged with the energy, but you'll find out later through a dream or other experience that it was effective. The relationship between you and astrological entities does not cease when the ritual ends!

Use the script, but be aware of the experience. At some point, you should be able to do certain aspects of these rituals by heart: the Openings, Closings, purifications and consecrations, and so on. But sometimes, even experienced magicians can get too caught up in looking at the script, leading to a disengagement with the purpose of the ritual itself. This can happen both with individuals and groups.

For individuals, be aware of what you are supposed to do next, but take the time to put the script down and feel what is happening. If you have to make a speech over the Venus Candle, then read the speech; but then put down the script and focus on turning the light of your aura the appropriate color, reinforce the Venusian emotions, place your hands around the flame and feel its warmth. Then pick up the script and resume. It's better to go slowly but do it well, than to rush around with your nose in the book, and miss out on everything you've spent time setting up for.

Likewise, when working in a group (see below), you should not be reading the script if you are not currently performing a role. Instead, put your finger on the page where your next speech or action is (such as tracing a special Hexagram or saying a short speech), and note what action or words immediately precede it. Close your eyes and focus on feeling the energy of the room and participating in the visualizations: as soon as that action is done or those words are spoken, you can stand up and do your part without having lost your place or panicking over what to do next.

Expanding the rituals for more than one person. We have designed the workings in this book for one person, especially the individual consecrations for particular Elements (and Signs and Planets). But you could easily adapt the rituals for more than one person, especially the culmination rituals. Divide up the ritual into various roles, and while each person performs a designated part, the others ought to visualize what is going on. For instance, perhaps one person could perform the Openings and Closings, while one or more people split up the duties in the middle of the ritual. But make sure that there is a reason for assigning each role, or allow for some symmetry: in a ritual using both active and passive Elements or Signs, one person should be in charge of the passive energies, and the other the active ones. This allows members to focus more consistently on one type of thing, rather than having to switch quickly and confusingly between too many types of thoughts or moods.

§5: Astrological elections for ritualists

In this section we'll talk about some ways to use traditional astrology to elect appropriate times for ritual. "Election" means "choice" (Lat. *electio*), and refers to choosing auspicious astrological times to begin some enterprise, whether initiating a business deal or consecrating a talisman.

Elections can get very complicated, but the instructions in this book will be easier to work with. The main reason for this is that elections are usually reserved for actions requiring special help, or which are unusual or risky or uncertain. But our rituals can be viewed more in terms of personal spiritual alignment, not achieving practical results like getting a job. Now, we will be doing some simple consecrations, and you might well try a more complicated election for the culmination rituals at the end of each Part. But it will not be like electing a time for a major talisman or angelic evocation. Still, we'll give you general advice for all sorts of things.

Some authors even eschew elections, at least for certain rituals. For example, the author of *The Book of Abramelin* argues that when dealing with the Holy Guardian Angel and the Abramelin system of magic, one does not need to use electional tools such as planetary hours.[14] This is partly because he (like others) assumes that the heavens *cause* earthly effects in the manner of physics: since he is interested in spiritual enlightenment, he believes that astrological concerns are therefore irrelevant. But there are two reasons not to follow this line of thought. First, instead of the causal theory of astrology, we could follow an alternative (and likewise ancient) view that the stars only *signify* things. So, instead of Virgo causing Virgoan things, Virgo *signifies* times in which the higher Virgoan principle is more accessible and ready to hand— not that Virgo itself somehow sends out special causal rays to cause them. This frees us from viewing astrological ritual in purely materialistic terms. Second, many traditional cosmologies agreed that spiritual beings operate *in harmony with* astrological configurations and indicate the influences of the Higher *in accordance with* them. Plato believed that our higher spiritual guardians were associated with, and indicated by, planets such as Mars or the Moon: that is, when we are speaking of beings such as angels, it is still appropriate to think of them as having something like Martial or Lunar qualities. So even for personal spiritual purposes, it is appropriate to match ritual actions to those very elemental and planetary configurations and rulerships, as they unfold astrologically in time.

Before moving to elections themselves, let us explain the chart design we have used below. There are many different house systems and ways to depict a chart, but we will be using a pared-down version which uses "whole-sign" houses and (for the most part) only shows the Ascendant and Descendant. In whole-sign houses, each sign is equivalent to a house: thus, if Taurus is rising (that is, the Ascendant is on Taurus), then all of Taurus is the first

---

[14] See von Worms III.5-6. The author even suggests that the use of geometric figures like Pentagrams are misleading tricks of the devil (III.4, p. 84).

house, all of Gemini the second house, and so on. There are no intermediary house cusps, and no intercepted signs. This was not only a traditional house system, but sidesteps the issue of which house system is best. So when we point out that some planet is in the eleventh house, we depict it as being in the eleventh sign; but if you prefer Placidus or Regiomontanus or anything else, feel free to use that.

At this point, let's introduce two general rules for astrological elections:

Rule #1: The more important the working, the more care should be put into it.

Rule #2: There is no perfect election, so do what you can in the time frame you have.

It is a bit hard to measure what makes a working "important," but here are some ideas. If you were performing an elaborate ritual such as an evocation, or consecrating a talisman for concrete practical effects, or making a serious personal commitment involving a particular planet, you would want a more carefully-timed ritual. That might involve a consideration of your natal chart, such as waiting for an important Jupiter transit to your Midheaven when consecrating a Jupiter talisman. Such transits of Jupiter do not come along every day, so it might mean planning a ritual months ahead of time.

In this book we will not be focusing on such workings: rather, we will focus on ongoing devotions, and more low-key consecrations and attunements. For example, suppose you want to perform daily planetary devotions before leaving for work: in that case, on Thursday (the day associated with Jupiter) you are really only trying to align with the general energy of Jupiter. You might even time the ritual for dawn on Thursday, which is the hour specifically assigned to Jupiter (see below). This sort of simple election is more appropriate for routine workings and the rituals in this book, when nothing very unusual is being planned.

Of course, you are certainly free to spend as much time as you want in finding a good election, which brings us to the second rule. You could wait for ages until you have the perfect election for connecting with the principle of Mercury, before consecrating the Mercury Candle in this book. You could make him be the lord of the Ascendant, outside the Sun's rays, in his own sign, trining Jupiter and sextiling Venus, out of any aspect with the malefic planets, in his own "domain" (see below), quick in speed, and so on. But this would be like taking a two-year cooking course and installing a new kitchen in your home just to boil the perfect egg. It might be years before you get such an election, and in the meantime you've neglected your spiritual path. There is no perfect election that is humanly possible, so instead you should do the best you can within the time frame you have. Do you want to consecrate a Mercurial Candle this week? Try Wednesday during the hour of Mercury, or better yet, identify a few days you have available, and see which day has Mercury in the best position during his planetary hour (we'll explain these things below). Do not make the perfect the enemy of the good.

If you do want more elaborate rules for elections, you can find them in works such as *Choices & Inceptions: Traditional Electional Astrology*. But in the spirit of this book, we are dividing the topic of elections into three broad categories:

1. **Simple alignments**. This is especially appropriate for rituals in this book, in which you are aligning with or becoming more formally attuned to astrological energies, focusing on a process in the soul rather than aiming at operational success (such as with practical talismans).
2. **Enhanced elections**. This is more appropriate for advanced techniques and practical operations, as well as for more thoughtfully designed programs of attunement, including the culmination rituals in this book.
3. **The Moon**. In all cases, we should be aware of the conditions of the Moon, and especially what conditions to avoid.

Elections for simple alignment

By "simple alignment" or attunement, we mean rituals and meditations that focus more on inner healing and awakening, making astrological principles more alive and present in your life overall. For as we suggested in our cosmological picture in §2, all of these principles are implicitly present in us already, but what we want is for them to become conscious, organized, and alive. Regular devotional practices would be examples of this kind of attunement, as well as the regular consecrations in this book. We've identified three ways to elect for this type of thing, ranging somewhat from what is more basic to what is more involved: (a) sect and rejoicing, (b) planetary days and hours, and (c) planets and signs in the angles (especially the Ascendant).

(a) Sect and rejoicing. Traditionally, the planets are divided into two groups, called "sects," and each group has a condition in which its members are said to "rejoice."[15] When we work with a Planet (or perhaps even an Element or Sign), it can help to know whether it is associated with the day or night sect, and to choose the time for the ritual accordingly.

The following diagram shows how the planets and signs and elements are divided according to sect. For the planets, each group contains a luminary, a benefic, and a malefic. The diurnal group or sect has the Sun, Jupiter, and Saturn, while the nocturnal group has the Moon, Venus, and Mars. For the signs and elements,[16] fiery and airy qualities are associated with the diurnal sect, while watery and earthy qualities are associated with the nocturnal sect.

Diurnal	**Nocturnal**
☉	☽
♃	♀
♄	♂
Masculine signs	Feminine signs
Fire, Air	Water, Earth

☿

Figure 2: Planets, signs, and elements grouped by sect

Mercury's membership has a little twist: it depends on what side of the Sun he is at the time. If he is in a degree that's earlier than the Sun (so that if it were morning, he would rise before the Sun), he belongs to the diurnal sect. But if he's in a degree later than the Sun (so that he would set after the Sun at sunset), he belongs to the nocturnal sect. For example, if the Sun were at 15° Gemini, then if Mercury were in any of the earlier degrees of Gemini and even into the degrees of Taurus, he would be earlier than the Sun, and be diurnal. But if he were in the later degrees of Gemini and even into those of Cancer, he would be nocturnal.

The use of these concepts is that if you are doing a ritual of some kind for a diurnal planet or sign or element, you might consider doing the ritual dur-

---

[15] See Dykes 2010, §III.2.

[16] For a list of the signs by elements and quadruplicity, see Appendix 1 or the Introduction to the Elemental rites in Part 1 below.

ing the day; but if you were doing it for a nocturnal planet or sign or element, try doing the ritual at night. That way, the general quality of the day or night will broadly match the sect membership of what you're focused on. This is extremely simple and flexible, and should accommodate most people's weekly or daily schedules.

For the planets, you can also take the this to the next level by electing a time in which they rejoice by sect position, or are in their own "domains." To begin with, each planet has a preferred position relative to the Sun, depending on its sect membership. The rule is simple: diurnal planets want to be in the same hemisphere (upper or lower) as the Sun, while nocturnal planets want to be on the opposite side of the Sun. The diagram below illustrates this idea:

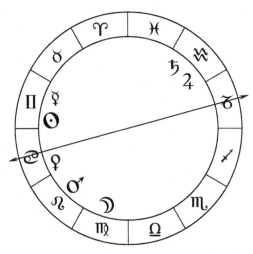

Figure 3: Planets in their domains in a diurnal chart

In this diagram, we have only shown the Ascendant, which tells us where the horizon is. The chart is diurnal or a "day" chart, because the Sun is above the horizon. All of the normal diurnal planets (the Sun, Jupiter, Saturn) are in the upper hemisphere, where the Sun is; all of the normal nocturnal planets (the Moon, Venus, Mars) are in the lower hemisphere, where the Sun is not. (You'll notice that the Sun by definition is always in the hemisphere he prefers, because he is always with himself.) Because Mercury is in an earlier degree than the Sun, he is counted as diurnal, and so he is also in the same hemisphere as the Sun.

The use of this idea, is that you might time your ritual for a period of the day or night when your planet is in its rejoicing condition. This will take a bit more planning. Suppose you wanted to perform a Saturn ritual with a chart such as this. The Sun is not far above the horizon, and as the heavens turn clockwise, Saturn will set within a few hours. This means that you would only have a few hours during the day to perform your Saturn ritual: namely, just after sunrise, and for a few hours afterwards until Saturn sets. If Saturn were much closer to the Sun, it would take most of the day before Saturn sets, so you would have a longer period to work with. But remember: with these rejoicing conditions, being a diurnal planet does not mean you must perform the ritual *during the day*, it means that you must time it so that a diurnal planet is in the *same hemisphere as the Sun*. So if it were nighttime (with the Sun below the horizon), Saturn would still be in his rejoicing condition, just so long as he were also below the horizon, in the same hemisphere as the Sun. Likewise, it's not that nocturnal planets rejoice at night, but that they rejoice whenever they are in the *hemisphere opposite the Sun*. You could still perform a ritual for a nocturnal planet during the daytime, since (in the case of this diagram), all of the nocturnal planets are in the hemisphere opposite the Sun, where they prefer to be.

The diagram also shows a further enhancement, called "domain." This means that in addition to being in the hemisphere where it rejoices, a planet is also in a sign of the same gender as itself. Thus, since all of the above feminine planets (Venus, Moon) are in feminine signs, while all of the masculine planets are in masculine signs, each planet is not only rejoicing by sect position, but is in its own domain. Again, this conveys the idea that the planet is in a suitable and joyful position, all things considered. But note that since each planet must be in a sign of the appropriate gender, it might take a while for slower planets to be in an appropriate sign.

(b) Planetary days and hours. These elections are also rather simple, but can be restrictive depending on the season of the year and the latitude of the place you are in. Planetary days are the simplest to understand: each of the seven days of the week is associated with a particular planet, *starting at sunrise and extending until sunset.*[17] In the diagram below, this assignment is shown by the planet which also rules the first "hour" of daylight (to be explained be-

---

[17] This is the scheme we will follow here. Other sources do not overtly restrict the planetary day to the daylight portion, but that might simply be because it was taken for granted. It is not a big deal if you perform a Sun ritual after the Sun has set on Sunday.

low). Thus, Sunday is assigned to the Sun, Monday to the Moon, and so on up to Saturday, which is assigned to Saturn. Since all of the daylight on a particular day is generally ruled by that planet, you will tend to have many hours to work with—but you will be restricted to working on that day. In this book, we recommend that you perform your Sun Candle consecration on Sunday or a period ruled by the Sun, the Moon Candle on Monday or a period ruled by the Moon, and so on.

Some traditional sources also assign special planets to the night: that is, *from sunset until the following sunrise.* In the diagram for planetary hours by night, you can identify these planets by looking at the row for the first hour after sunset. Thus, while the daylight on Sunday (from sunrise to sunset) is assigned to the Sun, the hours from sunset on Sunday to the following sunrise on Monday, are ruled by Jupiter; those from sunset on Monday to the following sunrise on Tuesday, by Venus; and so on.

You could certainly use these planetary days and nights to time rituals, both for planets and signs or even elements. Obviously, you could use the day or night of Venus to do a Venus working; but you could also use her day or night for a ritual involving Taurus or Libra, the two signs she rules. Likewise, if you were performing an Air ritual, you could decide to do it when an Air sign is rising on the Ascendant: if it happened to be Libra, you could perform it during the day or night of Venus; if Gemini, use the day or night of Mercury; if Aquarius, the day or night of Saturn. The point is that since you are trying to align yourself with various energies, it's useful to pick a time ruled by a planet associated with it.

Planetary "hours" are a bit more specialized than the days or nights. Traditionally, day and night referred to the periods of actual daylight and nighttime, not our standardized "civil" hours of 60 minutes apiece. As we mentioned above, "Sunday" refers especially to the period between sunrise and sunset on Sunday, but of course in everyday life we also refer to the period after sunset as being "Sunday *night.*"

With planetary hours, each period of daylight or nighttime is divided into twelve equal parts, known as "seasonal" or "planetary" hours. Each "hour" of the day and night is ruled by one of the planets, in descending order from Saturn, according to the planet's traditional distance from the earth (sometimes called the "Chaldean" order): Saturn, Jupiter, Mars, Sun, Venus, Mercury, Moon, then back to Saturn, Jupiter, and so on. But because the length of daylight and nighttime varies by season and latitude, these "hours" will be of different lengths from day to day. So for instance, in the depths of winter the actual period of daylight is rather short, and the period of darkness is rather long. Thus, since the period of daylight (the "day") is composed of 12 equal "hours," each will be less than 60 minutes long. The long, dark period between sunset and the next sunrise is called the "night," and is also divided into 12 equal parts, each a bit more than 60 minutes long. So in winter, each day hour will be much shorter than any night hour.

By revolving the planets in order like this, the first hour of the next day will always turn out to be ruled by the planet ruling the day itself. You can see below that by going in order, the series of planets on Sunday will automatically result in the Moon being the ruler of the first hour of daylight on Monday, which is assigned to her.

	Sunday	Monday	Tuesday	Wednesday	Thursday	Friday	Saturday
1	☉	☽	♂	☿	♃	♀	♄
2	♀	♄	☉	☽	♂	☿	♃
3	☿	♃	♀	♄	☉	☽	♂
4	☽	♂	☿	♃	♀	♄	☉
5	♄	☉	☽	♂	☿	♃	♀
6	♃	♀	♄	☉	☽	♂	☿
7	♂	☿	♃	♀	♄	☉	☽
8	☉	☽	♂	☿	♃	♀	♄
9	♀	♄	☉	☽	♂	☿	♃
10	☿	♃	♀	♄	☉	☽	♂
11	☽	♂	☿	♃	♀	♄	☉
12	♄	☉	☽	♂	☿	♃	♀

Figure 4: Planetary hours during day (from sunrise)

	Sunday	Monday	Tuesday	Wednesday	Thursday	Friday	Saturday
1	♃	♀	♄	☉	☽	♂	☿
2	♂	☿	♃	♀	♄	☉	☽
3	☉	☽	♂	☿	♃	♀	♄
4	♀	♄	☉	☽	♂	☿	♃
5	☿	♃	♀	♄	☉	☽	♂
6	☽	♂	☿	♃	♀	♄	☉
7	♄	☉	☽	♂	☿	♃	♀
8	♃	♀	♄	☉	☽	♂	☿
9	♂	☿	♃	♀	♄	☉	☽
10	☉	☽	♂	☿	♃	♀	♄
11	♀	♄	☉	☽	♂	☿	♃
12	☿	♃	♀	♄	☉	☽	♂

Figure 5: Planetary hours during night (from sunset)

Most astrology computer programs calculate planetary hours,[18] but to do it yourself you only need to know the times of sunrise and sunset on the day in question. Let's take an example. Suppose that on a Wednesday in your location, sunrise is at 7:32 AM and sunset is at 8:21 PM. This means that the day lasts for 12 hours and 49 minutes (or 769 minutes). If you divide these minutes by 12, then you know that each planetary hour last for 64.08 minutes. Since Mercury rules the first "hour" on Wednesday, the hour of Mercury will last from 7:32 AM – 8:36 AM. The next planetary hour is assigned to Moon, which will last from 8:36 AM – 9:40 AM, and so on, until sunset. For nighttime hours, divide the period of nighttime (from sunset to the following sunrise) by 12, and do the same. We recommend that you actually try to work a few of these out for yourself.

Just like the planetary days, planetary hours offer more focused times to elect a ritual. There is also no reason why you couldn't combine these hours with sect: for instance, since Mars is a nocturnal planet, why not perform a Mars ritual during the *night* of Mars (from sunset on Friday to sunrise on Saturday), and especially during one of his two planetary hours?

(c) The Ascendant and the angles. The last form of simple alignment brings in the houses, as well as some benefic/malefic considerations. Traditionally, the angles of the chart (the Ascendant, tenth, seventh, and fourth) are considered "strong," but for our purposes we should think of them more in terms of "presence" and "stimulation." Angular planets and signs are more present, ready-to-hand, active, and so on. The Ascendant and tenth are the most active, the seventh and the fourth less so. In practice, this means that if you are working with a planet or sign, try to put it in the Ascendant or the tenth, with the seventh and fourth being second-best. The following diagram is meant to show some possibilities for a working of Taurus or Venus:

---

[18] A free program may be downloaded at http://chronosxp.sourceforge.net/en/, but it is a good idea to check any program against the times for sunrise and sunset in your local newspaper to make sure it works correctly.

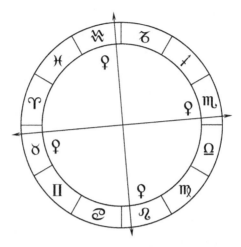

Figure 6: Angular possibilities for Taurus and Venus

You can see that we have put Taurus on the Ascendant for a Taurus working; and for a Venus working, she should be in any of the four angles. We have combined Taurus and Venus in this diagram, because she is the lord of Taurus, and it is always good to have the lord of the Ascendant in a powerful place. So although a Taurus working should have Taurus rising or on one of the angles, it is even better if Venus (its lord) is also in an angle. Likewise, a Venus working should have her in an angle, and even better if a sign she rules (Taurus) is on the Ascendant or tenth.

Another feature of this type of alignment is making the benefics angular, but the malefics cadent. Just as the angles suggests presence and stimulation, the cadent places (twelfth, ninth, sixth, third) suggest absence, receding, sluggishness. Thus, we normally prefer that the malefic planets (Mars, Saturn) be in cadent places, while the benefics (Jupiter, Venus, but also the Sun and Moon) be angular. Of course this sort of situation is not appropriate for a Saturn or Mars working, when we want them to be prominent: in that case, do make the malefic planet angular, but you should probably make the benefics angular or succeedent as well. (The succeedent places are all of the other houses: the second, fifth, eleventh, and eighth.) In the diagram below, we have imagined a Jupiter working. We have put Pisces (which he rules) on the Ascendant to emphasize his rulership of the time, and put him in an angle. We have also put the malefics in the third, a cadent place.

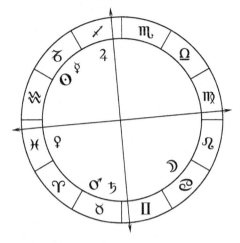

Figure 7: Jupiter election with cadent malefics

These benefic/malefic considerations start to take us away from mere alignments, and focus more on operational success and enhanced elections (below). You can probably already see that taking things to this level greatly limits your ritual times: for that reason, you should not go this far with something like simple daily meditations and devotions. But for more important ritual consecrations, and the culmination rituals in this book, it would be useful to follow these rules.

Enhanced elections

As we mentioned before, elections can be made very complicated indeed. So far we have looked at simple ways in which an Element, Planet, or Sign may be highlighted in the chart, and because we have focused on simple alignments and attunements, we have not dwelled on such things as operational results.

In this section we will go further into practical results and elections for more momentous rituals (including the culmination rituals in this book), by applying some of the categories of "planetary condition" to two of the most important things in the chart: the Ascendant and its lord. We've divided up the various planetary conditions into four categories: benefics and malefics (and their aspects), dignities, direct motion, and the Sun's rays. Once you begin to understand how these work, they should be pretty easy to implement. But in all cases, remember the rule we've already stated: there is no perfect election, so do what you can in the time frame you have.

In what follows, we will assume that we are electing for a ritual of Earth, or of Taurus, or of Venus. That is to say, for an Earth ritual we will choose an earthy sign, in this case Taurus; for a Taurus ritual, Taurus itself; and for Venus, we will focus on her but put one of her signs—Taurus—on the Ascendant. Of course we could do the same for any other combination: for a ritual of Fire, we could choose a fiery sign such as Leo, for a Leo ritual Leo itself, and for the Sun we would focus on the Sun, but also put his sign Leo on the Ascendant. The point of this is to show the close relationship between Elements, Signs, and Planets.

(a) Benefics and malefics, and their aspects. Generally speaking, we want benefics (especially Venus and Jupiter, but the Sun and Moon can also play this role) to be in or aspecting the Ascendant, and with or aspecting the lord of the Ascendant. But we want the malefics (Mars and Saturn) to be "in aversion" to the Ascendant and its lord—or at least, we want them only to be configured by a sextile or a trine. (We will explain "aversion" below.) Of course, if we are doing a Mars or Saturn ritual, then we want their signs (which should also be on the Ascendant), or the malefics themselves, to be well aspected by benefics. The following diagram gives an example of this:

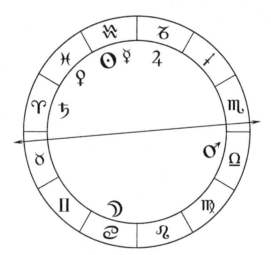

Figure 8: An election for Earth/Taurus/Venus

In this diagram, Taurus is rising as before. There is no planet in the Ascendant, but we can see that the benefics, Venus and Jupiter, each aspect the rising sign itself from the eleventh and the ninth. Please note that while aspects become more intensified by degree, it is often enough to note their whole-sign aspects. That is to say, because the sign of Pisces aspects Taurus by a sextile, then Venus aspects the rising sign itself simply by her being in Pisces. And because Capricorn aspects Taurus by a trine, Jupiter aspects the rising sign simply by his being in Capricorn. So, the rising sign has favorable aspects to it.

Now, although Venus has already been noted as being a benefic planet, in this case she is playing another important role: she is the lord of the Ascendant, because she rules Taurus. What this means is that Taurus itself is not only in a good condition, but Venus—who manages the affairs of Taurus—is also in a good condition, because Jupiter aspects her sign by sextile. Again, since Capricorn aspects Pisces by a sextile, any planet in it (such as Jupiter) will also sextile anything in Pisces. This configuration would be good not only for an Earth ritual (since Taurus is an earthy sign), but also one for Taurus itself, and for Venus in a Venus ritual. Whenever we elect for a sign, such as Taurus, we should always try to put its lord in a good condition, as well.

But what about the malefic planets? This diagram introduces an important concept in traditional astrology: aversion. Aversion means being "turned away," and it refers to signs or planets which *cannot* aspect some other sign or planet. For in most traditional astrology, planets and signs may only be related to certain other planets or signs, through the classical or "Ptolemaic" aspects: that is, a planet may be in the same sign as another planet, or be in a sextile, square, trine, or opposition. All other signs are considered "averse," as though there is no active relationship. The diagram below gives an example of signs which are averse to Mars in the Midheaven:

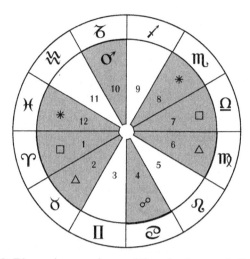

Figure 9: Places in aversion to Mars in the tenth (in white)

In this diagram, Mars is in the tenth house, in Capricorn. He is conjoined or assembled with anything in Capricorn itself, and is configured with or aspects any planets in places which he can aspect by sign. He aspects Scorpio and anything in it by a sextile, Aries and anything in it by a square, and so on. But he cannot aspect or see, or be directly related to, anything in Aquarius or Sagittarius, because there are no semi-sextiles; nor to anything in Gemini nor Leo, because there are no "inconjunct" aspects. The concept of aversion is described in detail in *Traditional Astrology for Today*, but the point here is that we *do not want* the malefics to aspect the Ascendant (or its lord). Rather, we want them to be in aversion to it, so that their malefic qualities are turned away. Thus, we want the malefics to be in the twelfth, eighth, sixth, or second, because these places are in aversion to the Ascendant. Moreover, we *do want* the lord of the Ascendant to aspect the Ascendant, rather than to be in aversion. Again, if we were doing a ritual for Mars or Saturn, then we would indeed want them to be in or aspecting the Ascendant, and we would want them to be favorably aspecting the benefics so as to take advantage of those benefic qualities.

In our election for Earth/Taurus/Venus, Mars and Saturn are in the twelfth and the sixth. Can either of them aspect the Ascendant? No, because those places are in aversion to the Ascendant. Can they aspect Venus herself? No, because those places happen to be in aversion to Pisces, where she is.

(b) Dignities. Dignities are rather straightforward, at least for our purposes here. Each planet rules at least one sign, and is exalted in exactly one sign.

Each planet is also in detriment in at least one sign, and in fall or descension in exactly one sign. The signs of rulership and detriment are opposite each other, as are the signs of exaltation and fall. Put another way, if you know what sign a planet rules, the sign of detriment is opposite it; if you know in what sign a planet is exalted, the sign of fall is opposite it. The table below illustrates this:

	Domicile	Exaltation	Detriment	Fall
♈	♂	☉	♀	♄
♉	♀	☽	♂	
♊	☿		♃	
♋	☽	♃	♄	♂
♌	☉		♄	
♍	☿	☿	♃	♀
♎	♀	♄	♂	☉
♏	♂		♀	☽
♐	♃		☿	
♑	♄	♂	☽	♃
♒	♄		☉	
♓	♃	♀	☿	☿

Figure 10: Table of major dignities and counter-dignities

For each sign on the left, we have listed what planet rules it (by "domicile"), is in detriment in it, and (if applicable) which one is exalted or in fall in it. Since there are seven traditional planets but twelve signs, not every sign has an exaltation and fall. You can see that Venus rules or has her domicile rulership in Taurus and Libra, but her detriment in Scorpio and Aries: these signs are opposite each other. The general rules for this kind of election are as follows:

- Do not put a planet in detriment or fall in the Ascendant, such as if Sagittarius is rising but Mercury is in it (detriment).
- Try to put the lord of the Ascendant in its own sign or exaltation, not in its detriment or fall, such as putting Venus in Libra or Pisces, not in Aries or Virgo.

- Try to put the malefic planets in their own signs or exaltations, and avoid putting the benefics in their detriments or falls.

The basic idea is that a planet in its own sign or exaltation will be especially empowered to be confident, authoritative, organized, prominent, and constructive. But planets in detriment or fall will be less confident or authoritative, disorganized, not prominent, or destructive. And so it follows that we want planets in the Ascendant or ruling it to be in their signs of rulership or exaltation, and we do not want planets in their detriments or fall to be strongly influencing the election. In our chart above with Taurus rising, you can see that the lord of the Ascendant, Venus, is strong in her own exaltation: this is a good indication for the election. It's true that Jupiter is in his fall, but he does not rule the Ascendant and is really only there to give whatever support he can. The malefics are in detriment, but that is all right because they have been marginalized already by being in aversion to the Ascendant. Actually, it is probably better that they are in detriment, because then they cannot act authoritatively in the houses in which they are. But if we were performing a Saturn or Mars ritual, we would indeed want them to be aspecting the Ascendant, and in one of their signs (domiciles) or exaltations.

Before looking at the third of our concepts, we should say something about the outer planets (Uranus, Neptune, and Pluto). We ourselves don't use them in our elections or chart reading or ritual work. You may use them if you like, but *do not give them rulerships over any sign*. They do not rule signs, nor are they exalted or in detriment or in fall in any of them. If anything, consider them only as providing supportive or troubling aspects to the seven traditional ones: preferably, let them only be in trines or sextiles, *closely by degree*. Do not pay attention to them if they are only related to the Ascendant or its lord by sign. For example, if Uranus were closely squaring Venus by degree in the above election, that would be something to avoid in an important Venus ritual (if you use Uranus at all). But if he were only squaring her by sign (that is, in Sagittarius or Gemini), or he was somewhere else in Pisces itself but still far away by degree, ignore him.

(c) Direct motion and retrogradation. It is best if the planet in question is moving in direct motion (forward in the zodiac) rather than being retrograde. Retrogradation generally means delay, diversion, or the later withdrawing of something which initially manifests.

(d) The Sun's rays. The fourth category for enhanced elections has to do with the Sun's rays. If you've watched the Sun rise or set in an area without

much light pollution, you've seen that as he rises in the east, stars and planets which were first visible before sunrise gradually get blotted out by his light until the whole sky is bright. Likewise, stars in the west gradually become more visible after he sets. Ancient astrologers assigned a standard distance from the Sun, at which planets are far away enough from him to be visible in the east before sunrise, and visible in the west just after sunset: that distance is 15° on either side of him. If planets are farther away from the Sun than this, then they are said by some astrologers to travel "in their own light," whereas if they are within this 15°, they are either said to be hidden and under his control, or else damaged by being "burned up" or "scorched" by proximity to him (usually called "combustion"). Some exceptions were made for planets which happened to be in their own signs or exaltations while under his rays: in those cases, while they may be covered up and obscured, they are at least not damaged.

The use of this concept is that we do not want the important planets in an election to be under the Sun's rays, because they become either less accessible and obscured, or actually harmed. Again, an exception was made for cases in which the action involved *required* secrecy, such as a business deal for which one does not want publicity, or making some kind of escape. In the Taurus election above, we have not assigned actual degrees to the planets. But it is most likely that Mercury is under the Sun's rays, because he is close to the Sun. But we have imagined that Venus, who is further away in the next sign, is greater than 15° away and therefore out of the rays. Even if she were within 15° of him, she would not necessarily be harmed because she is currently in her own exaltation; but she would still be more obscured, which takes away from her prominence and ability to act independently. For our purposes here, we should try to avoid having the lord of the Ascendant under the Sun's rays, because it makes the planet less accessible for what we want.

The Moon and her conditions

Finally, let us look at the Moon and her conditions. The Moon is a central planet in all elections, and lists of good and bad conditions of the Moon abounded in traditional literature.[19] Here we'll focus on just a few of them,

---

[19] See for example Dykes 2010, §IV.5.

but remember that a lot depends on exactly what your ritual is about. A paper or computerized ephemeris will come in handy here, because the Moon moves so swiftly that she changes her conditions often.

As for conditions in which the Moon *should* be, we will list four:

(a) Angular. Try to put the Moon in one of the angles, especially in the Ascendant or the tenth (see the diagram of Venus in the angles, above). Even if you use whole-signs, it is still good for you to put her immediately following the degree of the Midheaven. If you cannot do this, put her in one of the succeedent houses (except for the eighth), preferring the following, in order: the eleventh, the fifth, the second. Avoid putting her in a cadent house.

(b) In the sign or applying to the planet. Since the Moon is a general indicator of matters, she should be in the sign you are working with (or in a sign of its element), or applying to the relevant planet. So, for Fire she should be in a fiery sign, for Aries she should be in Aries, and for Venus she should be applying to Venus either by her body or a classical aspect—the closer, the more intense the relationship. Normally, she should not be in her sign of fall or descension (Scorpio), but of course if you are performing an alignment ritual for Scorpio, this would not be bad. (If this still makes you nervous, put her in Pisces or Cancer, so that she at least trines Scorpio.) If working with a malefic planet, make her aspect to it be by a sextile or trine. As we will mention below, this planet should also not be in its own fall.

(c) Applying to benefics. This condition pertains more to rituals which are devoted to a particular effect, which may include the culmination rituals in this book. The Moon should be applying to Venus or Jupiter by her body or a classical aspect, but even a trine to the Sun or a strong and unafflicted Mercury would be good.[20] Of course, you may disregard this rule when working with the malefics: in that case, make the aspect be by a sextile or trine. An exception would be her phase-based aspects to the malefics (see below).

(d) Waxing or increasing in light. Many people argue that rituals should not be performed when the Moon is waning (from the Full Moon to the New Moon), but we do not agree. It is true that Moon's waxing phase implies outward-oriented actions, growth, and development, while her waning phase implies inward-oriented actions, decay, and devolution. Based on that, it might seem as though we should only use the waxing phase: after all, who wants to connect with the principles of decay? But in terms of knowledge

---

[20] For example, Mercury should be direct (not retrograde), out of the Sun's rays, or in one of his own signs, or aspected by one of the benefics more closely so than by the malefics.

and experience, the waxing phase implies youth and gaining experience for the first time, while the waning phase implies wisdom and the assimilation of experience: so the waning phase is not necessarily a bad thing, provided that she is not also applying to Saturn (see below). But as a general rule, a waxing Moon is best.

As for bad conditions of the Moon to avoid, we have identified seven:

(a) *Being under the rays or scorched/combust.* As with the other planets, it is generally not favorable for the Moon to be under the rays (within 15° of the Sun): it implies hiddenness or a lack of manifestation. Or, in terms of the Moon's cycle, it implies either something coming to an end (as she enters the rays from her last quarter) or something not yet ready to be born (as she moves away from the Sun (after the New Moon), but before emerging from his rays. We could make an exception for this, if she is in Cancer or Taurus.

(b) *In her fall/descension, or applying to a planet in its own fall/descension.* Just as with the other planets, avoid ritual when the Moon is in her fall (Scorpio), unless you are doing a Scorpio ritual. Likewise, she should not be applying to a planet which is already in *its own* fall: thus, she should not apply to a Sun in Libra, Mercury in Pisces, Venus in Virgo, Mars in Cancer, Jupiter in Capricorn, or Saturn in Aries.

(c) *Besieged.* This condition is rather special, and refers to the Moon separating from one malefic planet, and applying to the other—particularly by conjunction, square or opposition. Actually, there were two versions of besiegement, one based solely on sign relationships, the other by degrees.[21] We'll focus on the degrees here, because it is more limited and rare (albeit worse). In the diagram below, the Moon is in Virgo, and she is being squared by both malefics. The rule is that the malefics must be casting their exact rays to no more than 7° on either side of her, *without* a ray of the Sun or a benefic planet intervening.[22] The Moon is at 15°. Saturn casts a square to 8° Virgo on one side of her, while Mars does so to 23° on her other side: thus, the rays are no more than 7° on either side of her. The gray areas show the 15° region in any sign where the Sun or a benefic planet would have to be, in order for them to cast a ray in between the malefics, and save her. Thus Jupiter is in Scorpio and does aspect Virgo by a sextile, but he is no longer in the gray region of Scorpio which would allow the ray of his exact degree to intervene

---

[21] See Dykes 2010, §IV.4.2.

[22] The notion that the Sun can break a besiegement seems to be a later adaptation of some earlier Greek views. See *The Book of Aristotle* II.6, in Dykes 2009.

in the gray, 15° region around the Moon. Likewise, Venus is in Pisces, but she is not yet in the region of it so as to cast her opposition into the besieged area of Virgo.

Besiegement does not happen very often, but it is something to note: it suggests being trapped, getting bad advice, or being surrounded by evil influences or people. It is probably more pertinent to rituals which strive for a practical result.

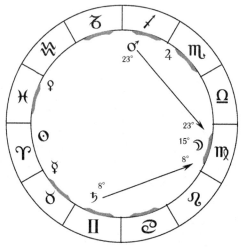

Figure 11: Malefic enclosure/besieging by degree

(d) Waning or decreasing in light, in rituals for results. As we suggested above, a decreasing Moon is not necessarily bad unless we are talking about a ritual for some kind of concrete results, or making something manifest and increase, for something new, *et cetera.*

(e) Applying to Mars while waxing, or Saturn while waning. Above, we said it was all right for the Moon to be applying to a malefic planet, provided that the malefic is the planet we are interested in, and that it was by a sextile or trine. But ancient authors also warned us about two specific kinds of application to the malefics: avoid applications to Mars when the Moon is waxing, and with Saturn when she is waning. There are two explanations for this. First, since the waxing phase is more akin to heat and light, an application to a hot planet like Mars would incline the Moon to extremes and imbalance in the realm of heat; likewise, since the waning phase is more akin to cold, an application to Saturn during that phase would also lead to imbalance in the realm of cold. But we might also put it in terms of sect: the waxing phase is more diurnal

and light-related, so it is all right for her to apply to the diurnal planet Saturn then, but not to Mars; the waning phase is more nocturnal and darkness-related, so it is all right for her to apply to the nocturnal planet Mars at that time, but not to Saturn.

(f) *Joined to a cadent planet.* This consideration is more pertinent to rituals for results. Just as angular (and generally, succeedent) houses imply presence, strength, and prominence, so cadent planets imply passing away or the past, absence, and obscurity. We have already suggested that you make the Moon angular or succeedent, so avoid too her application to a cadent planet, particularly to one in the twelfth or sixth.

(g) *Void in course.* Again, this pertains more for significant, result-oriented rituals. Like besieging, there were broadly two definitions of being void in course (or "emptiness of course"): a more frequent medieval type, and a rarer Hellenistic type.[23] We'll follow the medieval one here. The definition of emptiness or being void is that the Moon does not complete an exact conjunction or aspect to any other planet, *so long as she is her current sign.*

In the diagram below, the Moon has recently separated from a conjunction with Jupiter and a trine to the Sun. She is not even configured by sign to most of the other planets. And although she is approaching a square with Mercury, he is in the last degree of his own sign, and will cross over into Leo before she is able to perfect an exact aspect with him.[24] Therefore, she is void in course.

The meaning of a void-in-course Moon is roughly this: nothing new will happen. That is, in her current situation (her sign) she has already made all of the connections she can, and so the current state of affairs will continue in its own way without any change. Once she crosses into another sign, she will have new opportunities for further development. You can see why a void-in-course Moon is important in horary questions, because most questions are of the type, "Will this new thing happen"? Sometimes astrologers say that a void Moon means that "nothing will come of the matter," but this is not quite right. A void Moon doesn't mean that nothing *at all* will happen, but that nothing *new* will happen. Thus if you had a bad situation that was getting worse, a void Moon will generally mean that the bad trend will continue.

---

[23] See Dykes 2010, §III.9.
[24] Since the Moon moves about 13° per day, it will take her about that long to reach 29°. But since Mercury himself moves about a degree per day, by that time he will already have moved into Leo.

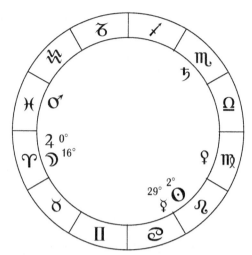

Figure 12: Medieval emptiness of course

We have covered a lot of ground in this section. Let us summarize these electional ideas in the following way.

On the one hand, there is little difficulty in electing for alignment rituals, daily devotions, and so on. For them, there is a variety of ways in which we simply want the time to harmonize with something very general about the natures of the elements, signs, and planets. For daily rituals in particular, one hardly needs to take these things into account.

But for more important rituals, there are approximately five major categories of difficulty which can effect planets, and which it is worth trying to overcome if you can. It is really impossible to say which is "worst," since each implies a different kind of undesirable thing:

1. *Harm from malefics.* For a sign, this especially refers to having a malefic in it (but also squaring or opposing it). For a planet, it means being in a conjunction, square, or opposition with the malefics. Try to improve this situation through aspects to benefics, or by putting the planet in a dignity.

2. *Weakness through cadence.* This refers to a planet being in a cadent house. This situation changes quickly, but waiting will likely prevent you from having the rising sign you want. Try to improve it by making the planet in question apply to an angular planet, or strengthen

the Moon by means of a dignity or having her apply to an angular planet.

3. *Lowliness and poor quality through fall.* For a sign, this means having a planet in fall within it (such as Capricorn having Jupiter in it). For a planet, this refers to the planet itself being in its fall. To improve this situation, make sure the lord of the sign is in a very good condition, and aspecting the sign itself: for example, in the case of Capricorn with Jupiter in it, try to put Saturn (the lord of Capricorn) in Libra or in some other good situation, aspecting Capricorn itself. One might also connect the fallen planet to other benefics, such as a trine to Venus or the Sun.

4. *Hiddenness through the sunbeams.* This refers to a planet being within 15° of the Sun. If you can, let this be only while the planet is in its own sign or exaltation, or let the Sun itself be in his sign or exaltation, or let the planet be aspecting the lord of the sign in question: for example, Saturn in Taurus under the rays, but aspected by Venus from a sextile.

5. *Reversal and change through retrogradation.* This refers to a planet being retrograde, but perhaps also to a retrograde planet in a sign for which you are electing (such as electing for a Libra ritual, while Libra has a retrograde Mercury in it). Try to support this retrograde planet by having it in a dignity, or being aspected by the lord of its sign, or aspected by strong benefics.

§6: Where to go from here: ongoing devotions and regular practice

If you enjoy these kinds of rituals and meditations, it is easy to adapt them and their concepts for daily alignments, meditations and blessings (or other occasions), such as before work or before going to bed. Following are a few of our suggestions for incorporating simple astrological magic into your life:

- For daily practice (using the Moon as an example): put the unlit blue Luna Candle and *The High Priestess* card on your Altar. Perform the purification and consecration from the Luna ritual, light the Candle, draw the Luna Hexagram, turn your aura to a bright blue, and recite a favorite short speech from the ritual. Feel the Lunar energy flow, and extinguish the Candle. This can be done in 5 minutes, which is a very reasonable time commitment for a daily practice.

- Use the ideas in the rituals, and the significations in the Appendices, to create a list of activities and places that match the Element, Planet, or Sign you are interested in. For Venus, take dancing lessons, watch a documentary about art, visit a beautiful garden, paint something. In this way, you will actively connect your daily life to these higher astrological principles.

- Again, use the significations and associations to create meals with certain spices, decorate your home or Altar with the appropriate stones, paint your walls or collect beautiful objects with the right colors, or wear a certain color or piece of jewelry. For Venus, burn rose incense on Fridays, wear green or a copper bracelet, eat a rich, sweet, greasy treat on Fridays or as an Altar offering, and so on.

- Create a work of art relating to the Element, Planet, or Sign you are interested in: a painting, a poem, song, or story. Write a story with characters whose body types and personalities match what you find in the Appendices or rituals.

- Attempt active dream work by performing a ritual or a meditation on a certain Tarot card or planet before bed, with the intention of having dreams about it. Keep a dream journal.

- Continue the Tarot meditations, using a Candle and Hexagram as described above, and try to go on regular imaginative journeys through the landscapes. Again, keep a journal of your experiences.

§7: The rituals and structure of this book

This book is structured to take you first through the Elements, then the Planets and the zodiacal Signs. Each set of rituals leads into the next, and while they become more complex as you advance, they can still be performed with ease. Also, please do not be intimidated by the length of the rites. For one thing, the font is larger than what is typically found in published books, and this makes for ease of reading while performing the rite, especially in candlelight or low lighting (which we recommend).

Anything worth doing takes time, and these rites, if worked correctly, will take anywhere from one half hour to an hour each, depending mostly on how long it takes you to build visualizations and perform the meditations. Advanced rituals can take longer to perform, and there is a reason for this. The longer you spend in ritual, the more you slip into a ritualized consciousness, and ritualized consciousness opens the gates to the higher levels of being. Conversely, this state of mind also makes it easy for time to pass without realizing it.

We have included diagrams for making the Pentagrams, Hexagrams, and other symbols, so that you will have all necessary information in front of you while you perform a rite. In time, we hope you will memorize them, since knowing them by heart enhances ritual further.

The ritual speeches themselves are written in boldface, headed by the title "Aspirant": this allows you to distinguish them from the "stage directions," which are either in normal typeface or italics. Speeches are just as important as making symbols in ritual. They do aid in understanding why you are doing what you are doing, but equally, their style helps elevate you so as to commune with the relevant Divine forces through the use of your own voice. When working in a group, speeches also elevate the consciousness of those working with you: hence the importance of using emotion when you speak.

The Elemental rituals culminate in a Spirit working, which utilizes all of the Elements. The Planetary rituals culminate in a ritual that uses them all, as do the Zodiacal rites. In the big picture, you are building a magical cosmos which will allow you to experience astrology in a more meaningful and fruitful way. The more you put into your cosmos, the more beautiful and expressive it will become.

PART 1: THE ELEMENTAL RITES

Introduction

The first five rites of this book are Elemental in nature. We start out with the Elements because they are "closer" to us and our experience (as opposed to purely spiritual and rational things), and because they provide the material context for the manifestation of higher things in the lower. So they are more familiar, and balancing them and getting them right will make it easier to consciously channel and manifest Planetary and Zodiacal energies into your experience and life. They are foundational for what is to come.

There were many ancient theories as to what the Elements are. Some, such as Plato, believed that the Elements are little, geometrically-shaped particles. But traditional magic and spirituality tends to think of them more as classes of energy types: as qualities rather than particles. So if we say something has an Airy or Watery quality, we don't expect to get a magnifying glass and see little bits of an "air" particle or a "water" particle there. We are describing classes of activity.

It is often hard to talk about the Elements, because they are applied to many different things, from physical events to very exalted classes of beings. This is partly because there are four of them, and whenever we have four types of something, it is easy to want to associate them with the Elements. (We will speak of one of these associations in a minute.) The same goes for the number Three. In fact, we might even say that because eternal beings like Numbers are very high up on the metaphysical ladder, sometimes we can confuse the down-to-earth, everyday four Elements, with other things that come in groups of four. Or, we might confuse the Elements themselves with *related* structures in other levels of reality. So for instance, the Hebrew Divine Name YHVH (Yod Heh Vav Heh) has four letters, and in Qabalism these letters are often associated with Fire, Water, Air, and Earth—but no one expects that God's name actually means the fire on your stove, with a shot glass of water, a puff of air, and a clod of earth. Rather, we may say that a relationship in these Divine letters (which describe something about God) is mirrored in a relationship between the Elements. So we have to be careful about what we're saying, even if in practice we can often get away with making these fast-and-loose associations between levels of reality.

Likewise, when we speak of the Elements, we are not really talking about the zodiacal Signs, although there is an association there. The Signs indicate the four energy types on a higher level, with each type split into three styles: movable, fixed, and common (often called "cardinal," fixed, and "mutable"): thus, four energy types with three styles apiece, yields twelve Signs. So, Aries is a fiery Sign, but it is the *movable* fiery Sign; Leo is the *fixed* fiery Sign. Neither Aries nor Leo is on fire in the way something down here is on fire, but they *indicate* activities and energy types which *manifest* down here.[25] So when we speak of the Elements here we are talking about lower realities, where the Elements pertain more to manifestation and the physical, everyday context of things.

The Elements are often grouped in different ways, and we will follow the mainstream classifications here. Now, with respect to higher realities, all of the Elements are considered passive. But amongst themselves, Fire and Air are considered masculine and active, and Water and Earth feminine and passive. Each of these suggests things about types of human behavior and psychology, which we'll look at in a moment. Each of the Elements has certain more primitive qualities, through which they are interrelated: Fire is hot and dry, Air is hot and moist, Water is cold and moist, and Earth is cold and dry. Actually, these should probably be understood in terms of activities and processes, which is how people like Ptolemy thought of them: for example, heat*ing* and dry*ing*, rather than simply "hot" and "dry."

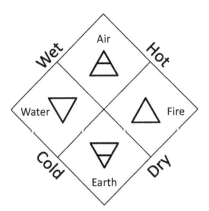

Figure 13: Elements and Elemental qualities

---

[25] See Part 3 for further discussion of the zodiacal Signs.

In this book we will also focus on the Elements in the context of the human soul and mind, rather than using them to explain weather or anything like that. To that end, we'll also take some shortcuts and speak of the Elements in terms of "energy" instead of "activities" and "processes." In Appendix 1 we have listed a lot of general characteristics (such as personality types and temperaments) for the Elements, but we can say a few other things here.[26]

For instance, Fire and Air are more projective energies, which are chiefly concerned with action and intellect. Water and Earth are receptive, and stand more for emotions and protective instincts. But in one sense this is only shorthand: we would normally associate anger (which is an emotion) with Fire, not with Water. What this really means is that Water is associated with the ability to respond emotionally to things which happen to us—which is a passive, receptive stance. When we come down to classifying emotional states, we might find that certain emotions like anger are a "fiery" type of emotion, perhaps a "fiery" aspect of Water: *this interplay and ambiguity among the Elements is typical of our manifest world.*

Taken all together, the Elements can be seen in the context of healing, which we discussed in the Introduction. From our "horizontal" perspective, they can be seen in terms of the temperaments or personality types: a complete circle or integrated whole of psychological features: a complete circle of creative, dynamic, energetic consciousness. We want to have appropriate, functional access to all sorts of styles of behavior, outlook, and emotional ranges, even if we normally tend to act more from the choleric (fiery) temperament, or the melancholic (earthy) temperament, or some other.

But if we look at them "vertically," they correspond to the different parts of our microcosmic being—that is, even though the Elements proper are *lower* realities which pertain primarily to our material existence, they can be stacked up hierarchically to correspond to levels in us, which match the whole macrocosm. So the Fiery aspect of us, considered the highest of the four, may correspond to a unifying spiritual drive and impulse for the Divine, an animating principle of each human individual. The next level, our Airy side, can indicate our rational mind which is especially good at dealing with ideas, concepts, language, but which is lower than the Divine. Then, Water may symbolize the emotional and instinctual soul, the purely emotional levels of love, hate, and many other conditions of sentient consciousness—this

---

[26] An excellent resource is Greenbaum's work on the temperaments, in the Bibliography.

corresponds to a combination of changeable physical realities and eternal values. Finally, Earth pertains to the actual physical being, the changeable physical context and manifestation of all of these energies which comprise us and our individuality.

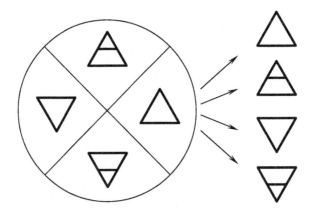

Figure 14: Horizontal and vertical balancing of Elements

So, these Elements are the bare bones of a magical cosmos. Their flexibility allows for many different operations, and they are foundational for expanding inner consciousness. But like anything in magic, they are not simply automatic in action, and they must be used consistently and persistently in order to get reliable and meaningful practical results.

Triplicities: the individual elements

Now that we've covered a few basic points, let's examine the Elements one at a time:

Fire: a projective, masculine, choleric energy
Fire means light and illumination in all possible senses. Controlled, Fire transmutes; uncontrolled, it devours all things and returns them to primal energy, to that principle which gave them being. Fire is the one Element we cannot touch directly in physical form.

Fire is thought of as clarity of consciousness, inner vision, and the Divine spark shining in the darkest parts of the human being. Elemental Fire corresponds to the clarity of inner sight. It represents all of the passions and is most definitely the fervent will to achieve. Fire drives through all obstacles and destroys them. It represents everything in and around you with enough energy to arouse your creative consciousness, and also represents all that may be accomplished by inspiration and desire.

Its time is noon, its direction is the South, and its season is the summertime. The energy of Fire is projective, as it flows outward; its color is red. The Element of Fire is consecrating, destructive, cleansing, energetic, sexual, and forceful. Sight, heat and light are manifestations of this Element. Rituals of Fire include ideas of consecration, destruction, protection, courage, sexual passion, energy, and strength. Its ritual forms are feeling heat from flames, burning, smoldering, or heating. Its natural symbols are flames, red-hot coals, or heated objects.

Water: receptive, feminine, phlegmatic energy

Water is a symbol of purity, capable of dissolving any impurity. It dissolves the solid elements of earth into a liquid state, which are then absorbed by other living organisms. Without Water, life would not exist. Therefore, Water is essentially the medium of fertility and germination.

As we emerged from the primeval ocean by the action of light upon Water, so must we be reborn on inner levels through ocean equivalents. On inner levels, Water is a container or carrier of consciousness, linking up conscious energies between all life forms. It is also the Element associated with psychism, the unconscious mind and dreams.

Water is pre-eminently the means of freeing oneself from extraneous impurities, revealing one's true aspect. The ability to reject the false and to preserve the truth is characteristic of Elemental Water.

Elemental Water and love go together. Love pours out, comforts, and cheers. Life begins in Water, and it represents the soul containing the light of the spirit. Thus, in Water is seen the principle of a container: the womb, receptivity, and the capacity for loving care. It is an icon of perfect purity and the greatest bliss that may be experienced by humans in spiritual safety.

Its time is dusk, its direction is the West, and its season is the autumn. The energy of Water is receptive, as it flows inward; its color is blue. The Element of Water is flowing, purifying, soothing, and loving. The sense of taste is a manifestation of this Element. Rituals of Water include ideas of the reception of a force, passive inspiration, self-reflection, skrying, purification, love, psychic awareness, dreams, sleep, and peace. Its ritual forms are drinking, dilution, placing in water, purifications such as bathing, and pouring libations. Its natural symbols are shells, cups and chalices, wells, bowls, and cauldrons.

Air: projective, masculine, sanguine energy

Elemental Air relates to the human intellect and thought processes, which are quick, changeable and abstract. Symbolically, Air is related to the creative breath which gave life to the world.[27] It is connected in many mythologies with the idea of creation as the medium for the development of life processes. Qabalistically, Air is considered to be the offspring of the Elements of Fire and Water, and it is the reconciler between these two Elements, balancing their extremes.

The Element of Air in the human is the conscious mind and the intellect. It is the great reconciler which seeks answers, decides issues, challenges stupidities, and defeats them through the intellect rather than through force or submission. Its time is the dawn, its direction is the East, and its season is the springtime. The energy of Air is projective, as it flows outward; its color is yellow. The Element of Air is moving, fresh, intelligent, restorative, and suspending. Hearing and smell are manifestations of this Element. Rituals of Air include healing, knowledge quests, enhancement of the imagination, and visions. Its ritual forms are visualization, the use of fans, and the inhalation of scents. Its natural symbols are feathers, incense smoke, and fragrant flowers.

Earth: receptive, feminine, melancholic energy

Qabalistically, Earth is the energy through which the three previous Elements come into manifestation to be expressed in the physical world. In Earth are the qualities of objectivity, solidity, gravity, weight, mass, incarnation, and definition. However, by itself Elemental Earth is cold and sterile, only acting as a kind of reservoir for the forces of which condense into it. It holds within itself all life preceding it, and all the life that will come forth from it.

Again, Qabalistically, Fire, Air or Water cannot manifest except by means of this Element, because Earth makes manifestation possible between individual units of existence. It has the property of conformability and resistance,

---

[27] This is discussed further in the *Logos & Light* audio series by Benjamin Dykes (www.bendykes.com/logos-light.php).

offering the necessary inertia to other energies for the interrelationship in the act of manifestation. Inertia is very much a power which keeps everything in proportion with everything else, and this is a magical value of Elemental Earth. In its perfect form, Elemental Earth is symbolic of the body about to receive the influx of Divine Light, and it is also the manifest expression of a complete thought and an act of the will.

If we combine these ideas, we encounter the concept of force embodied in form, and form ensouled by force. And here, we are dealing with the Principle of Polarity, the subtle interaction of the life force between two parts, the flow and return, the stimulus and the reaction. The Principle of Polarity runs through the whole of creation and is the basis for manifestation: hence the statement at the start of this section, that the Elements are the building blocks for all rituals designed to manifest an effect here in the physical world.

The Element of Earth in the human is the physical body. Its time is midnight, its direction is the North, and its season is winter. The energy of Earth is receptive, as it flows inward; its color is green. The Element of Earth is fertile, moist, nurturing, stabilizing, and grounding. Touch, gravity, and inertia are manifestations of this Element. Rituals of Earth include ideas of manifestation, construction, fertility, stability, and grounding. Its ritual forms are eating, burying, planting, making a physical image, and ritual action on the physical plane. Its natural symbols are salt, bread, clay dishes, soil, rocks, sheaves of wheat, and symbols of the harvest.

Quadruplicities

The quadruplicity of a sign has to do with how its element is expressed in terms of energetic movement and style. There are three categories: movable, fixed, or common (often called "cardinal," fixed or kerubic, or "mutable"), and each sign of a given element represents one of these. For example, of the earthy signs, Capricorn is movable, Taurus is fixed, and Virgo is common.

In traditional astrology, each quadruplicity is used for certain kinds of elections.[28] Movable signs imply initiative and beginning, and are used for things which we want to be completed or transform quickly: for example, travel or fighting or selling or getting engaged. Fixed signs imply what is lasting and stable, such as building something or getting married. Common signs

---

[28] For a fuller description of quadruplicities, see Dykes 2012 (*Choices & Inceptions*), such as Sahl's *On Elections* §§12a-17.

are so called because they partake of both change and stability, implying rep-
etition, partnership, combinations of things, and back-and-forth motion:
such as for ongoing business partnerships, and actions that involve routines
such as going back to school.

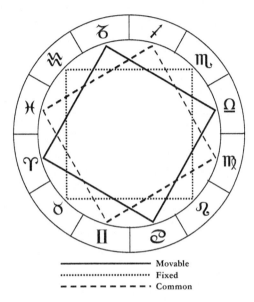

Figure 15: Quadruplicities

But if we're thinking more contemplatively and in terms of personal character and development, the quadruplicities are useful for understanding
different styles within the elements (and we have included some key words
for them in the Elemental rituals). So, if your Ascendant and other important
planets like the Moon are in fixed signs, it is useful to know how the fixed
quality works in your life. You might want to elect a time when the Moon or
Ascendant is in the quadruplicity you want to understand.

Here are some basic keywords for the quadruplicities, and the signs which
exhibit them:

Movable:

Initiating, quick, enterprising, readily engaged with others and the world, focused on the moment. (But can lead to hastiness, pushiness, and provocation.)

- **Aries** (movable fire): proclaiming self, asserting personal needs, triumph, single-minded, avoiding details and reflection
- **Cancer** (movable water): reaches out to nurture, desires and provokes emotional responses and connections
- **Libra** (movable air): engages and initiates on the basis of ideas and expression and beauty
- **Capricorn** (movable earth): leads by taking on responsibility, focusing on tasks and rules, needs organization and tradition

Fixed:

Patient, enduring, organized, methodical, often focusing on oneself and concentrating power from within. (But can stubbornly resist reasonable compromise or simpler solutions, and resent pressure from others.)

- **Leo** (fixed fire): confident, inner vitality, strong-willed, working long and hard to be recognized
- **Scorpio** (fixed water): interested in emotional complexity, holds onto emotions for a long time, sensitive to issues of weakness and insecurity, secretive, cut off from others
- **Aquarius** (fixed air): interested in organized ideas and mental structure, intelligibility and explanation, more emotionally detached and aloof, thoughtful
- **Taurus** (fixed earth): needing creature comforts, purposeful and patient, holding on, not wasting energy

Common:

Adaptability and versatility, comfortable with change, interested in details, observant and curious. (But can lead to indecision, feeling overwhelmed, easily bored or losing interest.)

- **Sagittarius** (common fire): multifaceted pursuit of truth, exploring and risk-taking, enthusiastic, can be sidetracked or change mind while still feeling certain
- **Pisces** (common water): emotionally observant, tendency to merge with others' emotional issues, humane, inconsistent

- **Gemini** (common air): curious and exploring, emotionally light, surface, wants interplay of information and expression and freedom
- **Virgo** (common earth): needs practical functioning, efficiency and neatness, clarity, making things fit together, concrete facts focused on results

But as there are four elements and three quadruplicities, there will not be an easy or perfect match between common ritual tools or symbols like incence (which naturally fits Air), and the quadruplicities. Nevertheless, we have assigned certain emblems to them even though their use overlaps with the Elements. So, in the Elemental rituals we will have a Fire Candle for consecration, but will also have a candle on the Altar to represent the movable aspect of each Element. Fire (that is, a candle flame) is a good representation of a movable Sign, as is water for fixed Signs and incense for common Signs. Fire is a catalyst; water in a motionless state is heavy and inert; incense changes form according to what is influencing it, *i.e.*, when unlit it is in solid form but when lit, it transforms into smoke.

Elemental Pentagrams

We have placed diagrams in the rites which show the proper way to draw the Elemental and Spirit Pentagrams. Starting with the number "1," draw in the direction of the arrows to finish with number "5." This will make a complete Pentagram. When the symbols of the Elements and Spirit are placed upon the Pentagram, it looks like this:

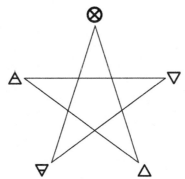

Figure 16: Elemental symbols on the Pentagram

The sign of the Pentagram represents the Four Elements (the triangles) crowned with Spirit (the wheel). You will notice that the triangles with lines in their middles indicate an Element that is a mixture or culmination of the others. The upward triangles indicate a projective energy. The downward triangles indicate a receptive energy. Therefore, the Pentagram is an illustration of the Hermetic Principle of Polarity. As you will see from the instructions in the rituals, the movement from point to point is related to the Element involved: for example, the Invoking Earth Pentagram begins from the Spirit point, and moves *towards* the Earth point. The other Pentagrams work in much the same way.

The Four Elemental Rituals

You may perform the four rituals in whatever order you choose. Nevertheless, we recommend that you start with Earth and then work through Water, Air, and Fire, as this is a standard ascending order of the Elements, and imitates a vertical ascension from lower types of reality to higher ones. Perform the Spirit working only after completing the first four, since the Spirit ritual requires the consecrated objects of the Elemental workings for a Feast of Spirit: a meal ritually eaten so as to take the consecrated Elements into the physical body.

Remember, if you find it hard to carry this book around during a ritual, then photocopy the relevant pages and use those instead.

A Brief Synopsis of the Elemental Rituals

We have designed these rituals to have only a few, well-defined parts. Each ritual has an Opening and a Closing, which are rather simple and short. In between these are three "Advancements," stages of the ritual formula. If doing the whole ritual at once seems challenging, then practice each part by itself until you feel comfortable. Remember, it's always good for beginners to practice an unfamiliar ritual first in street clothes, and without a ceremonial voice or attitude.

You will need the following supplies:

General Ritual Items

Temple space: A clean, comfortable space large enough to move around in, with room to comfortably put ritual objects in different places. If you need to clear your living room or even a 6x6 space at the foot of your bed, do that. The space should allow you to feel special and calm, without distractions.

Clothing: Clean, light, simple clothing, preferably something used only for devotional practices—not everyday street clothes.

Lighting: Lowered, but enough to read by. Have a few candles lit, preferably in one or more quarters of the room.

Altar: A small Altar, table, or other stable platform, short enough to be able to see the surface when seated. It should be big enough to hold the Tarot cards, Candles, and other itsems are listed below.

Spirit Lantern: For the Feast of Spirit, a lantern or candle holder with a white candle.

Altar cloth: Black or Green (Earth),[29] Blue (Water), Yellow (Air), Red (Fire), White (Spirit), preferably big enough to cover the surface of the Altar.

Tarot card: On the Altar, either *The Hanged Man* (Water), *The Fool* (Air), or *Judgment* (Fire). Earth has no card.

Incense/Water: A cup of water and stick of incense (lit) in the East, for purification and consecration. (These are not the *Elemental* Incenses, which will be on the Altar.)

Music: Suitable ambient music for the Element, including the forthcoming soundtracks by MjDawn.

Elemental Objects to Consecrate. Each ritual consecrates an object which embodies the Elements:

Earth consecration: Salt, in a dish.

Water consecration: A small vial of water, some of which will be poured into a larger Chalice of juice or wine.

Air consecration: Incense (preferably a stick or cone).

Fire consecration: Candle (preferably red).

---

[29] We typically use black, but many people prefer to use green for Earth, so we will use that color in the rituals.

Emblems of the Quadruplicities. Each ritual also employs three extra objects which stand for the quadruplicities:

Movable Signs: Candle (preferably white, to avoid confusion with the Fire Candle).

Fixed Signs: Cup of water.

Common Signs: Incense (lit), preferably a stick or cone.

Temple Arrangement

The Elemental Temple has the Altar in the center, with the extra cup of water and incense (for purifications and consecrations) in the East. Place a convenient seat just West of the Altar (or set it aside until it is needed), and arrange the surface of the Altar as described below.

In the Elemental rituals (and temporarily, in some others), the Elements themselves and their consecrated objects (the Fire Candle, *et cetera*) are associated with the cardinal directions in the following way:

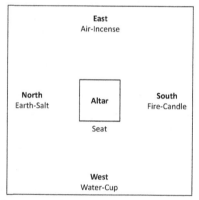

Figure 17: Elemental Temple, with Elemental attributions

That is to say, whenever we focus on a particular Element, we will focus upon that cardinal direction: thus when working with Earth, we will be especially interested in the North. Please note: this does not mean that the consecrated objects themselves should be distributed into these parts of the room as you perform the Elemental rituals—the diagram only illustrates the Elemental *associations* with the quarters. In the Feast of Spirit ritual, they will indeed be placed there, but in later rituals they will be given Zodiacal attributions, which will put them in different places.

Altar Arrangement

In each ritual, the quadruplicity emblems are placed on the Altar, in the form of a triangle whose apex points in the appropriate cardinal direction. The Elemental object to be consecrated is placed in the center. Please do not get confused by the fact that there is more than one of the same object. The Elements themselves are not identical with the quadruplicities, and it might be a good idea to have certain colors or scents to differentiate them. For example, since we consecrate a Fire Candle but in every ritual also have a Movable Candle, it would be a good idea to make the Fire Candle Red, and the Movable Candle some other color (probably white). Or you might want a special Airy Incense that reminds you of Elemental Air, but use some other, flexible incense for the Common Incense. As an illustration, here is the Altar arrangement for the Earth Consecration:

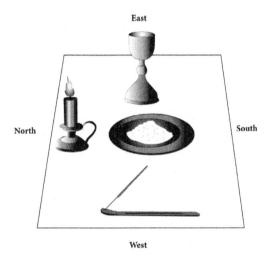

Altar arrangement for Salt consecration

You can see that the salt to be consecrated is in the center. Since Elemental Earth is associated with the North, the triangle of the quadruplicity emblems points North: the Movable Candle is the apex, and the other two emblems form the base. These show the three styles or modes of the energy of Earth, which will later be explicitly associated with zodiacal Signs: Capricorn (movable), Taurus (fixed), and Virgo (common).

Now let's turn to the stages of the rituals:

Preparation and Opening

After a short meditation, the room is ritually banished of unwanted influences, using a "banishing" Pentagram (see the diagram in each ritual). Then, the water and incense in the East are used to purify and consecrate the Temple in all four directions. The purpose of all of this is to create clean, empty, and devoted ritual vessel for the work to come.

Note that we make a cross over our bodies with the water and incense, as well: this is not a Christian cross, but a Qabalistic one. It represents Spirit (vertical line) manifesting in matter (horizontal). It also suggests just the sort of vertical and horizontal healing and balance that we have mentioned several times already: the power descending through the body from above, is balanced and maintained in the body by the horizontal line.

Second, the invoking Pentagram of the Element is created, which brings us and the Temple in contact with the powers of that Element. The Pentagram is drawn in the appropriate quarter of the room, visualized in its appropriate color. This completes the opening.

First Advancement

In the First Advancement, we begin to call on the quadruplicities and infuse the Element with them. Make an invoking Elemental Pentagram over the Altar in order to bring the power of Element to the Altar itself. Then draw a circle over each one of the quadruplicity emblems, tracing the symbol of the relevant zodiacal Sign, and visualize these sinking into each emblem. Then draw a line from this emblem to the Elemental item being consecrated, and do the same thing with the other emblems.

Second Advancement

Then, we perform a contemplative meditation on the Tarot card that pertains to the Element. After reading a brief explanation the card's meaning, visualize yourself inside of the card and note any thoughts or impressions that arise. In our rituals, Earth has no card; instead, perform a meditation on Earth as manifestation and crystallization, and visualize yourself in a crystal of salt. If you do not have a Tarot deck, we offer alternative visualizations. Of course, you are free to use these even with a Tarot meditation. If you like, record yourself reading the Tarot meditation beforehand, and listen to it as you visualize.

Third Advancement

Finally, the consecrated Element is taken into the body through the physical senses. That is, the warmth of the Fire is felt, the Water is tasted, Air is smelled, and Earth is likewise tasted. The ingestion of magical substances is a very old practice, certainly going back to ancient Egypt. The idea is that the integration and assimilation of a magical substance is completed by the act of swallowing and digesting it. In the *Pyramid Texts* it is written that the magician-king eats the magic of the gods and "enjoys himself when their magic is in his belly."[30] Only then may the king make his way through the spiritual world. This subject is reiterated in other sections of the *Pyramid Texts*, as for instance in this passage: "I will ascend and rise up to heaven. My magic is in my belly. I will ascend and rise up to heaven."[31]

Closing

To conclude, any spiritual beings or forces attracted to the ceremony are told to depart, and the purification and consecration is performed once again. The ritual concludes with the banishing Pentagram, returning the Elemental force whence it came.

The Ritual of a Feast of Spirit

The Ritual of the Feast of Spirit is rather different from the previous four. Here, the Elements are attributed to the different parts of the human being: Earth-body, Air-intellect, Water-soul and emotions, and Fire-higher inspiration and urges. While each one has a kind of integrity on its own, each is also only one Elemental phase of the life of Spirit. Ultimately we want to search for the One which unifies all things, and so they are ritually separated here, to show their inferior status as individual parts of the person below the level of Spirit. After a visualization of Divine Light to symbolize Spirit, the Elements are then reunited and ritually eaten, being absorbed and harmonized together in the context of realizing Spirit.

This ritual illustrates an important idea, related to the "double movement" which we mentioned in the Introduction to the book, as well as the vertical and horizontal concepts of healing. On the one hand, lower realities like the Elements receive their being from higher ones, from Divine Light and Spirit. In the changeable, material world, and in our human soul, each Elemental

---

[30] Naydler, *Pyramid Texts* Utterance 403, 411.
[31] *Ibid*, Utterance 1313.

type or faculty seems to conflict with the others, each sometimes wanting to control our actions and minds. This leads to confusion, imbalance, and unhappiness. But when we follow that spiritual impulse upwards, we must do two things. First, we must distinguish and purify each one separately: this is shown in the previous Elemental rituals, as well as through the ritual separation in this one. This separation allows us to clarify our relation to Spirit. Second, we must sacrifice their individuality and separateness by harmonizing and blending them together. But when doing so, the Elements are not really destroyed. Rather, together they become more than the sum of their parts, and we are able to realize the unifying Spirit which is responsible for them all. So although Spirit is always there, it is rarely evident to us until we perform these tasks on our personal Quest, and harmoniously subordinate the lower realities within Spirit, and in relation to the higher realities. This allows them to be more healthy, functional seats for the realization of higher Spirit in a life of happiness and personal enrichment.

Temple arrangement

On the Altar are placed the previously-consecrated Elemental objects: to the East, the Air Incense and the Tarot card *The Fool*; to the South, the Fire Candle and the Tarot card *Judgment*; to the West, a Chalice of wine or water containing a few drops of the previously consecrated Water, and the Tarot card *The Hanged Man*; to the North, the Earth Salt, with a piece of bread.

In the center of the Altar is a Spirit Lantern with a lit white candle, or a clear votive holder with a white candle. The lantern, a device which brings the Light to the Darkness, symbolizes Spirit. Water and incense are in the East for the purification and consecration of the Temple space.

Preparation and Opening

After a short meditation, prepare the Temple space as usual with the banishing Pentagram, purification by water, and consecration by fire (or rather, incense). Then make two invoking Spirit Pentagrams, drawing the powers of Spirit into the Temple space: the two Pentagrams represent impulses from both the active and passive energy of the Elements. Unlike other rituals, these invocations are performed in the center of the space, to indicate that Spirit is at the sacred center. You will face East as you form them, which is traditional to the art of magic.

The First Advancement

Trace invoking Pentagrams of Spirit over the Altar, to bring Spirit in relation to the Altar itself. Then separate the Elements and distribute them into their appropriate quarters (see diagram above). Again, this act symbolizes sacrificing of the personal self in the quest for the Divine Spirit. Return to the Altar and make the invoking Spirit Pentagrams over the Spirit Lantern, infusing it with this power.

Second Advancement

Sit, surrounding and permeating yourself with the Light. As your body fills with Light, visualize your physical body disappearing, so that all that is left is your consciousness, dwelling in the midst of Light.

The Third Advancement

Then, take the Spirit Lantern to each direction, beginning with the North (Earth, Bread, Salt). In each case, bless the Elemental emblem with the appropriate Spirit and Elemental Pentagrams, and bring it back to the Altar for unification.

Fourth Advancement

Now that the Elements are rejoined, perform an invocation requesting the gifts of the Elements while drawing the proper zodiacal symbols over each. Draw the Spirit Wheel over the Lantern while giving thanks and praise to Divine Spirit. Visualize the Light of the Lantern flowing over and blessing the individual Elements of your own being.

Fifth Advancement

Ritually consume the substance of the consecrated, reunited, magical Elements.

The Closing

Finally, perform the usual Closing, with a banishing Pentagram, license to depart, and purification and consecration.

A Ritual Consecration of Salt for Elemental Earth

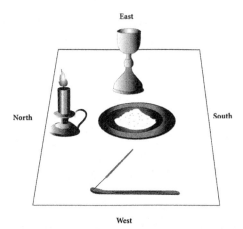

Figure 18: Altar arrangement for Salt consecration

Temple arrangement: Elemental Temple (see Introduction).
Altar cloth: Green (or Black).
Elemental emblem: Dish of Salt, in center of Altar.
Quadruplicity emblems: In a triangle pointing North: a Candle, water, and Earthy incense.
Tarot card: (None).
Incense, Water: In East, with incense lit.
Music: Suitable ambient or background music.

Preparation for the Rite

Sit for a moment at the Altar and contemplate the rite to come. Let the cares and worries of the day dissipate. ★ Focus on the top of your head and form a mental image of a ray of White Light permeating your body through the top of your head. Visualize this Light descending through the center of your body to your feet. Your body is now filled with Light. ★ Inhale and exhale this Light through the pores of your body until it is pulsing in and around you. ★ Imagine the Light extending from your body and filling the room. See the Light creating a barrier separating the room from the outer world. Let nothing exist for you outside of this special time and place.

OPENING

Go to the East of the Temple, and face the East.

Aspirant

I have come to this Temple to perform a ceremony of consecration upon this Salt that will become a Sacred Vessel of Earth. It is my sacred intention to consecrate this Earth as a manifesting link between the Spiritual World and my human soul, that I may more fully comprehend and thereby commune with the Powers of Earth. So mote it be. *Make the Banishing Pentagram to the East.*

Aspirant

Through the power of the banishing Pentagram, I expel all undesirable influences from this Temple. I say unto you now, depart and go in peace!

Make the Banishing Pentagram also in the South, the West, and the North. Return to the East.

Take up the Cup of Water and sprinkle three times in the East, then do the same in the South, the West, and the North. Return to the East. Dip your finger in the Cup and touch your forehead, then sprinkle Water toward your feet, and touch your right and left shoulders.

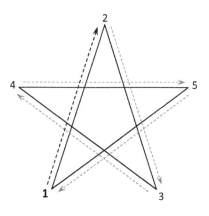

Banishing Elemental Pentagram

Aspirant

I am purified; the Temple is purified; all is purified by the Lustral Waters. *Replace the Cup.*

Take up the incense and wave it three times in the East, then do the same in the South, the West, and the North. Return to the East. Wave the incense toward your forehead, your feet and your right and left shoulders.

Aspirant

I am consecrated; the Temple is consecrated; all is consecrated by Holy Fire. *Replace the Incense.*

Aspirant

(*Facing center of Temple*) **Hear me, four quarters of the World, for I call out to thee! Grant me the strength to walk the hidden path and discover secret knowledge. Give me your eyes to see and your wisdom to understand, that I may be like you. Grant me your powers that I may command the powers of Earth.**

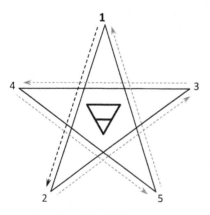

Invoking Earth Pentagram

Go to the North. Facing North, draw the green Invoking Earth Pentagram in the air.

Aspirant

In the Divine Name ADONAI (Ah-doh-nye), and in the Name of your great Archangel URIEL, I call forth the Powers of Earth. Yea, I seek thee, for I came forth from the primal Elements and to them shall I return. May the blessings of Earth be upon me. May I emulate the fruitful and productive Earth. May the power akin to the steady growth of the mountains move me forward and may the quiet Earth give me rest. O Great Spirits of the North, the manifestation of Spirit in the body, grant me the determination and resolve to keep steady on the Path, the power to manifest the spiritual in the physical, and the practicality to use these gifts for the good of all. I pray that I may be united with you, that your powers may flow through me and be expressed by me. So mote it be.

Visualize the Element as a GREEN light flowing through you, grounding you and giving you a sense of stability.

FIRST ADVANCEMENT

Stand on the Southern side of the Altar, facing North. Turn the color of your aura to GREEN.

Aspirant
In the Divine Name of Earth, ADONAI, and in the Name of its Archangel URIEL, O Great Ones of mystical Earth, give me your hands and your magic power, for I am made as you, by the Powers which formed my soul. Form in my spirit the power and might irresistible to compel the Forces of Elemental Earth to reveal themselves within this Temple, according to my words and aspirations, allowing me to bring them forth in full manifestation and power.

Draw the invoking Earth Pentagram in the air over the Altar, visualizing it in a vibrant green light.

Aspirant

Earth is called the Living Salt, because Salt is an essential nutrient of physical life. Physical life cannot endure without salt, and Spirit cannot manifest itself but ultimately through the physical. Earth is the body, the Temple of Divine Spirit, the container of mind, soul and spirit. It is the vehicle through which the Three Elements of Fire, Water and Air act in the material world. It is the outer shell of the Mysteries, the Temple and the Sacred Space, the forests and the fields; all that manifests from the Divine Light. With the power of Earth, I bless this Altar.

Visualize the green light of the Pentagram flowing into and charging the triangle and Salt.

♑   ♉   ♍

Capricorn Taurus   Virgo

Draw a circle around the Movable Candle. Trace the symbol of Capricorn in it, and visualize it sinking into the Candle. Draw a line from the Movable Candle to the Earth Salt, visualizing the energy of the flame flowing into and charging it.

Aspirant

Into this Salt I place the powers of movable Earth, the Sign of Capricorn, the force of Pragmatism. This energy will infuse this Salt with the qualities of ambition and practicality. Determination, accomplishment, authority, and self-control, shall be imbued in this vessel.

Make a circle around the Cup and draw the symbol of Taurus in it. Visualize the symbol sinking into the Cup, and draw a line from the Cup to the Earth Salt, visualizing the energy flowing into and charging it.

Aspirant

Into this Salt I place the powers of fixed Earth, the Sign of Taurus, the force of Preservation. This energy will infuse this Salt with the qualities of diligence and focus. Productiveness, stability, material pleasure, and perception, shall be imbued in this vessel.

Make a circle around the Incense and draw the symbol of Virgo in it. Visualize the symbol sinking into the Incense, and draw a line from the Incense to the Earth Salt, visualizing the energy flowing into and charging it.

Aspirant

Into this Salt I place the powers of common Earth, the Sign of Virgo, the force of Precision. This energy will infuse this Salt with the qualities of analysis and conservation. Service, regulation, and discrimination shall be imbued in this vessel.

Visualize all of the energies of the Triangle flowing into the Earth Salt, and hold the Salt aloft.

Aspirant

In the Divine Name ADONAI, and in the Name of the great Archangel URIEL, behold, all Powers of Earth now present in this Temple, I have consecrated this Salt with the forces that dwell in the realm of Earth. This Salt *shall* be for me a solid and tangible link, true and perfect, with all the Powers of Divine Manifestation that live within your realm. Empower this blessed Salt to be a perfect instrument of Materialization for the evolution of my Soul, and that through its use the Powers of the Divine shall manifest within me and be expressed in this Temple, and in the physical world. So mote it be.

SECOND ADVANCEMENT

Be seated, and contemplate the nature of the Element of Earth:

Aspirant
I am a child of the Elements, and Earth is my body. I am manifestation, and I dwell in the physical world. Through me filters the forces of the universe, for I am a part of the One, the Divine Creator of all things. My body is but an outward reflection of all that precedes it, for I come from the heavenly stars. I am accumulation. I am summation. I am established as the earthly Temple of Divine Spirit.

Close your eyes and visualize yourself in the center of a salt crystal. Feel its hardness and see its crystalline structure. Note any thoughts or sensations that arise. Before you end this visualization, make an offering of your own Light to the Powers of Earth.

Alternative Meditation

Visualize your body in front of you, as a three-dimensional image. See it turn to a vivid green, and then the other Elemental colors glowing around its aura, like concentric shells: the yellow light of Air in a luminous and shimmering yellow glow, then the blue light of Water flowing around it and illuminating your aura in a lovely and soft blue glow, then the red light of Fire flaming around that in a radiant and vibrant red glow, and finally the brilliant white light of Spirit, illuminating the outer edges.

You now have three rings of color surrounding your green aura, in order: yellow, blue, and red. Surrounding these is the white of Spirit. You have become concentric circles of Light. Make an offering of your own Light to the Powers of Earth before you leave this meditation.

THIRD ADVANCEMENT

Take up a small amount of the Earth Salt.

<u>Aspirant</u>
In the Divine Name ADONAI and in the Name of URIEL, the great Archangel of Earth, I now take into myself the Powers of Earth, that we may become as one.

Place a small amount of the Salt on your tongue. Through its taste, visualize the properties of Earth permeating your body, and the Powers of Earth crystallizing within you.

<u>Aspirant</u>
This consecrated Earth will serve as an agent of renewal and rebirth for my entire self: Body, Soul and Spirit, that I may prove a worthy vessel for the Divine Light. Let it be for me a true link with the Spiritual World, that through its use the Divine will manifest from its Source down through the levels of my essential being. Let this consecrated Earth create in me a committed heart and an awareness of the Divine Plan; and as a symbol of manifestation, grant it the power to aid my spiritual rebirth. Through such transformation, I will ever pursue the Pathway of Light and thus be better fit to aid my fellow humanity.

CLOSING

Go to the East and face the center of the room.

Aspirant

I now release any spirits that may have been attracted to this ceremony. Go in peace to your abodes and habitations and go with the blessings of ADONAI and URIEL.

Purify and consecrate the Temple and your body with the water and incense, as in the Opening. Banish with the banishing Pentagram in all four quarters, as in the Opening. Return to the East.

Aspirant

I now declare this ritual duly completed. So mote it be.

Extinguish the candles.

A Ritual Consecration of a Vial
for Elemental Water

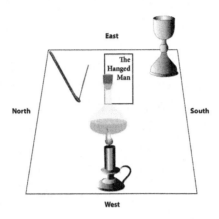

Figure 19: Altar arrangement for Water consecration

Temple arrangement: Elemental Temple (see Introduction).
Altar cloth: Blue.
Elemental emblem: Vial of water (on Altar), cup of wine/juice (to side).
Quadruplicity emblems: In a triangle pointing West: a Candle, water, and Watery incense.
Tarot card: *The Hanged Man.*
Incense, Water: In East, with incense lit.
Music: Suitable ambient or background music.

Preparation for the Rite

Sit for a moment at the Altar and contemplate the rite to come. Let the cares and worries of the day dissipate. ★ Focus on the top of your head and form a mental image of a ray of White Light permeating your body through the top of your head. Visualize this Light descending through the center of your body to your feet. Your body is now filled with Light. ★ Inhale and exhale this Light through the pores of your body until it is pulsing in and around you. ★ Imagine the Light extending from your body and filling the room. See the Light creating a barrier separating the room from the outer world. Let nothing exist for you outside of this special time and place.

Opening

Go to the East of the Temple, and face the East.

Aspirant

I have come to this Temple to perform a ceremony of consecration upon the contents of a Sacred Vessel of Water. It is my sacred intention to consecrate this Water as a purifying link between the Spiritual World and my human soul, that I may more fully comprehend and thereby commune with the Powers of Water. So mote it be. *Make the Banishing Pentagram to the East.*

Aspirant

Through the power of the banishing Pentagram, I expel all undesirable influences from this Temple. I say unto you now, depart and go in peace!

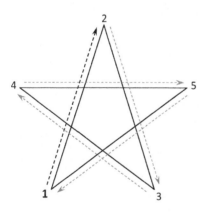

Banishing Elemental Pentagram

Make the Banishing Pentagram also in the South, the West, and the North. Return to the East.

Take up the Cup of Water and sprinkle three times in the East, then do the same in the South, the West, and the North. Return to the East. Dip your finger in the Cup and touch your forehead, then sprinkle Water toward your feet, and touch your right and left shoulders.

<u>Aspirant</u>

I am purified; the Temple is purified; all is purified by the Lustral Waters. *Replace the Cup.*

Take up the incense and wave it three times in the East, then do the same in the South, the West, and the North. Return to the East. Wave the incense toward your forehead, your feet and your right and left shoulders.

<u>Aspirant</u>

I am consecrated; the Temple is consecrated; all is consecrated by Holy Fire. *Replace the Incense.*

<u>Aspirant</u>

(*Facing center of Temple*) **Hear me, four quarters of the World, for I call out to thee! Grant me the strength to walk the hidden path and discover secret knowledge. Give me your eyes to see and your wisdom to understand, that I may be like you. Grant me your powers that I may command the powers of Water.**

Go to the West. Facing West, draw the blue Invoking Water Pentagram in the air.

<u>Aspirant</u>

In the Divine Name, EL, and in the Name of your great Archangel, GABRIEL, I call forth the Powers of Water. Yea, I seek thee for I came forth from the primal Waters and to them shall I return, like a drop of rain falling in the

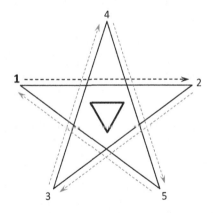

Invoking Water Pentagram

ocean. May the blessings of Water be upon me. May the mighty storms strengthen me. May the flowing waters cleanse me, and may the still waters bring me peace. O Great Spirits of the West, the deep matrix, the womb of all life, grant me your power to dissolve boundaries, to release what is held fast, to cleanse and to heal. I pray that I may be united with you, that your powers may flow through me and be expressed by me.

Visualize the Element as a BLUE light flowing through you, cleansing you and giving you a sense of peace.

First Advancement

Stand on the Eastern side of the Altar, facing West. Turn the color of your aura to BLUE.

Aspirant
In the Divine Name of Water, EL, and in the Name of its Archangel GABRIEL, O Great Ones of mystical Water, give me your hands and your magic power, for I am made as you, who formed my soul. Pour into my spirit the power and might irresistible to compel the Forces of Elemental Water to manifest within this Temple, according to my words and aspirations, allowing me to bring them forth in full manifestation and power. So mote it be.

Draw the invoking Water Pentagram in the air over the Altar, visualizing it in a vibrant blue light.

Aspirant

Water is called the Water of Life or the Living Water, for to the spiritual desert of the Soul, Living Water brings Life: it is the current of the Creative Word flowing outward into manifestation. For although one may seek the Divine Light in church and Temple, in reality it is within, in the precious inner Water of spiritual desire, which is the human Soul containing the Light of Spirit. Spiritual Water is the Ocean of Infinite Perfection, the vastness wherein all the rivers of Being seek to lose themselves, and within which are ever renewed. With the power of Water, I bless this Altar.

Visualize the blue light of the Pentagram flowing into and charging the triangle and Water.

Draw a circle around the Movable Candle. Trace the symbol of Cancer in it, and visualize it sinking into the Candle. Draw a line from the Movable Candle to the vial of Water, visualizing the energy of the flame flowing into and charging it.

♋ ♏ ♓

Cancer Scorpio Pisces

Aspirant

Into this vial I place the powers of movable Water, the Sign of Cancer, the force of Nurturing. This energy will infuse this vessel with the qualities necessary for growth and security, and encourage a deepening awareness of the emotions. Protection, sensitivity, and a sense of belonging shall be imbued in this vessel.

Make a circle around the Cup and draw the symbol of Scorpio in it. Visualize the symbol sinking into the Cup, and draw a line from the

Cup to the vial of Water, visualizing the energy flowing into and charging it.

Aspirant

Into this vial I place the powers of fixed Water, the Sign of Scorpio, the force of Disintegration. This energy will infuse this vessel with the qualities of transformation, determination and self -control. Intensity, power, secrecy, and depth of passion, shall be imbued in this vessel.

Make a circle around the Incense and draw the symbol of Pisces in it. Visualize the symbol sinking into the Incense, and draw a line from the Incense to the vial of Water, visualizing the energy flowing into and charging it.

Aspirant

Into this vial I place the powers of common Water, the Sign of Pisces, the force of the Visionary. This energy will infuse this vessel with the qualities of mysticism and imagination, and the power to move my soul into the spiritual realm. Creativity, the dissolution of boundaries, and the sense of oneness, shall be imbued in this vessel.

Visualize all of the energies of the Triangle flowing into the vial of Water, and hold the vial aloft.

Aspirant

In the Divine Name, EL, and in the Name of the great Archangel GABRIEL, behold, all Powers of Water now present in this Temple, I have consecrated this vial with the forces that dwell in the realm of Water. This vial of Water *shall* be for me a solid and tangible link, true and perfect, with all the Powers of Purity and Divine Love that live within your realm. Em-

power this blessed **Water** to be a perfect instrument of **Purity** for the evolution of my **Soul**, and that through its use the **Love** of the **Divine** shall descend into my heart and be expressed in this **Temple** and in the physical world. So mote it be.

SECOND ADVANCEMENT

Be seated, and contemplate the Tarot card *The Hanged Man*:

Aspirant
Spirit of the Mighty Waters, you of the Divine Death: the crucified Christ, the slain Osiris, Adonis, Tammuz, Ra, Odin, and Attis, the Dying God on the Tree of Life, the embodiment of sacrifice, death and rebirth, all who die and are resurrected to the greater life. Withdrawal from material life is necessary for the rebirth of all life; the Divine Spark sacrifices itself in the waters of the material universe in the act of becoming manifest. Between the Waters above and the Waters beneath, this is a force of transition. It is a time that cannot pass, for it has never been used and exists in constancy. Worldly things are left behind, and in a state of suspension I must prove myself worthy of continuing along the path. Like the Grail Knight, a trial must be passed, a choice or sacrifice made.

Close your eyes and visualize yourself in the place of *The Hanged Man*. Note any thoughts or sensations that arise. Before you end this visualization, make an offering of your own Light to the Powers of Water.

Alternative Meditation

Visualize yourself floating in blue, flowing water. Feel the water caress your skin, lift your hair, and move your body to and fro in its soft currents. Now visualize and feel the water move *through* you, cleansing you in body, soul, mind, and spirit. Your entire body becomes fluid, and merges with the water around you. Visualize yourself *as* flowing water, and watch as you flow with the currents, yielding to hard surfaces, flowing over and around them. You are languid and drift with the current of the water, for you and the water are one. You have become Elemental Water. Make an offering of your own Light to the Powers of Water before you leave this meditation.

THIRD ADVANCEMENT

Place a few drops of the consecrated Water into the cup of wine or juice.

Aspirant
In the Divine Name EL, and in the Name of GABRIEL, the great Archangel of Water, I now take into myself the Powers of Water, that we may become as one.

Drink the wine or juice, visualizing the Powers of Water flowing through your body.

Aspirant
This consecrated Water will serve as an agent of purification for the cleansing for my entire self: Body, Soul and Spirit, that I may prove a worthy vessel for the Divine Light. Let it be for me a true link with the Spiritual World, that through its use

Divine Love will flow from its Source down through the levels of my essential being. Let this consecrated Water create in me a clean heart and an awareness of Divine Love; and as a symbol of baptism, grant it the power to aid my spiritual rebirth. Through such transformation, I will ever pursue the Pathway of Light and thus be better fit to aid my fellow humanity. So mote it be.

CLOSING

Go to the East and face the center of the room.

Aspirant
I now release any spirits that may have been attracted to this ceremony. Go in peace to your abodes and habitations and go with the blessings of EL and GABRIEL.

Purify and consecrate the Temple and your body with the water and incense, as in the Opening. Banish with the banishing Pentagram in all four quarters, as in the Opening. Return to the East.

Aspirant
I now declare this ritual duly completed. So mote it be.

Extinguish the candles.

A RITUAL CONSECRATION OF INCENSE FOR ELEMENTAL AIR

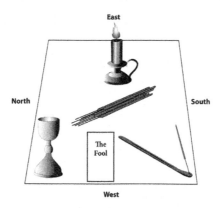

Figure 20: Altar arrangement for Incense consecration

Temple arrangement: Elemental Temple (see Introduction).
Altar cloth: Yellow.
Elemental emblem: Frankincense/Airy Incense, in center of Altar.
Quadruplicity emblems: In a triangle pointing East: a Candle, water, and Airy incense.
Tarot card: *The Fool.*
Incense, Water: In East, with incense lit.
Music: Suitable ambient or background music.

PREPARATION FOR THE RITE

Sit for a moment at the Altar and contemplate the rite to come. Let the cares and worries of the day dissipate. ★ Focus on the top of your head and form a mental image of a ray of White Light permeating your body through the top of your head. Visualize this Light descending through the center of your body to your feet. Your body is now filled with Light. ★ Inhale and exhale this Light through the pores of your body until it is pulsing in and around you. ★ Imagine the Light extending from your body and filling the room. See the Light creating a barrier separating the room from the outer world. Let nothing exist for you outside of this special time and place.

OPENING

Go to the East of the Temple, and face the East.

Aspirant

I have come to this Temple to perform a ceremony of conse-cration upon this Incense that will become a Sacred Vessel of Air. It is my sacred intention to consecrate this Air as an intel-lectual link between the Spiritual World and my human soul, that I may more fully comprehend and thereby commune with the Powers of Air. So mote it be. *Make the Banishing Penta-gram to the East.*

Aspirant

Through the power of the banishing Pentagram, I expel all undesirable influences from this Temple. I say unto you now, depart and go in peace!

Make the Banishing Pentagram also in the South, the West, and the North. Return to the East.

Take up the Cup of Water and sprinkle three times in the East, then do the same in the South, the West, and the North. Return to the East. Dip your finger in the Cup and touch your fore-head, then sprinkle Water to-ward your feet, and touch your right and left shoulders.

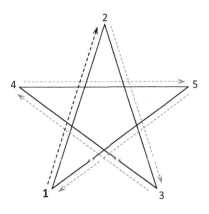

Banishing Elemental Pentagram

Aspirant

I am purified; the Temple is purified; all is purified by the **Lustral Waters.** *Replace the Cup.*

Take up the incense and wave it three times in the East, then do the same in the South, the West, and the North. Return to the East. Wave the incense toward your forehead, your feet and your right and left shoulders.

Aspirant

I am consecrated; the Temple is consecrated; all is consecrated by Holy Fire. *Replace the Incense.*

Aspirant

(Facing center of Temple) Hear me, four quarters of the World, for I call out to thee! Grant me the strength to walk the hidden path and discover secret knowledge. Give me your eyes to see and your wisdom to understand, that I may be like you. Grant me your powers that I may command the powers of Air.

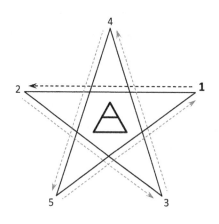

Invoking Air Pentagram

Go to the East. Facing East, draw the yellow Invoking Air Pentagram in the air.

Aspirant

In the Divine Name YHVH (Yod Heh Vav Heh) and in the Name of your great Archangel RAPHAEL, I call forth the Powers of Air. Yea, I seek thee for I came forth from the primal Airs and to them shall I return, like a breath in the Heavenly Ether. May the blessings of Air be upon me.

May the inner Air enlighten me. May the rushing Air enliven my mind, and may the quiet Air lead me inward. O Great Spirits of the East, Breath of Spirit in the soul, grant me the curiosity to ask the relevant questions, the power to perceive and to know hidden things, and the intuition and foresight to use this knowledge wisely. I pray that I may be united with you, that your powers may flow through me and be expressed by me. So mote it be.

Visualize the Element as a YELLOW light flowing through you, refreshing and revitalizing your mind.

FIRST ADVANCEMENT

Stand on the Western side of the Altar, facing East. Turn the color of your aura to YELLOW.

<u>Aspirant</u>
In the Divine Name of Air, YHVH, and in the Name of its Archangel RAPHAEL, O Great Ones of mystical Air, give me your hands and your magic power, for I am made as you, who formed my soul. Revitalize my spirit with the power and might irresistible, to compel the Forces of Elemental Air to manifest within this Temple, according to my words and aspirations, allowing me to bring them forth in full manifestation and power.

Draw the invoking Air Pentagram in the air over the Altar, visualizing it in a vibrant yellow light.

Aspirant

Air is called the Breath of Life, and the Divine Breath is the Source of all Life. Just as physical life cannot exist without air or breath, the essence of human life, which is Consciousness, cannot exist without Divine Inspiration. Spirit is never joined to a body except through the pathway of a Soul, and it was the Breath of Spirit into the soul that brought consciousness into being. Spirit and Soul create the Mind, and when I see through Mind, I see myself to be all and am present everywhere and in everything. With the power of Air I bless this Altar.

Visualize the yellow light of the Pentagram flowing into and charging the triangle and Incense.

Libra   Aquarius   Gemini

Draw a circle around the Movable Candle. Trace the symbol of Libra in it, and visualize it sinking into the Candle. Draw a line from the Movable Candle to the Air Incense, visualizing the energy of the flame flowing into and charging it.

Aspirant

Into this Incense I place the powers of movable Air, the Sign of Libra, the force of Balance. This energy will infuse this Incense with the qualities of intuition and foresight. Harmony, beauty, equilibrium, and grace, shall be imbued in this vessel.

Make a circle around the Cup and draw the symbol of Aquarius in it. Visualize the symbol sinking into the Cup, and draw a line from the Cup to the Air Incense, visualizing the energy flowing into and charging it.

Aspirant

Into this Incense I place the powers of fixed Air, the Sign of Aquarius, the force of Deep Counsel. This energy will infuse this Incense with the qualities of independence and freedom of thought. Intellect, inspiration, rationality and sound judgment shall be imbued in this vessel.

Make a circle around the Commmon Incense and draw the symbol of Gemini in it. Visualize the symbol sinking into the Air Incense, and draw a line from the Common Incense to the Air Incense, visualizing the energy flowing into and charging it.

Aspirant

Into this Incense I place the powers of common Air, the Sign of Gemini, the force of the Inquirer. This energy will infuse this Incense with the qualities of investigation and curiosity. Swift action, the ability to change, communication, and expressive speech shall be imbued in this vessel.

Visualize all of the energies of the Triangle flowing into the Air Incense, and hold the Incense aloft.

Aspirant

In the Divine Name YHVH (Yod Heh Vav Heh) and in the Name of the great Archangel RAPHAEL, behold, all Powers of Air now present in this Temple, that I have consecrated this Incense with the forces that dwell in the realm of Air. This Incense *shall* be for me a solid and tangible link, true and perfect, with all the Powers of Divine Thought and Wisdom that live within your realm. Empower this blessed Incense to be a perfect instrument of Mind for the evolution of my Soul, and that through its use the Inspiration of the Divine shall de-

scend into my heart and be expressed in this Temple and in the physical world. So mote it be.

SECOND ADVANCEMENT

Be seated, and contemplate the Tarot card *The Fool*:

Aspirant

Spirit of Ether, fashioned from the Limitless Light, you are the life-breath from which comes First Thought. You are Harpocrates, the Babe in the Egg of Blue on the Lotus flower of the Nile, the God of Silence, and the Truth found only in Silence. Divine Innocence is your name. You are the Spirit in search of inner experience, quitting reason for childlike wonder. Standing on the precipice and thence stepping into the unknown, you are the beginning and the end, the neither and the otherwise, the betwixt and between, on the threshold linking that which was, to that which will be. Beyond thought, beyond knowing, all that is and all that is not. The beginning that was unknown is now standing on the edge of the Great Mystery, about to step into the world of creation and manifestation.

Close your eyes and visualize yourself in the imagery of the card. Note any thoughts or sensations that arise. Before you end this visualization, make an offering of your own Light to the Powers of Air.

Alternative Meditation

Inhale and exhale deeply with your stomach. Feel the air fill your lungs as you inhale, and then feel your lungs empty again as you exhale. Do this for four breaths. Then as you inhale and exhale, visualize and feel the pores of your body expand. Feel the air permeating your body through its pores. As you continue, your pores become larger and larger, until there is little left of your body but empty space filled with air. You are consciously aware, but your physical body begins to disappear as you become the Element of Air. Feel the weightlessness of your body as Elemental Air. You expand throughout the confines of the room. You fill the room because you are Elemental Air. Make an offering of your own Light to the Powers of Air before you leave this meditation.

THIRD ADVANCEMENT

Light one stick of the consecrated Incense from the Candle on the Altar.

Aspirant
In the Divine Name YHVH and in the Name of RAPHAEL, the great Archangel of Air, I now take into myself the Powers of Air, that we may become as one.

Inhale the scent of the consecrated Incense, and feel the scent permeate your body with its fragrance. Visualize the Powers of Air gently wafting through you.

Aspirant

This consecrated Air will serve as an agent of renewal and rebirth for my entire self: Body, Soul and Spirit, that I may prove a worthy vessel for the Divine Light. Let it be for me a true link with the Spiritual World, that through its use Divine Inspiration will flow from its Source down through the levels of my essential being. Let this consecrated Air create in me a meditative heart and an awareness of Divine Reason; and as a symbol of intellect, grant it the power to aid my spiritual rebirth. Through such transformation, I will ever pursue the Pathway of Light and thus be better fit to aid my fellow humanity.

CLOSING

Go to the East and face the center of the room.

Aspirant

I now release any spirits that may have been attracted to this ceremony. Go in peace to your abodes and habitations and go with the blessings of YOD HEH VAV HEH and RAPHAEL.

Purify and consecrate the Temple and your body with the water and incense, as in the Opening. Banish with the banishing Pentagram in all four quarters, as in the Opening. Return to the East.

Aspirant

I now declare this ritual duly completed. So mote it be.

Extinguish the candles.

A RITUAL CONSECRATION OF A CANDLE FOR ELEMENTAL FIRE

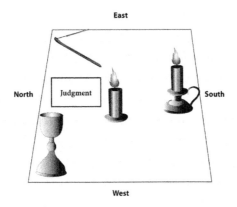

Figure 21: Altar arrangement for Fire Candle consecration

Temple arrangement: Elemental Temple (see Introduction).

Altar cloth: Red.

Elemental emblem: Red Fire Candle, in center of Altar.

Quadruplicity emblems: In a triangle pointing South: a Candle, water, and Fiery incense.

Tarot card: *Judgment*.

Incense, Water: In East, with incense lit.

Music: Suitable ambient or background music.

PREPARATION FOR THE RITE

Sit for a moment at the Altar and contemplate the rite to come. Let the cares and worries of the day dissipate. ★ Focus on the top of your head and form a mental image of a ray of White Light permeating your body through the top of your head. Visualize this Light descending through the center of your body to your feet. Your body is now filled with Light. ★ Inhale and exhale this Light through the pores of your body until it is pulsing in and around you. ★ Imagine the Light extending from your body and filling the room. See the Light creating a barrier separating the room from the outer world. Let nothing exist for you outside of this special time and place.

OPENING

Go to the East of the Temple, and face the East.

Aspirant

I have come to this Temple to perform a ceremony of consecration upon a Candle that will become a Sacred Vessel of Fire. It is my sacred intention to consecrate this Fire as a catalytic link between the Spiritual World and my human soul, that I may more fully comprehend and thereby commune with the Powers of Fire. So mote it be. *Make the Banishing Pentagram to the East.*

Aspirant

Through the power of the banishing Pentagram, I expel all undesirable influences from this Temple. I say unto you now, depart and go in peace!

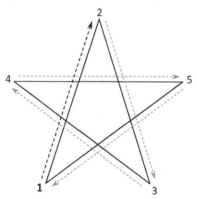

Banishing Elemental Pentagram

Make the Banishing Pentagram also in the South, the West, and the North. Return to the East.

Take up the Cup of Water and sprinkle three times in the East, then do the same in the South, the West, and the North. Return to the East. Dip your finger in the Cup and touch your fore-head, then sprinkle Water toward your feet, and touch your right and left shoulders.

<u>Aspirant</u>

I am purified; the Temple is purified; all is purified by the Lustral Waters. *Replace the Cup.*

Take up the incense and wave it three times in the East, then do the same in the South, the West, and the North. Return to the East. Wave the incense toward your forehead, your feet and your right and left shoulders.

<u>Aspirant</u>

I am consecrated; the Temple is consecrated; all is consecrated by Holy Fire. *Replace the Incense.*

<u>Aspirant</u>

(Facing center of Temple) **Hear me, four quarters of the World, for I call out to thee! Grant me the strength to walk the hidden path and discover secret knowledge. Give me your eyes to see and your wisdom to understand, that I may be like you. Grant me your powers that I may command the powers of Fire.**

Go to the South. Facing the South, draw the red Invoking Fire Pentagram in the air.

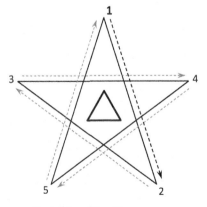

Invoking Fire Pentagram

<u>Aspirant</u>

In the Divine Name ELOHIM (El-oh-heem) and in the Name of your great Archangel MICHAEL, I call forth the Powers of Fire. Yea, I seek thee for I came forth from the primal Fires and to them shall I return, like a flash in the

Heavenly Fires. May the blessings of Fire be upon me. May the inner Fires impassion me. May the raging Fires destroy the dross, and may the hearth Fires sustain me. O Great Spirits of the South, Light of Spirit in the soul, grant me the power to clear and cleanse all places of darkness, burn away all barriers and achieve victory in my endeavors, fulfilling my true potential. I pray that I may be united with you, that your powers may flow through me and be expressed by me. So mote it be.

Visualize the Element as a RED light flowing through you, burning away all impurities and giving you strength.

FIRST ADVANCEMENT

Stand on the Northern side of the Altar, facing South. Turn the color of your aura to RED.

Aspirant

In the Divine Name of Fire, ELOHIM, and in the Name of its Archangel, MICHAEL, O Great Ones of mystical Fire, give me your hands and your magic power, for I am made as you, who formed my soul. Ignite my spirit with the power and might irresistible to compel the Forces of Elemental Fire to manifest within this Temple, according to my words and aspirations, allowing me to bring them forth in full manifestation and power.

Draw the invoking Fire Pentagram in the air over the Altar, visualizing it in a vibrant red light.

Aspirant

Fire is called the Living Fire, the Source of Life, for Life is the hidden Light in humanity. It is the Spiritual Light at the heart of everything that lies within, the Light that shines in the darkness though the darkness comprehends it not. Fire is the dynamic, expansive and fiery principle, the passionate urge which motivates life, the desire for change through vital heat. Fire is the benefit of the World for its power brings forth the flowers, herbs and trees: it is birth, it is resurrection and new life. The act of transformation depends upon the Fires for it is the essential Soul. With the power of Fire I bless this Altar.

Visualize the red light of the Pentagram flowing into and charging the triangle and Candle.

Draw a circle around the Movable Candle. Trace the symbol of Aries in it, and visualize it sinking into the Candle. Draw a line from the Movable Candle to the Fire Candle, visualizing the energy of the flame flowing into and charging it.

♈ ♌ ♐
Aries Leo Sagittarius

Aspirant

Into this Candle I place the powers of movable Fire, the Sign of Aries, the force of the Initiator. This energy will infuse this Candle with the qualities of the fiery impulse and the thrust necessary for new life. New beginnings, the direct release of energy, individualism, will, and self-assertion shall be imbued in this vessel.

Make a circle around the Cup and draw the symbol of Leo in it. Visualize the symbol sinking into the Cup, and draw a line from the

Cup to the Fire Candle, visualizing the energy flowing into and charging it.

Aspirant

Into this Candle I place the powers of fixed Fire, the Sign of Leo, the force of Inner Glory. This energy will infuse this Candle with the qualities of self-awareness, self-confidence, and a great capacity to love. Generosity, charisma, and radiance shall be imbued in this vessel.

Make a circle around the Incense and draw the symbol of Sagittarius in it. Visualize the symbol sinking into the Incense, and draw a line from the Incense to the Fire Candle, visualizing the energy flowing into and charging it.

Aspirant

Into this Candle I place the powers of common Fire, the Sign of Sagittarius, the force of the Adventurer. This energy will infuse this Candle with the qualities of seeking what lies beyond the horizon, answering the ultimate questions, and knowing no fear. Aspiration, the sense of seeking, action, and spiritual ideals shall be imbued in this vessel.

Visualize all of the energies of the Triangle flowing into the Fire Candle, and hold the Candle aloft.

Aspirant

In the Divine Name ELOHIM, and in the Name of the great Archangel MICHAEL, behold, all Powers of Fire now present in this Temple, that I have consecrated this Candle with the forces that dwell in the realm of Fire. This Candle *shall* be for me a solid and tangible link, true and perfect, with all the Powers of Divine Will and Passion that live within your realm.

Empower this blessed Fire to be a perfect instrument of magical transformation for the restoration of my Soul, and that through its use, the Will of the Divine shall descend into my heart and be expressed in this Temple and in the physical world. So mote it be. *Light the Fire Candle.*

SECOND ADVANCEMENT

Be seated, and contemplate the Tarot card *Judgment.*

<u>Aspirant</u>
Spirit of Primal Fire, the Divine Initiator who awakens us to the Holy Presence within: through you comes rebirth and renewal. Your power is the reawakening of Nature under the influence of Spirit, the mystery of birth in death. Baptism by Fire is your name. O Consecrating Fire, who eternally refines the impure within your holy flames, leaving only the right and good, I enter upon your path. Test and try me, that I may be victorious in my spiritual rebirth. Awaken me from my long slumber, that I may be ever renewed in your Light. I seek the way, I yearn to know. The path of Fire calls to me and says, "Let the fires rise, let the flames consume, and the dross shall be burned away." I will tread the way of Fire and welcome the descending Spirit, that it may enter my heart and set me alight in a holy Fire.

Close your eyes and visualize yourself in the imagery of the card. Note any thoughts or sensations that arise. Before you end this visualization, make an offering of your own Light to the Powers of Fire.

Alternative Meditation

Visualize the flames of fire in front of you. See the light and illumination of the fire, as its flames rise higher and higher. See and feel the heat of the flames. Now move the flames over you, and visualize yourself encompassed in fire, but it does not burn you. As you sit in the center of the fire, you are within a bright white light, in the center of the fire, with the red flames dancing around you. Smokes rises from your skin as any spiritual impurities are burned away. As the smoke clears, visualize your body turning a bright red that glows, like hot coals. Then visualize your body turning from red to a bright white light. You radiate light in all directions, radiance shoots out from your own body of light, and you become a being of purest illumination. Make an offering of your own Light to the Powers of Fire before you leave this meditation.

THIRD ADVANCEMENT

Cup your hands around the Candle flame.

Aspirant
In the Divine Name ELOHIM and in the Name of MICHAEL, the great Archangel of Fire, I now take into myself the Powers of Fire, that we may become as one.

Feel the warmth of the flame, and imagine its heat lighting you in a Holy Fire, the Powers of Fire flowing from your hands throughout your body.

Aspirant
This consecrated Fire will serve as an agent of renewal and rebirth for my entire self: Body, Soul and Spirit, that I may

prove a worthy vessel for the Divine Light. Let it be for me a true link with the Spiritual World, that through its use Divine Power will flow from its Source down through the levels of my essential being. Let this consecrated Fire create in me a victorious heart and an awareness of the Divine Will; and as a symbol of consecration, grant it the power to aid my spiritual rebirth. Through such transformation, I will ever pursue the Pathway of Light and thus be better fit to aid my fellow humanity.

CLOSING

Go to the East and face the center of the room.

Aspirant
I now release any spirits that may have been attracted to this ceremony. Go in peace to your abodes and habitations and go with the blessings of ELOHIM and MICHAEL.

Purify and consecrate the Temple and your body with the water and incense, as in the Opening. Banish with the banishing Pentagram in all four quarters, as in the Opening. Return to the East.

Aspirant
I now declare this ritual duly completed. So mote it be.

Extinguish the candles.

A RITUAL OF A FEAST OF SPIRIT

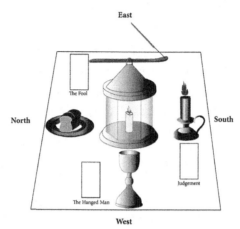

Figure 22: Altar arrangement for Feast of Spirit

Temple arrangement: Elemental Temple (see Introduction).
Altar cloth: White.
Elemental emblems on Altar: Air Incense, *The Fool* (East); Fire Candle, *Judgment* (South); Cup of wine (or juice) with a little of the consecrated Water, *The Hanged Man* (West); Bread and consecrated Earth Salt (North); a Spirit Lantern or small votive holder, with white candle (center).
Incense, Water: In East, with incense lit.
Music: Suitable ambient or background music.

PREPARATION FOR THE RITE

Sit for a moment at the Altar and contemplate the rite to come. Let the cares and worries of the day dissipate. ★ Focus on the top of your head and form a mental image of a ray of White Light permeating your body through the top of your head. Visualize this Light descending through the center of your body to your feet. Your body is now filled with Light. ★ Inhale and exhale this Light through the pores of your body until it is pulsing in and around you. ★ Imagine the Light extending from your body and filling the room. See the Light creating a barrier separating the room from the outer world. Let nothing exist for you outside of this special time and place.

OPENING

Standing West of the Altar facing East, say:

Aspirant

O Thou single source of truth and wisdom, who has taught us that we shall be lamps unto ourselves, let me ascend up to the Supreme Light as if on the Chariot of Truth. Carry me over all gulfs and abysses, bear me upward out of canyons and valleys, become to me a harbor of liberation so that I may repose in the arms of Light. *Make the Banishing Pentagram to the East.*

Aspirant

Through the power of the banishing Pentagram, I expel all undesirable influences from this Temple. I say unto you now, depart and go in peace!

Make the Banishing Pentagram also in the South, the West, and the North. Return to the East.

Take up the Cup of Water and sprinkle three times in the East, then do the same in the South, the West, and the North. Return to the East. Dip your finger in the Cup and touch your forehead, then sprinkle Water toward your feet, and touch your right and left shoulders.

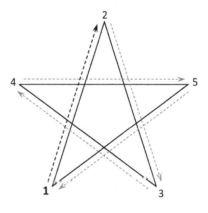

Banishing Elemental Pentagram

Aspirant

I am purified; the Temple is purified; all is purified by the Lustral Waters. *Replace the Cup.*

Take up the incense and wave it three times in the East, then do the same in the South, the West, and the North. Return to the East. Wave the incense toward your forehead, your feet and your right and left shoulders.

Aspirant

I am consecrated; the Temple is consecrated; all is consecrated by Holy Fire. *Replace the Incense.*

Aspirant

(Facing center of Temple) **Hear me, four quarters of the World, for I call out to thee! Grant me the strength to walk the hidden path and discover secret knowledge. Give me your eyes to see and your wisdom to understand, that I may be like you. Grant me your powers that I may command the powers of Spirit.**

Go to the West of the Altar. Facing East, draw both invoking Spirit Pentagrams in the air, and visualize them in a brilliant white Light.

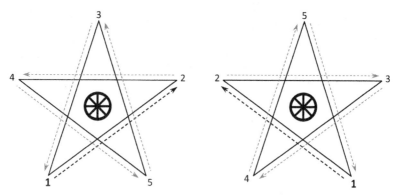

Invoking Passive Spirit Pentagram   Invoking Active Spirit Pentagram

<u>Aspirant</u>

In the Divine Names of EHEIEH (Eh-heh-yeh) and AGLA (Ah-gah-lah), I call forth the Powers of Spirit. Yea, I seek thee for I came forth from thee and to thee shall I return. You are the Fire of my being, the Water of my soul, the Air of my mind, and the Earth of my body. With Your Divine Presence, all that is not known is now made known, and all that is feared is no longer feared. Through You, I receive the gift of hope and dispel all shadows. O Divine Mystery, weave for me a Veil, molded from the Celestial Fire which You conceal, that will sever me from all things which only belong to the outer world, that in this chamber of Light I may see and hear nothing that comes not from on High. Come forward and be an advocate unto me, for I am one who has searched the whole of the worlds for You. O Great Ones of the realm of Spirit, give me your hands and your magic power, for I am made as you, who gave life to my soul. Infuse into my being the power and might irresistible, to compel the Divine Forces of Spirit to manifest within this Temple, according to my words and aspirations, allowing me to bring them forth in full manifestation and power. I pray that I may be united with You, that Your powers may flow through me and be expressed by me. So mote it be.

Stand for a moment and imagine Spirit flowing into every part of you, and alighting your entire being in a Divine white Light.

First Advancement

Go to the West of the Altar and face the East. Turn the your aura to a bright WHITE light, and draw the invoking Spirit Pentagrams of Spirit over the Altar, in a vibrant white light.

Aspirant

Upon this Altar are the consecrated Elements of my being, the universe, and the natural world. The Bread and Salt are my body, the Incense my thought, the Cup emotions, and the Flame my will. And in the center of these is the Lamp of Divine Spirit: for all Elements proceed from the One Divine Spirit, whose Light brings life to all that exists, to the Gods and the Angels, to humans, to the lower creatures who dwell upon the earth, even unto the very ground upon which I walk. All that has been, is now, and ever will be, comes forth from the One.

O Divine Light, implanted into my being before all beginnings, and enduring after all endings, blessed be. Open unto me the inner paths I seek, and guide me toward the fulfillment of my true potential. Be born within me, and bear within Yourself the intentions of my truest Will, that You and I may grow together in flowing of eternal Light from which every living entity has come forth.

To that end, I must first strip my lower being away, to reveal the Indwelling One, the mystic Love which dwells within the hearts of humanity, and within the secret soul of the universe.

Remove the Bread and Salt to the North, and face North.

Aspirant

I set aside my corruptible body in my search for the Divine Light.

Return to the Altar, remove the Incense to the East, and face East.

Aspirant

I set aside my inferior thoughts in my search for the Divine Light.

Return to the Altar, remove the Wine to the West, and face West.

Aspirant

I set aside my lesser emotions in my search for the Divine Light.

Return to the Altar, remove the Candle to the South, and face South.

Aspirant

I set aside my lower will in my search for the Divine Light.

Return to the West of the Altar, and face East. Trace a circle around the Lantern, and draw the invoking Spirit Pentagrams in it.

Aspirant

Spirit of all-perfect purity, before whose Light humanity's face is veiled, purify my body, mind, heart, and will, in my quest to know You. Divine Spirit, aid me that I may walk lightly on the path of life, and inflame within me the sacred spark of Your immortal Light. Great fountain of Life and Love, may I continue to flourish and grow as I walk within Your glorious

garden. As I continually invoke You with praise and love, may my invocation ever ascend unto You like sweet-smelling incense, until the light of my love becomes one with Your infinite Light.

SECOND ADVANCEMENT

Sit for a moment and let your being be permeated with white Light. Breathe this Light until your entire self glows in all directions and your body disappears, so that only the bright White Light remains. Note any thoughts or sensations that arise. When the meditation is complete, say:

Aspirant

Divine Spirit, You are a lamp to those who behold You, a mirror to those who perceive You, and a door to those who knock. You are the way for the wayfarer, and I am a traveler on the road of life. May your Light dwell within me and shine through me, so that every being I encounter will feel Your presence and know Your love. Let them look upon me and see only the Light Divine. So mote it be.

THIRD ADVANCEMENT

Take the Lantern to the North, and use it to trace the invoking Passive Spirit Pentagram and invoking Earth Pentagram over the Bread and Salt:

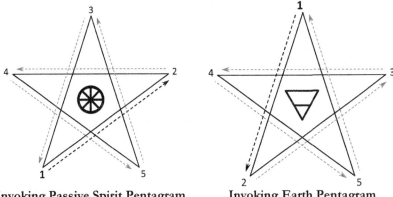

Invoking Passive Spirit Pentagram   Invoking Earth Pentagram

Aspirant

I bless this Bread and Salt with the power of Spirit moving through the Earth. *Return the Bread and Salt to the Northern side of the Altar.*

Take the Lantern to the West, and use it to trace the invoking Passive Spirit Pentagram and invoking Water Pentagram over the Cup of Wine:

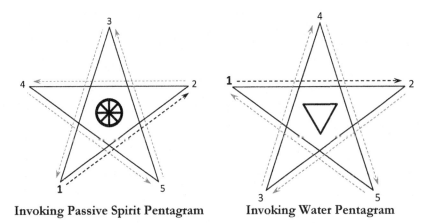

Invoking Passive Spirit Pentagram   Invoking Water Pentagram

Aspirant

I bless this Cup with the power of Spirit moving through the Waters. *Return the Cup to the Western side of the Altar.*

Take the Lantern to the East, and use it to trace the invoking Active Spirit Pentagram and invoking Air Pentagram over the Air Incense:

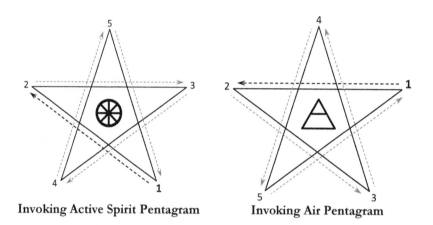

Invoking Active Spirit Pentagram   **Invoking Air Pentagram**

Aspirant

I bless this Incense with the power of Spirit moving through the Air. *Return the Incense to the Eastern side of the Altar.*

Take the Lantern to the South, and use it to trace the invoking Active Spirit Pentagram and invoking Fire Pentagram over the Fire Candle:

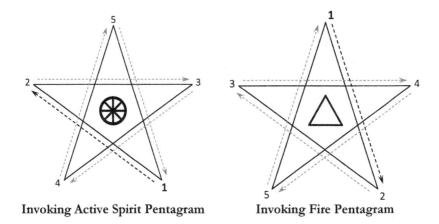

Invoking Active Spirit Pentagram   **Invoking Fire Pentagram**

Aspirant

I bless this Flame with the power of Spirit moving through Fire. *Return the Candle to the Southern side of the Altar, and place the Lantern in the center.*

FOURTH ADVANCEMENT

Stand to the West of the Altar, facing East.

Aspirant

The Elements of my mortal self have been set aside in my quest for the Divine Spirit. I have communed in silence, for I can only know Spirit through the silence. Now I must rejoin the Elements, that I may be whole again and remit this Light to the outer world.

Draw a circle around the Bread and Salt, tracing in it the symbols of the Earthy Signs.

♑   ♉   ♍

Capricorn Taurus Virgo

Divine Earth, bring prosperity and security to my world. Like the yearning roots of the tree as they burrow into the depths of the earth, may I be a grounding of the Divine Light whose rays shine forth to heal the world.

♎   ♒   ♊

Libra   Aquarius   Gemini

Draw a circle around the Incense, tracing in it the symbols of the Airy Signs.

Divine Air, bring imagination and creativity to my world. Like the unfettered winds, may I breathe in the freshness of new and inspired possibilities.

♋   ♏   ♓

Cancer   Scorpio   Pisces

Draw a circle around the Cup, tracing in it the symbols of the Watery Signs.

Divine Water, bring compassion and love to my world. Like the purifying erosion of the water on the stone, cleanse and wear away all that is unnecessary to my spiritual growth.

♈   ♌   ♐

Aries   Leo   Sagittarius

Draw a circle around the Candle and draw in that circle the symbols of Aries, Leo and Sagittarius.

Divine Fire, bring clarity and passion to my world. Like the light of the Sun, may I see clearly the way forward to tread the path of Light.

Draw a circle over the Lantern, and in it the eight-spoked Wheel of Spirit: first the clockwise circle, then the cross, then the diagonal X.

Divine Spirit, First Beginning of my beginning, First Element of the Fire within me,
First Element of the Water within me, First
Element of the Air within me, First Element
of the Earth within me. I, a mortal born of a
mortal womb, have beheld today with Immortal Eyes the wonder of Your glory. I have

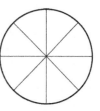

Wheel of Spirit

been united with Your Sacred Form. I have been empowered
by Your Sacred Names. I have received the influence of Your
Goodness. I give you thanks. Blessed be. *Visualize the Light from
the Lantern flowing over and blessing the Elements around it.*

FIFTH ADVANCEMENT

Take a moment to visualize yourself surrounded and permeated
with a bright WHITE Light.

Aspirant

To all beings now present within this Temple, I invite you to
partake with me the Elements of Spirit. To inhale with me the
perfume of this Incense, as a consecrated emblem of Air.
(*Take and smell the Incense.*) To feel with me the warmth of this
Fire, as a consecrated emblem of Fire. (*Cup hands around the
flame.*) To eat with me this Bread and Salt, as a consecrated
emblem of Earth. (*Eat the Bread and Salt*). And finally, to drink
with me this Wine, as a consecrated emblem of Water. (*Drink
the Wine*).

Aspirant

Hail to Thee, immensity of subtle Spirit, extending from the heights of the heavens to the depths of the earth! Hail to Thee, invisible Spirit, who enters into me and clings to me in goodness! Hail to Thee, beginning and end of Nature, the brightness of the Sun and the night-shining Moon. Hail to Thee! I give you thanks and praise, and may I continue to walk in your Light now and forever more. So mote it be.

CLOSING

Go to the East and face the center of the room.

Aspirant

I now release any spirits that may have been attracted to this ceremony. Go in peace to your abodes and habitations and go with the blessings of EHEIEH (Eh-Heh-Yeh) and AGLA (Ah-Gah-Lah).

Purify and consecrate the Temple and your body with the water and incense, as in the Opening. Banish with the banishing Pentagram in all four quarters, as in the Opening. Return to the East.

Aspirant

I now declare this ritual duly completed. So mote it be.

Extinguish the candles.

PART 2: THE PLANETARY RITES

Introduction

In Part 1, we worked with the forces of the Elements. There were several reasons for this. First, they are the material for the manifestation of all spiritual forces. Without the presence of the Elements, our magic would not manifest within or around us. Second, the Elements represent—in the lower, manifest world—the human being. They are arranged in the shape of a Pentagram, which illustrates the microcosmic world as a whole, as well as the manifest world of the human being. Now, the Aspirant is the medium of manifestation of all forces brought into the physical world: in other words, the powers invoked in magic are manifested through the human being. Because of this, we must first activate, stimulate and purify the Elements within our own being in order to approach the higher forces that dwell in the macrocosm. To work with the Planets before first working with the Elements invites failure.

But when working with the Planets, one is working with the macrocosm or the larger universe. The root word "cosmos" (Gr. *kosmos*) means an orderly and harmonious system, and can be used as a synonym for "the universe." When adding the prefixes *macro* and *micro*, the word cosmos takes on the meaning of a larger universe (macrocosm) and a smaller universe (microcosm). As we described in the Introduction, the microcosm is a mirror of the macrocosm, and holds within it all of the forces that make up the greater universe. Because we all have a Divine origin and are ultimately made up of the same spiritual properties as the Divine world, we can access the macrocosm, experiencing it in our microcosmic lives, and we will do this here through Planetary and Zodiacal magic.

Just as the Pentagram represents the microcosm, the Hexagram represents the macrocosm and is therefore used as the symbol of the Planets. The Hexagram is a six-pointed star consisting of two superimposed triangles, one whose apex is up and with the other apex down. In the diagram below, you will notice that the Planets are placed at the angles of the Hexagram, with the Sun in the center. Ritual magic uses the seven Planets of the ancients, but not the modern, "outer" planets (Uranus, Neptune, and Pluto). Note, too, that the upper three Planets are the traditional superior Planets, and the lower ones the inferiors, again with the Sun in the center.

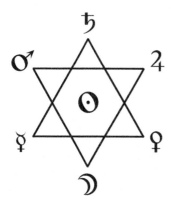

**Figure 23: Macrocosmic
Hexagram**

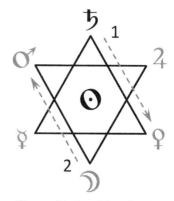

**Figure 24: Invoking Saturn
Hexagram**

When drawing the Hexagram, draw each triangle separately, in a clockwise fashion. Start at the angle of the Planet being worked with, draw the triangle clockwise, and then draw the second triangle starting at the opposite angle. For example, if invoking Saturn, we begin the first triangle from the Saturn angle, then the second triangle from the Moon angle.

Likewise, a Jupiter Hexagram begins with the Jupiter angle, then that of Mercury; a Mars Hexagram from Mars, then Venus; a Venus Hexagram from Venus, then Mars; a Mercury Hexagram from Mercury, then Jupiter; a Moon Hexagram from the Moon, then Saturn. *However*, because the Sun is in the midst of, and is a ruler and mediator of all the Planets, Solar Hexagrams must be drawn using *all six* of the Hexagrams, in order: first the entire Saturn Hexagram, then the entire Jupiter Hexagram, and so on through Mars, Venus, Mercury, and the Moon. Don't worry: you'll only have to do this a couple of times in this book.

The Natures of the Planets

Following are some brief descriptions of the seven traditional Planets, with their typical significations. You can find more information on them in Appendix 2.

The Moon is a feminine planet, representing the female principle and women generally. She governs the instincts, moods, tides, phases, receptivity, fluctuations, feelings, habit patterns, and reflex actions. Her action fluctuates and is changeable. She signifies personal interests, desires, needs, magnetism, growth and fertility, impressionability, and the subconscious.

Mercury is considered ambiguous as to gender. Mercury rules sense and reason, the ability to communicate, awareness, dexterity, rationalization, transmission and exchanges, teaching and learning, numbers and counting and measuring, interpreting, and philosophizing. His action is quick and subject to alteration.

Venus is a feminine planet, and is called the lesser benefic. Venus rules culture, art and beauty, cleanliness, relationships and love, good taste, friendliness, playfulness and games, typically feminine pursuits, jewelry, clothing, music and singing. Her action is gentle and harmonious.

The Sun is a masculine planet, representing the male principle and men in general. The Sun signifies leadership, success, glory and strength, authority, health and vital principles, dignity, and the deep impulses of the soul.

Mars is a masculine planet, and is known as the lesser malefic. Mars indicates courage, lust, competition, wanderlust and adventuring. He governs surgeries and blood, weapons, warfare and conflict, a dislike for authorities over him, fire and burning, crafts using metal tools and other things worked with heat, and hunting. His action is sudden, self-assertive and often disruptive, but is helpful for making decisive changes.

Jupiter is a masculine planet, and is called the greater benefic. Jupiter suggests wealth and assets, abundance, the priesthood or initiatory revelations, wisdom and higher education (especially in law or religion), social advancement and visibility, morality, patience. Jupiter is the judge, the lawmaker, ally, priest. Jupiter's action is orderly and promotes health and growth.

Saturn is a masculine planet, and is known as the greater malefic. Saturn rules form and organization, convention and tradition, discipline, responsibility and burdens, sorrows, and delays. He indicates deep thought, solitude, wise counsel, great age, speaking few words, as well as actions that are solitary or difficult or abject, the sea, and fishing. His action is slow and lasting.

The seven planetary rituals

Some of our readers are astrologers or have astrology programs, others not. Therefore we suggest two options for setting up the Temple.

If you know how to locate your desired planet in the heavens before the rite, then use the East to represent the Ascendant at the time of the ritual. When invoking the Planet itself, go to that part of the Temple and face that direction, or face that direction while still at the Altar, standing on the opposite side. The rituals will instruct you as to when to do each of these. For example, suppose you are performing a Venus ritual, and Venus is towards the Northeast at the time of the ritual. At the appropriate stages of the ritual, you will either go to the Northeast of the room and face Venus, or else stand on the Southwest side of the Altar, facing the Northeast and Venus herself from across the Altar (the Altar will be between you and Venus).

But if you do not know how to locate the planet itself, then note where your planet falls in the following diagram of the Temple (with the Hexagram superimposed upon it), and face that direction instead, standing on the opposite side. Again, if you are working with Venus but do not know where she is in the heavens, then go to the Northeast of the Altar and face Venus's symbolic position in the Hexagram, towards the Southwest (see diagram).

Please note that the positions of the planetary glyphs in the diagram only show where the planet is *symbolically* located if you do not know how to locate the actual planet in the heavens. These symbolic planetary stations will also be used in the culmination ritual (see below). The Planetary Candles will not actually be placed in these positions in the room, but they will be so on the Altar.

In the first part of the Planetary rituals, the Elemental tools you have already consecrated will be used to mark the cardinal points in the room. But on the macrocosmic level which we are now symbolically operating on, the attributions of the directions and Elements change to their Zodiacal form. In the Elemental Temple, we assigned East to Air, South to Fire, West to Water, and North to Earth. But now, when working with the Planets and the Signs, we have "risen above" the merely microcosmic level, and so the attributions are aligned with Signs instead. Therefore, we have included a section in these rituals, in which the Elemental tools are moved to their new positions as seen in the second figure below. Since not everyone may be familiar with these attributions, we have labeled them as optional (albeit recommended).

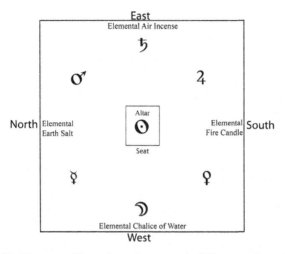

Figure 25: Planetary Temple, microcosmic/Elemental attributions and Hexagrammatic positions of Planets

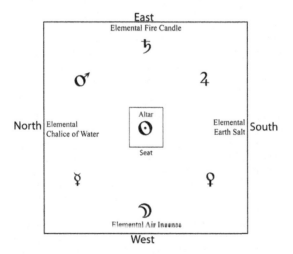

Figure 26: Planetary Temple, new macrocosmic/Zodiacal attributions and Hexagrammatic positions of Planets

East (Ascendant): Aries, Fire

South (Midheaven): Capricorn, Earth

West (Descendant): Libra, Air

North (the IC or lower heaven): Cancer, Water

Following are the special ritual tools necessary for performing each Planetary ritual, and its basic structure:

Ritual Items:

- Consecrated Elemental objects, in appropriate *micro*cosmic quarters (see first diagram above).
- Altar cloth of the appropriate Planetary color (seven total): Blue-violet (Saturn), Violet (Jupiter), Red (Mars), Orange (Sol), Green (Venus), Yellow (Mercury), Blue (Moon).
- Orange Sol Candle (all rites).[1]
- Planetary Candle of the appropriate color (six besides the Sol Candle), of the same colors as the Altar cloths, placed on the Altar as each ritual instructs. See the figure below.
- Tarot card corresponding to the appropriate Planet (seven total).

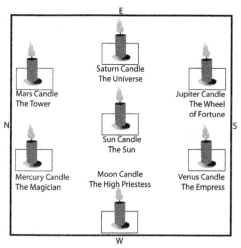

Figure 27: Planetary Altar, with all Candles and Tarot cards

---

[1] In our rituals, we refer to the Sun and Moon by their Latin names, *Sol* and *Luna*. In this way, they have personal names like the other planets.

Remember, if you find it hard to carry this book around during a ritual, then photocopy the relevant pages and use those instead.

Preparation and Opening

The Preparation for the Rite, and its Opening, are the same as in the Elemental rites.

Invocation of Elements

The Elements are invoked through their Pentagrams in the usual Elemental quarters. This allows the Planetary energy to manifest more fully in the microcosmic world. But please note that the consecrated Elemental tools will later rest in the quarters according to the new, macrocosmic arrangement. Thus the Air Incense (for example) will begin in the East, but will later be moved to its macrocosmic, zodiacal position in the West. Again, this is optional but recommended.

Invocation of Spirit

Elemental Spirit is invoked, because it is the culmination and crown of the other Elements.

First Advancement: Invocation of the Planet

In this first major portion of the ritual, advance to the location of the planet[2] and face it in the heavens. Using the unlit Planetary Candle,[3] draw the invoking Hexagram of the Planet and make one rotation around the Temple. (The only ritual that does not use this rotation is the Sun ritual.) Return to the Hexagram, and use the Candle to touch the symbol of the Planet within it.

Then, move to the Altar, and face the planet from the opposite side. Place the Candle in its appropriate place on the Altar. Give an oration which defines the Planet's nature and calls to its powers. Draw a circle around the Candle, and draw the Planetary Hexagram in its proper color within it, visual-

---

[2] This will apply to every planet except the Sun. Again, if you know the location of the planet in the heavens, face that; otherwise, face its symbolic position according to the Planetary Hexagram.

[3] For all planets after the Sun ritual, the Sol Candle will remain lit from the beginning of the ritual.

izing the Hexagram sinking into the Candle. The circle around the Candle limits the force of the Hexagram to that Candle alone.

Then, take the Planetary Candle and go to each of the cardinal points, drawing the symbol of the Planet there: this establishes the power of the Planet as it relates to each of those points. Return to the West of the Altar, and light the Planetary Candle using the flame of the Sol Candle.

Second Advancement: Planetary Meditation

In the second portion, perform a contemplative meditation on the Tarot card pertaining to the Planet. After reading a brief explanation of what the card signifies, visualize yourself inside the imagery of the card, and note any thoughts or impressions that arise. For those without a Tarot deck, we provide alternative astrological landscapes for meditation, drawn from William Lilly's *Christian Astrology*. If you like, record yourself reading the Tarot meditation beforehand, and listen to it as you visualize.

Closing

The Closing is the same as in the Elemental Rituals.

Culmination ritual: Creating a Magical Universe

The Opening

The Preparation, Opening, and initial Invocations of the Elements and Spirit are the same as in the previous Planetary Rites.

First Advancement: Creation of a Magical Universe

Invoke Sol as the creator of the universe. Then, in descending order from Saturn to the Moon, recreate the magical universe of Light and Life under the power and sovereignty of the Sun.

Second Advancement: Climbing the Ladder of Lights & Forming the Six-Rayed Star

Climb the Ladder of Lights from the Moon up to Saturn, always walking from the center where the Sun is symbolically located, to the positions of the planets. This walking to and fro creates the Six-Rayed Star of the Planetary Hexagram in the Temple. At each station, sacrifice the negative aspects of the Planetary forces within yourself, and pledge to embody the positive aspects. The gate of each Planet is opened by visualizing the symbol of the Planet in the heart. Having climbed to the highest heaven in Saturn, return to the Altar and recite a song of praises to the Planetary powers.

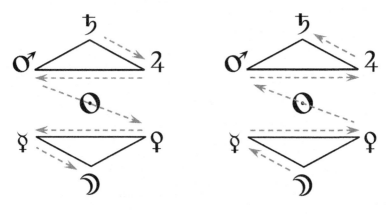

Figure 28: Descending movement of Creation (1st Advancement)

Figure 29: Ascending movement of Ladder (2nd Advancement)

The Closing

The Closing is the same as in the Planetary rites.

CONSECRATION OF A CANDLE OF SOL

To be Performed on the Day of Sol (Sunday)

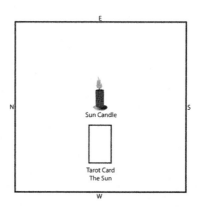

Figure 30: Altar arrangement for Sol

Temple arrangement: Planetary Temple 1st Part (see Introduction), with Air Incense and Fire Candle lit.

Altar cloth: Orange.

Candles: Unlit orange Sol Candle (center of Altar), with a lighter nearby.

Tarot Card: *The Sun.*

Incense, Water: In the East, with incense lit (frankincense or other Solar incense).

Music: Suitable ambient or background music.

PREPARATION FOR THE RITE

Sit for a moment at the Altar and contemplate the rite to come. Let the cares and worries of the day dissipate. ✱ Focus on the top of your head and form a mental image of a ray of White Light permeating your body through the top of your head. Visualize this Light descending through the center of your body to your feet. Your body is now filled with Light. ✱ Inhale and exhale this Light through the pores of your body until it is pulsing in and around you. ✱ Imagine the Light extending from your body and filling the room. See the Light creating a barrier separating the room from the outer world. Let nothing exist for you outside of this special time and place.

OPENING

Standing West of the Altar, facing East, say:

<u>Aspirant</u>
I banish all worldly influences dwelling within this Temple by the Flaming Star of the Five Elements. I say unto you now, depart!

Go to the East. Make the Banishing Pentagram to the East, then do the same in the South, the West, and the North. Return to the East.

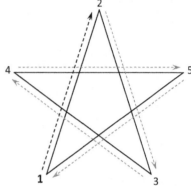

Take up the Cup of Water and sprinkle three times in the East, then do the same in the South, **Banishing Elemental Pentagram**

the West, and the North. Return to the East. Dip your finger in the Cup and touch your forehead, then sprinkle Water toward your feet, and touch your right and left shoulders.

<u>Aspirant</u>
I am purified; the Temple is purified; all is purified by the Lustral Waters. *Replace the Cup.*

Take up the incense and wave it three times in the East, then do the same in the South, the West, and the North. Return to the East. Wave the incense toward your forehead, your feet and your right and left shoulders.

Aspirant

I am consecrated; the Temple is consecrated; all is consecrated by Holy Fire. *Replace the Incense.*

Aspirant

(*In East, facing East*) I have purified and consecrated this Temple for the invocation of Sol, and in so doing have created a Temple, that the heavenly forces of Sol may dwell here for a time. So mote it be.

INVOKING THE ELEMENTS

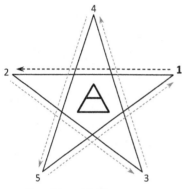

Invoking Air Pentagram

Go to the East and take up the consecrated Elemental Air Incense. Face the East, and with the Incense draw the Invoking Air Pentagram in the air.

Aspirant

Through the power of the Pentagram, I call forth the spirits of Air!

Invoking Fire Pentagram

Replace the Incense. Using the index finger, touch the center of the Air Pentagram and draw a line in the air, walking towards the South.

In the South and facing South, take up the consecrated Elemental Fire Candle. With the Candle draw the Invoking Fire Pentagram.

Aspirant
Through the power of the Pentagram, I call forth the spirits of Fire!

Replace the Candle. Touch the center of the Fire Pentagram and draw a line in the air towards the West.

In the West and facing West, take up the consecrated Elemental Chalice of Water. With the Chalice draw the Invoking Water Pen-Pentagram.

Invoking Water Pentagram

Aspirant
Through the power of the Pentagram, I call forth the spirits of Water!

Replace the Chalice. Touch the center of the Water Pentagram and draw a line in the air towards the North.

In the North and facing North, take up the consecrated Elemental Salt. With the Salt draw the Invoking Earth Pentagram.

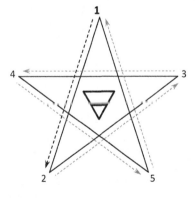

Invoking Earth Pentagram

Aspirant
Through the power of the Pentagram, I call forth the spirits of Earth!

Replace the Salt. Touch the center of the Earth Pentagram and draw a line in the air towards the East. While standing in the East, turn and face the center of the room.

Aspirant

Hear me, four quarters of the World, for I call out to thee! Grant me the strength to walk the hidden path and discover secret knowledge. Give me your eyes to see and your wisdom to understand, that I may be like you. Grant me your powers that I may call the powers of Sol.

INVOCATION OF SPIRIT

Go to the West of the Altar and face East. In the air before you, draw the two Invoking Spirit Pentagrams:

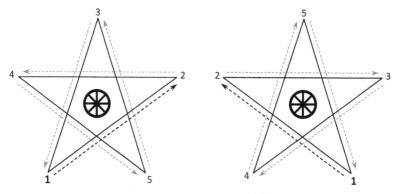

Invoking Passive Spirit Pentagram   Invoking Active Spirit Pentagram

Aspirant

O Thou supreme Life-Spirit, Cause of all Creation, Origin of all, and single Source of every living soul. Of Thee alone is my beginning, and in Thee alone have I no ending. O Thou single source of truth and wisdom, let me ascend to the Higher

Realms on the Chariot of Truth. Bring me over the gulfs and abysses, bear me upward out of gorges and valleys; become for me the source of liberation. Let Thy great brightness cause the path to be lit before me. Let me ascend to the Heavens as if upon a ship of Light, that I may come to know the Planetary Spheres. So mote it be. *Pause for a moment and visualize your aura filled with White Light.*

Optional: Elevating the Temple into the Heavens

Aspirant
All is now in readiness to ascend to the Planetary Powers. I shall quit the material world and enter the higher realms by placing the consecrated Elemental Powers in their zodiacal stations.

Go clockwise to the South, take up the Candle, and go clockwise to the East. Face the East.

Aspirant
In the earthly realm, the East is the station of Elemental Air. However, in the higher realms, the East is the station of Aries, the movable Sign of Fire. (*Place the Candle in the East.*) Through the power of this consecrated emblem of Fire, this quarter is now elevated to the heavens. *Take up the Incense and go clockwise to the West, facing the West.*

Aspirant
In the earthly realm, the West is the station of Elemental Water. However, in the higher realms, the West is the station of Libra, the movable Sign of Air. (*Place the Incense in the West.*) Through the power of this consecrated emblem of Air, this

quarter is now elevated to the heavens. *Take up the Chalice. Go clockwise to the North and face the North.*

Aspirant

In the earthly realm, the North is the station of Elemental Earth. However, in the higher realms, the North is the station of Cancer, the movable Sign of Water. (*Place the Chalice in the North.*) Through the power of this consecrated emblem of Water, this quarter is now elevated to the heavens. *Take up the Salt. Go clockwise to the South and face the South.*

Aspirant

In the earthly realm, the South is the station of Elemental Fire. However, in the higher realms, the South is the station of Capricorn, the movable Sign of Earth. (*Place the Salt in the South.*) Through the power of this consecrated emblem of Earth, this quarter is now elevated to the heavens. *Go to the West of the Altar, and face East.*

FIRST ADVANCEMENT: THE INVOCATION OF SOL

Aspirant

(*West of Altar, facing East.*) I have opened this Temple to perform a consecration of a Candle of Sol. Unseen Watchers over the sacred Magic, watch over this ceremony of the Light Divine. So mote it be.

Take up the unlit orange Sol Candle. Turn towards Sol in the heavens, with the Altar in between (or focus on the center of the Altar).

<u>Aspirant</u>

By the authority of the Six-Rayed Star, the Mystical Seal of Solomon the King and the Symbol of Life, I call forth the Powers of Sol! *With the Candle, draw the six Invoking Hexagrams for Sol above the Altar, tracing the symbol of Sol in the center of the last one.*

Invoking Solar Hexagram
(from Saturn)

Invoking Solar Hexagram
(from Jupiter)

Invoking Solar Hexagram
(from Mars)

Invoking Solar Hexagram
(from Venus)

Invoking Solar Hexagram
(from Mercury)

Invoking Solar Hexagram
(from Luna)

Aspirant

(*Holding Candle of Sol aloft.*) **In the Divine Name YHVH ELOAH V'DAATH (Yod Heh Vav Heh, El-oh-ah, Veh-Dah-ath), and in the name of the great Archangel, MICHAEL, I call to the Sun, the Lord of Love, He who is permanently benign and youthful. You are the one who travels through the underworld in the darkest of night, to be reborn in the dawn. You are the beneficent one, he who endures in well-being. The ruler of days and the mediator of the Planetary powers are you. Through you come the forces of magical ascendance and mystical endeavor, and your power is now present in the working of this rite.**

Touch the Sol Candle to the symbol of Sol in the center of the Hexagram. Put the Sol Candle in the center of the Altar.

Aspirant

I have called to the Sun, the lord of the sky and the master of eternity. It is you who remains perfect, and it is you who fills the heavens with rays of golden fire. It is through your power that that the inner nature finds perfect equilibrium, true fulfillment, and magical selfhood. You are the glorious lord of the day, the measure of time, and the one who bestows timeless gifts. The giver of life and the joy of life renewed, are your titles. For you are the divine bearer of healing and of hope, the one who gives jubilation to all the worlds. Your torch of mighty flame manifests the invisible, and you are the lord of the city of the Sun, the dwelling place of the Phoenix. Through the Radiant Glory of the presence of the Sol, I consecrate this Candle of the Sun.

Make a circle around the Candle and draw in the circle the Invoking Hexagrams of Sol, placing the sigil of Sol in the center of the last Hexagram. Visualize the Orange Hexagram sink into the Candle.

Take the Sol Candle to the East, and face East. Make an ORANGE symbol of Sol in the air to the East, with the Candle.

Symbol of Sol

Aspirant

I stand before the rising Sun. The Powers of Sol dawn within my mind, and I breathe in the mystery of Solar Magic. (*Visualize the symbol of the Sun rising out of darkness while its rays fill your body with its bright orange color.*) **I establish the Power of the Sun in the East.** *Go to the South and face the South. Make the orange symbol of Sol.*

Aspirant

The Sun reaches his zenith and shines brightly in the heavens. I project the Powers of Sol through the Magic of the Light. (*Visualize the orange light of the Sun raying out of your body in brilliant streams of light.*) **I establish the Power of Sun in the South.** *Go to the West and face the West. Make the orange symbol of Sol.*

Aspirant

The Sun is setting and now sheds an inner Light. I take the Solar Powers within me and they dwell within my soul. (*Visualize the orange symbol of the Sun glowing in your heart.*) **I establish the Power of Sun in the West.** *Go to the North and face the North. Make the orange symbol of Sol.*

Aspirant

The Sun is at his nadir, now dwelling in the hidden realms. I will explore the worlds of mystery in the Light of Sol. (*Visualize the symbol of the Sun on an orange door in front of you; see the door begin to open.*) **I establish the Power of Sun in the North.** *Return to the West of the Altar and sit, facing East.*

Light the Sol Candle, and visualize it glowing in a vibrant ORANGE light. Place the Sol Candle in its proper position on the Altar.

SECOND ADVANCEMENT:
MEDITATION ON *THE SUN* CARD

Turn the color of your aura to ORANGE. Take up the Tarot card The Sun and study its image, saying:

Aspirant

Lord of the Fire of the World, Splendor of the Firm Basis. From your Light, the astrologers deduce the movement of the Stars and the Celestial Signs. You are the center of our universe and the giver of life to the earth through your warming rays. Each day you travel across the sky, and in the night you pass through the underworld. Daily are you reborn, for in the dawn you are the newborn child, at the noontide you are matured and at the sunset you are the elder, ready for death. Each sunrise is a celebration of your rebirth, a victory of life over the forces of death and darkness. Through your power, which dawns after the darkest of nights, innocence is rediscovered and therefore renewed, bringing hope for the future. Through your powers, accomplishment is assured. You are optimism, enlightenment and vitality. Happiness, enthusiasm, and joy are yours to impart.

Close your eyes and visualize yourself within the imagery of the card. Note any thoughts or sensations that arise. Before you end this visualization, make an offering of your own Light to the Powers of the Sun.

Alternative Meditation

It is daytime, hot and dry. You are sitting in a lovely, sunlit orchard, beneath an orange tree situated in an orange grove of a thousand sun-drenched fruit trees. The pungent aroma of the blooming oranges fills your senses. Off in the distance, in the shade of some of the trees, sits a large lion with several lionesses close by. Baby cubs frolic with each other in the light of the glowing sunbeams. As you stand there in the meadow, you watch the seasons pass. First spring comes with its moistening showers. Then the summer heat blooms hot and dry. After the summer come the autumn mists and then, in the winter, the gentle snows fall. The snows then turn to the showers of spring once again.

You walk through the sunlit orchard until you come upon a glittering palace of gold with high towers topped with rubies; the gold and rubies glitter in the sunlight. As you approach the palace you see peacocks of brilliant hues proudly walking the paths that weave through the well-manicured gardens which make up the entrance to the large estate. Swans rest on still waters in small ponds.

As you approach the palace, ruby doors swing wide and you look inside to find a great dining hall, with glowing candle-filled chandeliers hung high from the ceiling. An enormous table is set with golden tableware, and crystal goblets are filled with golden honey mead. Upon the table is a feast of many and varied dishes of great delight and wonderful aromas. The room is warm, opulent and comfortable. You hear the sound of music and laughter coming from another room.

You turn and leave the palace and return to the orange grove. Before you quit this visualization, make an offering of your own Light to the Powers of the Sun.

Aspirant

The Sol Candle has been consecrated and holds within it the force of the Sun. With this power, the Temple of the Sun has been created. So mote it be.

CLOSING

Go to the East and face the center of the room.

Aspirant

I now release any spirits that may have been attracted to this ceremony. Go in peace to your abodes and habitations and go with the blessings of the Sun.

Purify and consecrate the Temple and your body with the water and incense, as in the Opening. Banish with the banishing Pentagram in all four quarters, as in the Opening. Return to the East.

Aspirant

I now declare this ritual duly completed. So mote it be.

Extinguish the candles.

CONSECRATION OF A CANDLE OF LUNA

To be Performed on the Day of Luna (Monday)

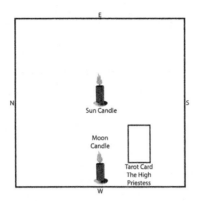

Figure 31: Altar arrangement for Luna

Temple arrangement: Planetary Temple 1st Part (see Introduction), with Air Incense and Fire Candle lit.

Altar cloth: Blue.

Candles: Orange Sol Candle (lit), blue Luna Candle (unlit).

Tarot Card: *The High Priestess.*

Incense, Water: In the East, with incense lit (jasmine or other Lunar incense).

Music: Suitable ambient or background music.

PREPARATION FOR THE RITE

Sit for a moment at the Altar and contemplate the rite to come. Let the cares and worries of the day dissipate. ✱ Focus on the top of your head and form a mental image of a ray of White Light permeating your body through the top of your head. Visualize this Light descending through the center of your body to your feet. Your body is now filled with Light. ✱ Inhale and exhale this Light through the pores of your body until it is pulsing in and around you. ✱ Imagine the Light extending from your body and filling the room. See the Light creating a barrier separating the room from the outer world. Let nothing exist for you outside of this special time and place.

OPENING

Standing West of the Altar, facing East, say:

Aspirant

I banish all worldly influences dwelling within this Temple by the Flaming Star of the Five Elements. I say unto you now, depart!

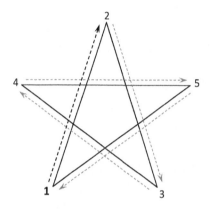

Banishing Elemental Pentagram

Go to the East. Make the Banishing Pentagram to the East, then do the same in the South, the West, and the North. Return to the East.

Take up the Cup of Water and sprinkle three times in the East, then do the same in the South, the West, and the North. Return to the East. Dip your finger in the Cup and touch your forehead, then sprinkle Water toward your feet, and touch your right and left shoulders.

Aspirant

I am purified; the Temple is purified; all is purified by the Lustral Waters. *Replace the Cup.*

Take up the incense and wave it three times in the East, then do the same in the South, the West, and the North. Return to the East. Wave the incense toward your forehead, your feet and your right and left shoulders.

Aspirant

I am consecrated; the Temple is consecrated; all is consecrated by Holy Fire. *Replace the Incense.*

Aspirant

(*In East, facing East*) I have purified and consecrated this Temple for the invocation of Luna, and in so doing have created a Temple, that the heavenly forces of Luna may dwell here for a time. So mote it be.

INVOKING THE ELEMENTS

Go to the East and take up the consecrated Elemental Air Incense. Face the East, and with the Incense draw the Invoking Air Pentagram in the air.

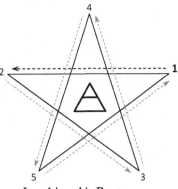

Invoking Air Pentagram

Aspirant

Through the power of the Pentagram, I call forth the spirits of Air!

Replace the Incense. Using the index finger, touch the center of the Air Pentagram and draw a line in the air, walking towards the South.

In the South and facing South, take up the consecrated Elemental Fire Candle. With the Candle draw the Invoking Fire Pentagram.

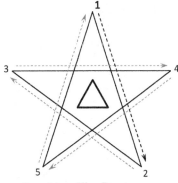

Invoking Fire Pentagram

Aspirant

Through the power of the Pentagram, I call forth the spirits of Fire!

Replace the Candle. Touch the center of the Fire Pentagram and draw a line in the air towards the West.

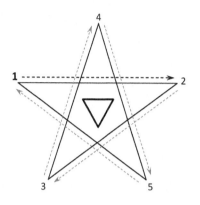

Invoking Water Pentagram

In the West and facing West, take up the consecrated Elemental Chalice of Water. With the Chalice draw the Invoking Water Pentagram.

Aspirant

Through the power of the Pentagram, I call forth the spirits of Water!

Replace the Chalice. Touch the center of the Water Pentagram and draw a line in the air towards the North.

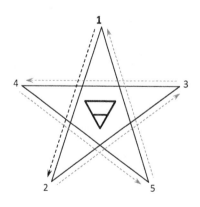

Invoking Earth Pentagram

In the North and facing North, take up the consecrated Elemental Salt. With the Salt draw the Invoking Earth Pentagram.

Aspirant

Through the power of the Pentagram, I call forth the spirits of Earth!

Replace the Salt. Touch the center of the Earth Pentagram and draw a line in the air towards the East. While standing in the East, turn and face the center of the room.

Aspirant

Hear me, four quarters of the World, for I call out to thee! Grant me the strength to walk the hidden path and discover secret knowledge. Give me your eyes to see and your wisdom to understand, that I may be like you. Grant me your powers that I may call the powers of Luna.

INVOCATION OF SPIRIT

Go to the West of the Altar and face East. In the air before you, draw the two Invoking Spirit Pentagrams:

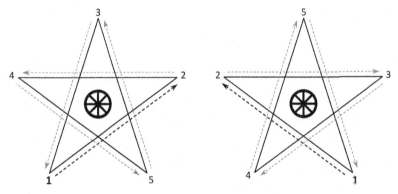

Invoking Passive Spirit Pentagram   Invoking Active Spirit Pentagram

Aspirant

O Thou supreme Life-Spirit, Cause of all Creation, Origin of all, and single Source of every living soul. Of Thee alone is my beginning, and in Thee alone have I no ending. O Thou single source of truth and wisdom, let me ascend to the Higher

Realms on the Chariot of Truth. Bring me over the gulfs and abysses, bear me upward out of gorges and valleys; become for me the source of liberation. Let Thy great brightness cause the path to be lit before me. Let me ascend to the Heavens as if upon a ship of Light, that I may come to know the Planetary Spheres. So mote it be. *Pause for a moment and visualize your aura filled with White Light.*

Optional: Elevating the Temple into the Heavens

Aspirant
All is now in readiness to ascend to the Planetary Powers. I shall quit the material world and enter the higher realms by placing the consecrated Elemental Powers in their zodiacal stations.

Go clockwise to the South, take up the Candle, and go clockwise to the East. Face the East.

Aspirant
In the earthly realm, the East is the station of Elemental Air. However, in the higher realms, the East is the station of Aries, the movable Sign of Fire. (*Place the Candle in the East.*) Through the power of this consecrated emblem of Fire, this quarter is now elevated to the heavens. *Take up the Incense and go clockwise to the West, facing the West.*

Aspirant
In the earthly realm, the West is the station of Elemental Water. However, in the higher realms, the West is the station of Libra, the movable Sign of Air. (*Place the Incense in the West.*) Through the power of this consecrated emblem of Air, this

quarter is now elevated to the heavens. *Take up the Chalice. Go clockwise to the North and face the North.*

Aspirant

In the earthly realm, the North is the station of Elemental Earth. However, in the higher realms, the North is the station of Cancer, the movable Sign of Water. (*Place the Chalice in the North.*) **Through the power of this consecrated emblem of Water, this quarter is now elevated to the heavens.** *Take up the Salt. Go clockwise to the South and face the South.*

Aspirant

In the earthly realm, the South is the station of Elemental Fire. However, in the higher realms, the South is the station of Capricorn, the movable Sign of Earth. (*Place the Salt in the South.*) **Through the power of this consecrated emblem of Earth, this quarter is now elevated to the heavens.** *Go to the West of the Altar, and face East.*

FIRST ADVANCEMENT: THE INVOCATION OF LUNA

Aspirant

(*West of Altar, facing East.*) **I have opened this Temple to perform a consecration of a Candle of Luna. Unseen Watchers over the sacred Magic, watch over this ceremony of the Light Divine. So mote it be.**

Take up the unlit blue Luna Candle. Advance to the location of Luna in the Temple (or her symbolic, Hexagrammatic location), facing her.

<u>Aspirant</u>

By the authority of the Six-Rayed Star, the Mystical Seal of Solomon the King and the Symbol of Life, I call forth the Powers of Luna!

Invoking Luna Hexagram

With the Candle, draw the Invoking Hexagram of Luna. Draw the symbol of Luna in the center.

Holding the blue Candle of Luna, walk clockwise around the room once slowly while saying:

<u>Aspirant</u>

In the Divine Name SHADDAI EL CHAI, and in the name of the great Archangel, GABRIEL, I call to the Moon, the Lunar Powers that scatter silver Light throughout the world. Through the Heavens you ride, wandering in the darkness of the Night, the stars dancing in your radiance. You are the force of the night's holy enchantments, and your Power, which governs the tides of the great oceans and all growing things, is now present in the working of this rite.

Return to the Luna Hexagram, touch the Candle to the symbol of Luna in the center, and move clockwise back to the Altar. Place the Candle in its proper position on the Altar, still facing Luna.

<u>Aspirant</u>

I have called to the Moon, the Shining Guide through the realm of dreams and the gracious opener to the hidden worlds. O Luna, you are the giver of dreams and the maker of enchantments. It is you who brings all things to birth and

growth and to their earthly fulfillment. Ruler of the sacred light, wherein all that is manifest is first perfected. You are the Changeful One, the Lady of Life and of the green crops. Through the Purifying Glory of the Moon's presence, I consecrate this Candle of Luna.

Make a circle around the Luna Candle, draw in the circle the Invoking Hexagram of Luna, and place the sigil of Luna in the center. Visualize the BLUE Hexagram sink into the Candle.

Take the Luna Candle to the East, and face East. Make the BLUE symbol of Luna in the air to the East, with the Candle.

Symbol of Luna

<u>Aspirant</u>
I stand before the rising Moon. The Powers of Luna dawn within my mind, and I breathe in the mysteries of the Magic of the Moon. (*Visualize the symbol of the Moon rising out of darkness while its rays fill your body with its bright blue color.*) **I establish the Power of Luna in the East.** *Go to the South and face the South. Make the blue symbol of Luna.*

<u>Aspirant</u>
The Moon reaches her zenith and shines brightly in the heavens. I project the Powers of Luna through the Magic of the Light. (*Visualize the blue light of the Moon raying out of your body in brilliant streams of light.*) **I establish the Power of Luna in the South.** *Go to the West and face the West. Make the blue symbol of Luna.*

Aspirant

The Moon is in her setting and now sheds an inner Light. I take the Lunar Powers within me, and they dwell within my soul. (*Visualize the blue symbol of the Moon glowing in your heart.*) I establish the Power of Luna in the West. *Go to the North and face the North. Make the blue symbol of Luna.*

Aspirant

The Moon is at her nadir, now dwelling in the hidden realms. I will explore the worlds of mystery in the Light of the Moon. (*Visualize the symbol of the Moon on a blue door in front of you; see the door begin to open.*) I establish the Power of Luna in the North. *Return to the West of the Altar and sit, facing the East.*

Light the Luna Candle from the Sol Candle. Visualize the Luna Candle glowing in a vibrant BLUE light. Place the Luna Candle in its proper position on the Altar.

SECOND ADVANCEMENT:
MEDITATION ON *THE HIGH PRIESTESS*

Turn the color of your aura to BLUE. Take up the Tarot card *The High Priestess* and study its image while saying:

Aspirant

Priestess of the Silver Star, The Crown of Beauty, she who is the beginning of consciousness and the guardian of the unconscious mind. You are the Veiled One who receives creative force and initiates form. You are Diana, Goddess of the Hunt, who has laid aside her bow and is now at peace. You are the Shekinah, the spiritual Bride and Mother, the female indwelling presence of the Divine. Union with you is the reward of the slain and resurrected God. You are intuition, introspection, mystical vision and the experience of the inner worlds, for through you comes the knowledge of how to access these worlds. You are wisdom, serenity, spiritual enlightenment and inner illumination. You are the keeper of the sacred Scrolls of Divine Knowledge and Wisdom. The world is purified in the Light of your lustral waters.

Close your eyes and visualize yourself in the imagery of the card. Note any thoughts or sensations that arise. Before you end the visualization, make an offering of your own Light to the Powers of the Moon.

Alternative Meditation

It is nighttime, and the air is cool and moist. You are sitting beneath a very large, round tree with great-spreading branches and leaves. Around you on the ground are many mushrooms popping up out of the cool, wet soil. High above you in the branches of the tree, a night owl hoots a soft greeting. A frog jumps on your lap, startling you, but you gently brush it away. You hear the honking of geese and you look up to see a flock outlined against the full moon overhead. The night is calm and peaceful, and you feel free from the cares of the day.

You walk down a moonlit path and eventually come upon a quiet port town, a sea harbor with golden-hued, lamp-lit sailing ships, whose bare masts stand straight against the nighttime sky. Everyone has gone home for the night. You hear the waves of the ocean crash against the many docks that line the shore, and watch as the ships gently rock in the surf. A cool wind strokes your face and body. As you walk along the docks, you see stacked crates bearing novelties of all kinds from distant and mysterious lands. One crate holds a bunch of melons and you stop and eat one, savoring its soft and moist fruit. As you eat your melon, you notice another crate filled with silver jewelry, candlesticks and goblets. Wind chimes tinkle in the distance as a moonbeam shines down over you, revealing a small, clear stone crystal lying on the dock. You pick up the stone and see within its crystalline structure the reflection of the Moon shimmering on the ocean. You stand for a while, savoring the peace and quiet and serenity of the night.

You leave the port town and return to the large tree. Before you quit this visualization, make an offering of your own Light to the Powers of the Moon.

Aspirant
The Luna Candle has been consecrated and holds within it the force of the Moon. With this power, the Temple of the Moon has been created. So mote it be.

CLOSING

Go to the East and face the center of the room.

Aspirant
I now release any spirits that may have been attracted to this ceremony. Go in peace to your abodes and habitations and go with the blessings of Luna.

Purify and consecrate the Temple and your body with the water and incense, as in the Opening. Banish with the banishing Pentagram in all four quarters, as in the Opening. Return to the East.

Aspirant
I now declare this ritual duly completed. So mote it be.

Extinguish the candles.

CONSECRATION OF A CANDLE OF MARS
To be Performed on the Day of Mars (Tuesday)

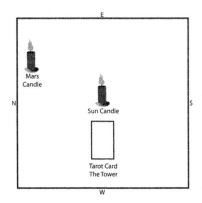

Figure 32: Altar arrangement for Mars

Temple arrangement: Planetary Temple 1st Part (see Introduction), with Air Incense and Fire Candle lit.

Altar cloth: Red.

Candles: Orange Sol Candle (lit), red Mars Candle (unlit).

Tarot Card: *The Tower.*

Incense, Water: In the East, with incense lit (spicy or other Martial incense).

Music: Suitable ambient or background music.

PREPARATION FOR THE RITE

Sit for a moment at the Altar and contemplate the rite to come. Let the cares and worries of the day dissipate. ✶ Focus on the top of your head and form a mental image of a ray of White Light permeating your body through the top of your head. Visualize this Light descending through the center of your body to your feet. Your body is now filled with Light. ✶ Inhale and exhale this Light through the pores of your body until it is pulsing in and around you. ✶ Imagine the Light extending from your body and filling the room. See the Light creating a barrier separating the room from the outer world. Let nothing exist for you outside of this special time and place.

OPENING

Standing West of the Altar, facing East, say:

Aspirant

I banish all worldly influences dwelling within this Temple by the Flaming Star of the Five Elements. I say unto you now, depart!

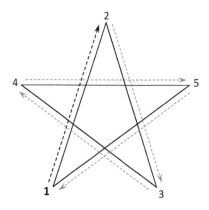

Banishing Elemental Pentagram

Go to the East. Make the Banishing Pentagram to the East, then do the same in the South, the West, and the North. Return to the East.

Take up the Cup of Water and sprinkle three times in the East, then do the same in the South, the West, and the North. Return to the East. Dip your finger in the Cup and touch your forehead, then sprinkle Water toward your feet, and touch your right and left shoulders.

Aspirant

I am purified; the Temple is purified; all is purified by the Lustral Waters. *Replace the Cup.*

Take up the incense and wave it three times in the East, then do the same in the South, the West, and the North. Return to the East. Wave the incense toward your forehead, your feet and your right and left shoulders.

Aspirant

I am consecrated; the Temple is consecrated; all is consecrated by Holy Fire. *Replace the Incense.*

Aspirant

(*In East, facing East*) **I have purified and consecrated this Temple for the invocation of Mars, and in so doing have created a Temple, that the heavenly forces of Mars may dwell here for a time. So mote it be.**

INVOKING THE ELEMENTS

Go to the East and take up the consecrated Elemental Air Incense. Face the East, and with the Incense draw the Invoking Air Pentagram in the air.

Invoking Air Pentagram

Aspirant

Through the power of the Pentagram, I call forth the spirits of Air!

Replace the Incense. Using the index finger, touch the center of the Air Pentagram and draw a line in the air, walking towards the South.

In the South and facing South, take up the consecrated Elemental Fire Candle. With the Candle draw the Invoking Fire Pentagram.

Invoking Fire Pentagram

Aspirant
Through the power of the Pentagram, I call forth the spirits of Fire!

Replace the Candle. Touch the center of the Fire Pentagram and draw a line in the air towards the West.

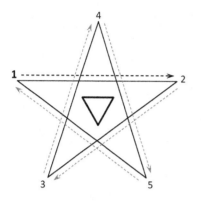

Invoking Water Pentagram

In the West and facing West, take up the consecrated Elemental Chalice of Water. With the Chalice draw the Invoking Water Pentagram.

Aspirant
Through the power of the Pentagram, I call forth the spirits of Water!

Replace the Chalice. Touch the center of the Water Pentagram and draw a line in the air towards the North.

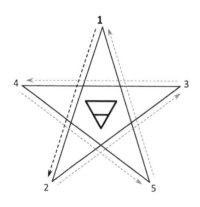

Invoking Earth Pentagram

In the North and facing North, take up the consecrated Elemental Salt. With the Salt draw the Invoking Earth Pentagram.

Aspirant
Through the power of the Pentagram, I call forth the spirits of Earth!

Replace the Salt. Touch the center of the Earth Pentagram and draw a line in the air towards the East. While standing in the East, turn and face the center of the room.

Aspirant

Hear me, four quarters of the World, for I call out to thee! Grant me the strength to walk the hidden path and discover secret knowledge. Give me your eyes to see and your wisdom to understand, that I may be like you. Grant me your powers that I may call the powers of Mars.

INVOCATION OF SPIRIT

Go to the West of the Altar and face East. In the air before you, draw the two Invoking Spirit Pentagrams:

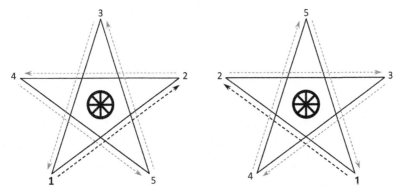

Invoking Passive Spirit Pentagram   Invoking Active Spirit Pentagram

Aspirant

O Thou supreme Life-Spirit, Cause of all Creation, Origin of all, and single Source of every living soul. Of Thee alone is my beginning, and in Thee alone have I no ending. O Thou single source of truth and wisdom, let me ascend to the Higher

Realms on the Chariot of Truth. Bring me over the gulfs and abysses, bear me upward out of gorges and valleys; become for me the source of liberation. Let Thy great brightness cause the path to be lit before me. Let me ascend to the Heavens as if upon a ship of Light, that I may come to know the Planetary Spheres. So mote it be. *Pause for a moment and visualize your aura filled with White Light.*

Optional: Elevating the Temple into the Heavens

<u>Aspirant</u>
All is now in readiness to ascend to the Planetary Powers. I shall quit the material world and enter the higher realms by placing the consecrated Elemental Powers in their zodiacal stations.

Go clockwise to the South, take up the Candle, and go clockwise to the East. Face the East.

<u>Aspirant</u>
In the earthly realm, the East is the station of Elemental Air. However, in the higher realms, the East is the station of Aries, the movable Sign of Fire. (*Place the Candle in the East.*) Through the power of this consecrated emblem of Fire, this quarter is now elevated to the heavens. *Take up the Incense and go clockwise to the West, facing the West.*

<u>Aspirant</u>
In the earthly realm, the West is the station of Elemental Water. However, in the higher realms, the West is the station of Libra, the movable Sign of Air. (*Place the Incense in the West.*) Through the power of this consecrated emblem of Air, this

quarter is now elevated to the heavens. *Take up the Chalice. Go clockwise to the North and face the North.*

Aspirant

In the earthly realm, the North is the station of Elemental Earth. However, in the higher realms, the North is the station of Cancer, the movable Sign of Water. (*Place the Chalice in the North.*) **Through the power of this consecrated emblem of Water, this quarter is now elevated to the heavens.** *Take up the Salt. Go clockwise to the South and face the South.*

Aspirant

In the earthly realm, the South is the station of Elemental Fire. However, in the higher realms, the South is the station of Capricorn, the movable Sign of Earth. (*Place the Salt in the South.*) **Through the power of this consecrated emblem of Earth, this quarter is now elevated to the heavens.** *Go to the West of the Altar, and face East.*

FIRST ADVANCEMENT: THE INVOCATION OF MARS

Aspirant

(*West of Altar, facing East.*) **I have opened this Temple to perform a consecration of a Candle of Mars. Unseen Watchers over the sacred Magic, watch over this ceremony of the Light Divine. So mote it be.**

Take up the unlit red Mars Candle. Advance to the location of Mars in the Temple (or his symbolic, Hexagrammatic location), facing him.

Aspirant

By the authority of the Six-Rayed Star, the Mystical Seal of Solomon the King and the Symbol of Life, I call forth the Powers of Mars!

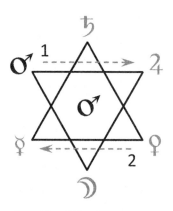

Invoking Mars Hexagram

With the Candle, draw the Invoking Hexagram of Mars. Draw the symbol of Mars in the center.

Holding the red Candle of Mars, walk clockwise around the room once slowly while saying:

Aspirant

In the Divine Name ELOHIM GIBOR, and in the name of the great Archangel ZAMAEL, I call to the mighty guardian, he who enchains the forces of darkness. You are the all-powerful defender of justice and truth, and the noble inspirer of courage, endurance and bold resolve. It is you who motivates loyalty and confirms the steadfast heart and the unfaltering hand. You are the powerful adversary of all malevolent Forces, be they human or not, and your power is now present in the working of this rite.

Return to the Mars Hexagram, touch the Candle to the symbol of Mars in the center, and move clockwise back to the Altar. Place the Candle in its proper position on the Altar, still facing Mars.

Aspirant

It is you who restrains the serpent; your splendor consumes the enemy. Furious you are in combat, for you are the victorious one. You are the pure flame of valor and infuse strong

resolve into the blood of all who aspire. **Fearless champion are you, whose domain is the abode of the fearless and whose might is protection for the good. It is your light that emboldens, for you are the defender of the just cause. Your arm is above me, your shield is before me, and your sword strikes down all barriers. Through the Valiant Glory of the Martial presence, I consecrate this Candle of Mars.**

Make a circle around the Mars Candle, draw in the circle the Invoking Hexagram of Mars, and place the sigil of Mars in the center. Visualize the RED Hexagram sink into the Candle.

Take the Mars Candle to the East, and face East. Make the RED symbol of Mars in the air to the East, with the Candle.

Symbol of Mars

Aspirant
I stand before the rising of Mars. The Martial Powers dawn within my mind, and I breathe in the mysteries of the Magic of the Mars. (*Visualize the symbol of Mars rising out of darkness while its rays fill your body with its bright red color.*) **I establish the Power of Mars in the East.** *Go to the South and face the South. Make the red symbol of Mars.*

Aspirant
Mars reaches his zenith and shines brightly in the heavens. I project the Martial Powers through the Magic of the Light. (*Visualize the red light of Mars raying out of your body in brilliant streams of light.*) **I establish the Power of Mars in the South.** *Go to the West and face the West. Make the red symbol of Mars.*

Aspirant

Mars is in his setting and now sheds an inner Light. I take the Martial Powers within me, and they dwell within my soul. (*Visualize the red symbol of Mars glowing in your heart.*) **I establish the Power of Mars in the West.** *Go to the North and face the North. Make the red symbol of Mars.*

Aspirant

Mars is at his nadir, now dwelling in the hidden realms. I will explore the worlds of mystery in the Martial Light. (*Visualize the symbol of the Mars on a red door in front of you; see the door begin to open.*) **I establish the Power of Mars in the North.** *Return to the West of the Altar and sit, facing the East.*

Light the Mars Candle from the Sol Candle. Visualize the Mars Candle glowing in a vibrant RED light. Place the Mars Candle in its proper position on the Altar.

SECOND ADVANCEMENT: MEDITATION ON *THE TOWER*

Turn the color of your aura to RED. Take up the Tarot card *The Tower* and study its image while saying:

Aspirant

Lord of the Hosts of the Mighty, you who are an avenging force. Through your power comes the sudden and complete destruction of false thoughts and habits, and what follows is the rebuilding and reconstruction of the self which reveals the Higher Self to those who walk your path. To some you are the force of failure, ruin and catastrophe, but to others you are the Tower struck by lightning, wherein reality alters convictions

which lack the essence of truth. **Through you comes the destruction of the lies of life, and what is left is the foundation of truth. Clarity of vision is given and resistance to change finally is broken. The Tower is ambition built on false principles, now destroyed by the inception of the true and full idea of the Good. Through you is the sudden inspiration of truth, a message sent from heaven to earth, from the Spirit to the material, that the time for change is now.**

Close your eyes and visualize yourself in the imagery of the card. Note any thoughts or sensations that arise. Before you quit this visualization, make an offering of your own Light to the Powers of Mars.

Alternative Meditation

It is nighttime, and the air is hot and dry. You are standing on rather barren ground beside a tree with many thorns. When you reach out to touch one of the thorns, you find it is very sharp. Its point pricks your finger, which begins to bleed slightly. Looking up into the sky, you see red clouds with streaks of lightning; the silhouette of a hawk is outlined in the flashing light. You hear a rumbling in the distance and cannot tell if it is thunder or the sound of cannon. To your left is a wolf stalking prey, and you hear the growl of a bear close by as it crashes through the underbrush.

You walk down a red and dusty path and eventually come upon a red brick building; the bricks are fiery hot, and glow in the darkness of the night. As you approach the door, it opens wide and you look inside. A blast of hot air blows your hair and invades your nostrils with an acrid odor. Within the brick building is an enormous forge with large bellows driving hot air into iron furnaces, which are alight with great red flames. Molten metals flow in glowing red rivers, emptying into molds of fierce weapons of war: swords, spear heads, hatchets, and spiked maces.

You turn and leave the building and return to the thorn tree. Before you quit this visualization, make an offering of your own Light to the Powers of Mars.

Aspirant
The Martial Candle has been consecrated and holds within it the force of Mars. With this power, the Temple of Mars has been created. So mote it be.

CLOSING

Go to the East and face the center of the room.

Aspirant
I now release any spirits that may have been attracted to this ceremony. Go in peace to your abodes and habitations and go with the blessings of Mars.

Purify and consecrate the Temple and your body with the water and incense, as in the Opening. Banish with the banishing Pentagram in all four quarters, as in the Opening. Return to the East.

Aspirant
I now declare this ritual duly completed. So mote it be.

Extinguish the candles.

CONSECRATION OF A CANDLE OF MERCURY
To be Performed on the Day of Mercury (Wednesday)

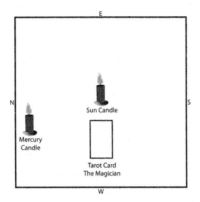

Figure 33: Altar arrangement for Mercury

Temple arrangement: Planetary Temple 1st Part (see Introduction), with Air Incense and Fire Candle lit.

Altar cloth: Yellow.

Candles: Orange Sol Candle (lit), yellow Mercury Candle (unlit).

Tarot Card: *The Magician.*

Incense, Water: In the East, with incense lit (lavender or other Mercurial incense).

Music: Suitable ambient or background music.

PREPARATION FOR THE RITE

Sit for a moment at the Altar and contemplate the rite to come. Let the cares and worries of the day dissipate. ✶ Focus on the top of your head and form a mental image of a ray of White Light permeating your body through the top of your head. Visualize this Light descending through the center of your body to your feet. Your body is now filled with Light. ✶ Inhale and exhale this Light through the pores of your body until it is pulsing in and around you. ✶ Imagine the Light extending from your body and filling the room. See the Light creating a barrier separating the room from the outer world. Let nothing exist for you outside of this special time and place.

OPENING

Standing West of the Altar, facing East, say:

<u>**Aspirant**</u>

I banish all worldly influences dwelling within this Temple by the Flaming Star of the Five Elements. I say unto you now, depart!

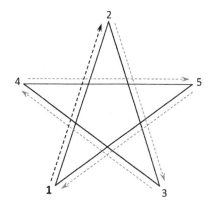

Banishing Elemental Pentagram

Go to the East. Make the Banishing Pentagram to the East, then do the same in the South, the West, and the North. Return to the East.

Take up the Cup of Water and sprinkle three times in the East, then do the same in the South, the West, and the North. Return to the East. Dip your finger in the Cup and touch your forehead, then sprinkle Water toward your feet, and touch your right and left shoulders.

<u>**Aspirant**</u>

I am purified; the Temple is purified; all is purified by the Lustral Waters. *Replace the Cup.*

Take up the incense and wave it three times in the East, then do the same in the South, the West, and the North. Return to the East. Wave the incense toward your forehead, your feet and your right and left shoulders.

Aspirant

I am consecrated; the Temple is consecrated; all is consecrated by Holy Fire. *Replace the Incense.*

Aspirant

(*In East, facing East*) **I have purified and consecrated this Temple for the invocation of Mercury, and in so doing have created a Temple, that the heavenly forces of Mercury may dwell here for a time. So mote it be.**

INVOKING THE ELEMENTS

Go to the East and take up the consecrated Elemental Air Incense. Face the East, and with the Incense draw the Invoking Air Pentagram in the air.

Aspirant

Through the power of the Pentagram, I call forth the spirits of Air!

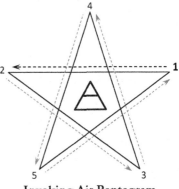

Invoking Air Pentagram

Replace the Incense. Using the index finger, touch the center of the Air Pentagram and draw a line in the air, walking towards the South.

In the South and facing South, take up the consecrated Elemental Fire Candle. With the Candle draw the Invoking Fire Pentagram.

Invoking Fire Pentagram

Aspirant
Through the power of the Pentagram, I call forth the spirits of Fire!

Replace the Candle. Touch the center of the Fire Pentagram and draw a line in the air towards the West.

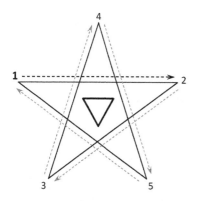

Invoking Water Pentagram

In the West and facing West, take up the consecrated Elemental Chalice of Water. With the Chalice draw the Invoking Water Pentagram.

Aspirant
Through the power of the Pentagram, I call forth the spirits of Water!

Replace the Chalice. Touch the center of the Water Pentagram and draw a line in the air towards the North.

Invoking Earth Pentagram

In the North and facing North, take up the consecrated Elemental Salt. With the Salt draw the Invoking Earth Pentagram.

Aspirant
Through the power of the Pentagram, I call forth the spirits of Earth!

Replace the Salt. Touch the center of the Earth Pentagram and draw a line in the air towards the East. While standing in the East, turn and face the center of the room.

Aspirant

Hear me, four quarters of the World, for I call out to thee! Grant me the strength to walk the hidden path and discover secret knowledge. Give me your eyes to see and your wisdom to understand, that I may be like you. Grant me your powers that I may call the powers of Mercury.

INVOCATION OF SPIRIT

Go to the West of the Altar and face East. In the air before you, draw the two Invoking Spirit Pentagrams:

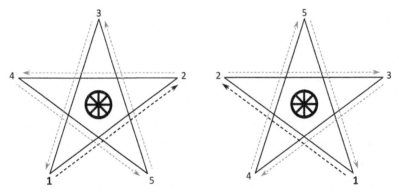

Invoking Passive Spirit Pentagram   Invoking Active Spirit Pentagram

Aspirant

O Thou supreme Life-Spirit, Cause of all Creation, Origin of all, and single Source of every living soul. Of Thee alone is my beginning, and in Thee alone have I no ending. O Thou single source of truth and wisdom, let me ascend to the Higher

Realms on the Chariot of Truth. Bring me over the gulfs and abysses, bear me upward out of gorges and valleys; become for me the source of liberation. Let Thy great brightness cause the path to be lit before me. Let me ascend to the Heavens as if upon a ship of Light, that I may come to know the Planetary Spheres. So mote it be. *Pause for a moment and visualize your aura filled with White Light.*

Optional: Elevating the Temple into the Heavens

Aspirant

All is now in readiness to ascend to the Planetary Powers. I shall quit the material world and enter the higher realms by placing the consecrated Elemental Powers in their zodiacal stations.

Go clockwise to the South, take up the Candle, and go clockwise to the East. Face the East.

Aspirant

In the earthly realm, the East is the station of Elemental Air. However, in the higher realms, the East is the station of Aries, the movable Sign of Fire. (*Place the Candle in the East.*) Through the power of this consecrated emblem of Fire, this quarter is now elevated to the heavens. *Take up the Incense and go clockwise to the West, facing the West.*

Aspirant

In the earthly realm, the West is the station of Elemental Water. However, in the higher realms, the West is the station of Libra, the movable Sign of Air. (*Place the Incense in the West.*) Through the power of this consecrated emblem of Air, this

quarter is now elevated to the heavens. *Take up the Chalice. Go clockwise to the North and face the North.*

Aspirant

In the earthly realm, the North is the station of Elemental Earth. However, in the higher realms, the North is the station of Cancer, the movable Sign of Water. (*Place the Chalice in the North.*) Through the power of this consecrated emblem of Water, this quarter is now elevated to the heavens. *Take up the Salt. Go clockwise to the South and face the South.*

Aspirant

In the earthly realm, the South is the station of Elemental Fire. However, in the higher realms, the South is the station of Capricorn, the movable Sign of Earth. (*Place the Salt in the South.*) Through the power of this consecrated emblem of Earth, this quarter is now elevated to the heavens. *Go to the West of the Altar, and face East.*

FIRST ADVANCEMENT: THE INVOCATION OF MERCURY

Aspirant

(*West of Altar, facing East.*) I have opened this Temple to perform a consecration of a Candle of Mercury. Unseen Watchers over the sacred Magic, watch over this ceremony of the Light Divine. So mote it be.

Take up the unlit yellow Mercury Candle. Advance to the location of Mercury in the Temple (or his symbolic, Hexagrammatic location), facing him.

Aspirant

By the authority of the Six-Rayed Star, the Mystical Seal of Solomon the King and the Symbol of Life, I call forth the Powers of Mercury!

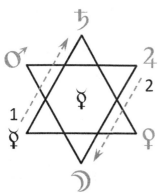

Invoking Mercury Hexagram

With the Candle, draw the Invoking Hexagram of Mercury. Draw the symbol of Mercury in the center.

Holding the yellow Candle of Mercury, walk clockwise around the room once slowly while saying:

Aspirant

In the Divine Name ELOHIM TZABAOTH (El-oh-heem Tzah-bah-oth), and in the name of the great Archangel RAPHAEL, I call to the Mercury, who is the traveler between the Worlds. It is you who bears secret tidings to both gods and humans alike. It is you who speaks the Words of Power. You are the Great Magician of the Magical Art; knowledge and skill are yours to impart to those who seek them. You are the keeper of the signs, the sigils, and the secret names. The Great Scribe you are, and your Power is now present in the working of this rite.

Return to the Mercury Hexagram, touch the Candle to the symbol of Mercury in the center, and move clockwise back to the Altar. Place the Candle in its proper position on the Altar, still facing Mercury.

Aspirant

You are the Lord of Divine Words. I shall hear now the words you impart, and I shall be raised from the darkness to the Light. With your power you are the far-seeing and sure guide of souls, the true Counselor to those of the magical arts. You are the keeper of the words of power and the might of Number. You are sought amongst the children of High Magic, for in your hands are the hidden ways of life and death, and of every mystery. You are the giver of knowledge, the giver of power. Through the enlightening glory of the Mercurial presence, I consecrate this Candle of Mercury.

Make a circle around the Mercury Candle, draw in the circle the Invoking Hexagram of Mercury, and place the sigil of Mercury in the center. Visualize the YELLOW Hexagram sink into the Candle.

Take the Mercury Candle to the East, and face East. Make the YELLOW symbol of Mercury in the air to the East, with the Candle.

Symbol of Mercury

Aspirant

I stand before the rising of Mercury. The Mercurial Powers dawn within my mind, and I breathe in the mysteries of the Magic of the Mercury. (*Visualize the symbol of Mercury rising out of darkness while its rays fill your body with its bright yellow color.*) **I establish the Power of Mercury in the East.** *Go to the South and face the South. Make the yellow symbol of Mercury.*

<u>**Aspirant**</u>

Mercury reaches his zenith and shines brightly in the heavens. I project the Mercurial Powers through the Magic of the Light. (*Visualize the yellow light of Mercury raying out of your body in brilliant streams of light.*) **I establish the Power of Mercury in the South.** *Go to the West and face the West. Make the yellow symbol of Mercury.*

<u>**Aspirant**</u>

Mercury is in his setting and now sheds an inner Light. I take the Mercurial Powers within me, and they dwell within my soul. (*Visualize the yellow symbol of Mercury glowing in your heart.*) **I establish the Power of Mercury in the West.** *Go to the North and face the North. Make the yellow symbol of Mercury.*

<u>**Aspirant**</u>

Mercury is at his nadir, now dwelling in the hidden realms. I will explore the worlds of mystery in the Mercurial Light. (*Visualize the symbol of Mercury on a yellow door in front of you; see the door begin to open.*) **I establish the Power of Mercury in the North.** *Return to the West of the Altar and sit, facing the East.*

Light the Mercury Candle from the Sol Candle. Visualize the Mercury Candle glowing in a vibrant YELLOW light. Place the Mercury Candle in its proper position on the Altar.

SECOND ADVANCEMENT:
MEDITATION ON *THE MAGICIAN*

Turn the color of your aura to YELLOW. Take up the Tarot card *The Magician* and study its image while saying:

Aspirant

Great Magus of Power, architect and carpenter of the house in which Divine spirit dwells. It is you who directs magical energy, and yet you also are the energy that is directed. You are Hermes, the God of wisdom, magic and communication. Through you all magical acts are manifested. You have transcended duality and you have mastered the Elements of the universe. You are the divine motive in the human being, because you are the unity of the individual on all levels of existence. Above your head is the sign of infinite life, life unending. The lesson you teach is "As above, so below," which shows that mastery in one realm brings mastery in yet another. In you is the potential for a new adventure, a journey undertaken in the light of day, for you bring Mystery out of darkness into the light.

Close your eyes and visualize yourself in the imagery of the card. Note any thoughts or sensations that arise. Before you quit this visualization, make an offering of your own Light to the Powers of Mercury.

Alternative Meditation

It is dusk, the time between the day and the night. You are leaning against a large walnut tree, whose leaved branches resemble a multitude of ferns growing out of wood. A walnut drops from the tree beside you and you bend down and pick it up. You break the shells and take a bite, chewing thoughtfully as you try to discern a taste you can identify. As you savor the treat you notice a fox run quickly past you, followed closely by a sprinting greyhound. Both disappear in the dusky light.

You follow a long pathway that continues for quite a while. A boisterous wind picks up, pushing you forward, moving you more swiftly and lightly; you almost fly through the air. Eventually the path leads to a marketplace. There is no one in the marketplace, but all of the booths are set up for coming day.

You approach one booth and find clothing of all kinds for both men and women. When you try on the men's clothing, you feel quite masculine; however, when you try on the women's clothing, your nature becomes much more feminine. You approach another booth and find Tarot cards and divination pendulums, along with occult books of all sorts. An astrolabe sits on the counter, and sky maps are hung from the ceiling. You move on to another booth and find books of poetry and philosophy, along with other books of learning. Maps of foreign lands line the walls.

You leave the marketplace and return to the walnut tree. Before you quit this visualization, make an offering of your own Light to the Powers of Mercury.

Aspirant
The Mercurial Candle has been consecrated and holds within it the force of Mercury. With this power, the Temple of Mercury has been created. So mote it be.

CLOSING

Go to the East and face the center of the room.

Aspirant
I now release any spirits that may have been attracted to this ceremony. Go in peace to your abodes and habitations and go with the blessings of Mercury.

Purify and consecrate the Temple and your body with the water and incense, as in the Opening. Banish with the banishing Pentagram in all four quarters, as in the Opening. Return to the East.

Aspirant
I now declare this ritual duly completed. So mote it be.

Extinguish the candles.

CONSECRATION OF A CANDLE OF JUPITER

To be Performed on the Day of Jupiter (Thursday)

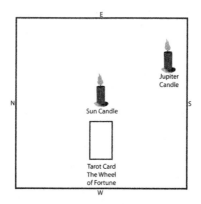

Figure 34: Altar arrangement for Jupiter

Temple arrangement: Planetary Temple 1st Part (see Introduction), with Air Incense and Fire Candle lit.

Altar cloth: Violet.

Candles: Orange Sol Candle (lit), violet Jupiter Candle (unlit).

Tarot Card: *The Wheel of Fortune.*

Incense, Water: In the East, with incense lit (cedar or other Jupiterian incense).

Music: Suitable ambient or background music.

PREPARATION FOR THE RITE

Sit for a moment at the Altar and contemplate the rite to come. Let the cares and worries of the day dissipate. ✹ Focus on the top of your head and form a mental image of a ray of White Light permeating your body through the top of your head. Visualize this Light descending through the center of your body to your feet. Your body is now filled with Light. ✹ Inhale and exhale this Light through the pores of your body until it is pulsing in and around you. ✹ Imagine the Light extending from your body and filling the room. See the Light creating a barrier separating the room from the outer world. Let nothing exist for you outside of this special time and place.

Opening

Standing West of the Altar, facing East, say:

Aspirant
I banish all worldly influences dwelling within this Temple by the Flaming Star of the Five Elements. I say unto you now, depart!

Go to the East. Make the Banishing Pentagram to the East, then do the same in the South, the West, and the North. Return to the East.

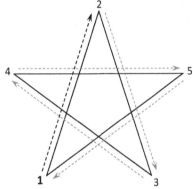

Banishing Elemental Pentagram

Take up the Cup of Water and sprinkle three times in the East, then do the same in the South, the West, and the North. Return to the East. Dip your finger in the Cup and touch your forehead, then sprinkle Water toward your feet, and touch your right and left shoulders.

Aspirant
I am purified; the Temple is purified; all is purified by the Lustral Waters. *Replace the Cup.*

Take up the incense and wave it three times in the East, then do the same in the South, the West, and the North. Return to the East. Wave the incense toward your forehead, your feet and your right and left shoulders.

Aspirant

I am consecrated; the Temple is consecrated; all is consecrated by Holy Fire. *Replace the Incense.*

Aspirant

(In East, facing East) **I have purified and consecrated this Temple for the invocation of Jupiter, and in so doing have created a Temple, that the heavenly forces of Jupiter may dwell here for a time. So mote it be.**

INVOKING THE ELEMENTS

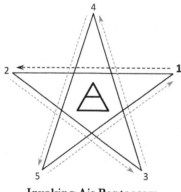

Invoking Air Pentagram

Go to the East and take up the consecrated Elemental Air Incense. Face the East, and with the Incense draw the Invoking Air Pentagram in the air.

Aspirant

Through the power of the Pentagram, I call forth the spirits of Air!

Replace the Incense. Using the index finger, touch the center of the Air Pentagram and draw a line in the air, walking towards the South.

Invoking Fire Pentagram

In the South and facing South, take up the consecrated Elemental Fire Candle. With the Candle draw the Invoking Fire Pentagram.

Aspirant
Through the power of the Pentagram, I call forth the spirits of Fire!

Replace the Candle. Touch the center of the Fire Pentagram and draw a line in the air towards the West.

In the West and facing West, take up the consecrated Elemental Chalice of Water. With the Chalice draw the Invoking Water Pen-Pentagram.

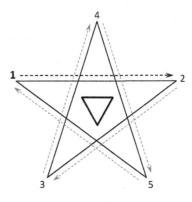

Invoking Water Pentagram

Aspirant
Through the power of the Pentagram, I call forth the spirits of Water!

Replace the Chalice. Touch the center of the Water Pentagram and draw a line in the air towards the North.

In the North and facing North, take up the consecrated Elemental Salt. With the Salt draw the Invoking Earth Pentagram.

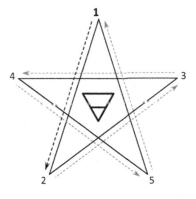

Invoking Earth Pentagram

Aspirant
Through the power of the Pentagram, I call forth the spirits of Earth!

Replace the Salt. Touch the center of the Earth Pentagram and draw a line in the air towards the East. While standing in the East, turn and face the center of the room.

Aspirant

Hear me, four quarters of the World, for I call out to thee! Grant me the strength to walk the hidden path and discover secret knowledge. Give me your eyes to see and your wisdom to understand, that I may be like you. Grant me your powers that I may call the powers of Jupiter.

INVOCATION OF SPIRIT

Go to the West of the Altar and face East. In the air before you, draw the two Invoking Spirit Pentagrams:

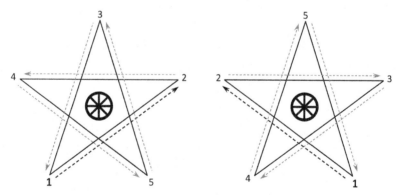

Invoking Passive Spirit Pentagram   Invoking Active Spirit Pentagram

Aspirant

O Thou supreme Life-Spirit, Cause of all Creation, Origin of all, and single Source of every living soul. Of Thee alone is my beginning, and in Thee alone have I no ending. O Thou single source of truth and wisdom, let me ascend to the Higher

Realms on the Chariot of Truth. **Bring me over the gulfs and abysses, bear me upward out of gorges and valleys; become for me the source of liberation. Let Thy great brightness cause the path to be lit before me. Let me ascend to the Heavens as if upon a ship of Light, that I may come to know the Planetary Spheres. So mote it be.** *Pause for a moment and visualize your aura filled with White Light.*

Optional: Elevating the Temple into the Heavens

Aspirant

All is now in readiness to ascend to the Planetary Powers. I shall quit the material world and enter the higher realms by placing the consecrated Elemental Powers in their zodiacal stations.

Go clockwise to the South, take up the Candle, and go clockwise to the East. Face the East.

Aspirant

In the earthly realm, the East is the station of Elemental Air. However, in the higher realms, the East is the station of Aries, the movable Sign of Fire. (*Place the Candle in the East.*) **Through the power of this consecrated emblem of Fire, this quarter is now elevated to the heavens.** *Take up the Incense and go clockwise to the West, facing the West.*

Aspirant

In the earthly realm, the West is the station of Elemental Water. However, in the higher realms, the West is the station of Libra, the movable Sign of Air. (*Place the Incense in the West.*) **Through the power of this consecrated emblem of Air, this**

quarter is now elevated to the heavens. *Take up the Chalice. Go clockwise to the North and face the North.*

Aspirant

In the earthly realm, the North is the station of Elemental Earth. However, in the higher realms, the North is the station of Cancer, the movable Sign of Water. (*Place the Chalice in the North.*) Through the power of this consecrated emblem of Water, this quarter is now elevated to the heavens. *Take up the Salt. Go clockwise to the South and face the South.*

Aspirant

In the earthly realm, the South is the station of Elemental Fire. However, in the higher realms, the South is the station of Capricorn, the movable Sign of Earth. (*Place the Salt in the South.*) Through the power of this consecrated emblem of Earth, this quarter is now elevated to the heavens. *Go to the West of the Altar, and face East.*

FIRST ADVANCEMENT: THE INVOCATION OF JUPITER

Aspirant

(*West of Altar, facing East.*) I have opened this Temple to perform a consecration of a Candle of Jupiter. Unseen Watchers over the sacred Magic, watch over this ceremony of the Light Divine. So mote it be.

Take up the unlit violet Jupiter Candle. Advance to the location of Jupiter in the Temple (or his symbolic, Hexagrammatic location), facing him.

Aspirant

By the authority of the Six-Rayed Star, the Mystical Seal of Solomon the King and the Symbol of Life, I call forth the Powers of Jupiter!

With the Candle, draw the Invoking Hexagram of Jupiter. Draw the symbol of Jupiter in the center.

Holding the violet Candle of Jupiter, walk clockwise around the room once slowly while saying:

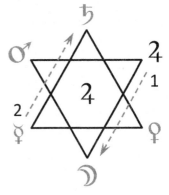

Invoking Jupiter Hexagram

Aspirant

In the Divine Name EL, and in the name of the great Archangel
SACHIEL (Sah-khee-el), I call to the glorious dispenser of mercy, and the divine Patron of brotherhood and sisterhood, he who blesses peace and amity between all beings. He is the lord of benevolent rule and the enlightened wisdom which underlies noble authority. The bringer of order in the midst of chaos is his name, and his power is now present in the working of this rite.

Return to the Jupiter Hexagram, touch the Candle to the symbol of Jupiter in the center, and move clockwise back to the Altar. Place the Candle in its proper position on the Altar, still facing Jupiter.

Aspirant

You are harmony, integrity, and truth. You are he who disposes with true wisdom all matters which fall within your judgment, for you uphold the law and dispense justice. You

are the far-seeing one, and the divine order established at the creation of the world. No one reaches enlightenment unless their heart is righteous by following your ways. You are the lord of benevolence, for you have given bread to the hungry and clothed the naked. You are a husband to the widow, and father to the orphan. Through the benevolent glory of your presence, I consecrate this **Candle of Jupiter.**

Make a circle around the Jupiter Candle, draw in the circle the Invoking Hexagram of Jupiter, and place the sigil of Jupiter in the center. Visualize the VIOLET Hexagram sink into the Candle.

Take the Jupiter Candle to the East, and face East. Make the VIOLET symbol of Jupiter in the air to the East, with the Candle.

4

Symbol of Jupiter

Aspirant
I stand before the rising of Jupiter. The Jovial Powers dawn within my mind, and I breathe in the mysteries of the Magic of the Jupiter. (*Visualize the symbol of Jupiter rising out of darkness while its rays fill your body with its bright violet color.*) **I establish the Power of Jupiter in the East.** *Go to the South and face the South. Make the violet symbol of Jupiter.*

Aspirant
Jupiter reaches his zenith and shines brightly in the heavens. I project the Jovial Powers through the Magic of the Light. (*Visualize the violet light of Jupiter raying out of your body in brilliant streams of light.*) **I establish the Power of Jupiter in the South.** *Go to the West and face the West. Make the violet symbol of Jupiter.*

Aspirant

Jupiter is in his setting and now sheds an inner Light. I take the Jovial Powers within me, and they dwell within my soul. (*Visualize the violet symbol of Jupiter glowing in your heart.*) **I establish the Power of Jupiter in the West.** *Go to the North and face the North. Make the violet symbol of Jupiter.*

Aspirant

Jupiter is at his nadir, now dwelling in the hidden realms. I will explore the worlds of mystery in the Jovial Light. (*Visualize the symbol of Jupiter on a violet door in front of you; see the door begin to open.*) **I establish the Power of Jupiter in the North.** *Return to the West of the Altar and sit, facing the East.*

Light the Jupiter Candle from the Sol Candle. Visualize the Jupiter Candle glowing in a vibrant VIOLET light. Place the Jupiter Candle in its proper position on the Altar.

SECOND ADVANCEMENT:
MEDITATION ON *THE WHEEL*

Turn the color of your aura to VIOLET. Take up the Tarot card *The Wheel* and study its image while saying:

Aspirant

Lord of the Forces of Life, you who are the Mercy and Magnificence of Sovereignty, the Intelligence of Conciliation. You are the *Rota Fortunae*, the wheel of the Goddess Fortuna, the goddess of luck and Fate, and Fate decrees a fixed and natural order in the cosmos. You are the Greek *Moirai*, the Roman *Parcae* and the Norse *Norns*, who determine the events of the

world through the mystic spinning of the threads of human fate. Your spinning wheel changes positions for those still bound to it. For some it is tribulations, and for others it is blessings, according to the higher Order of Fate. You are the symbol of time, bringing past deeds to the present and on to the future. You are the wheel of life, death and rebirth, the extremes of light and darkness, and the exchanges between these ever turn the Wheel.

Close your eyes and visualize yourself in the imagery of the card. Note any thoughts or sensations that arise. Before you quit this visualization, make an offering of your own Light to the Powers of Jupiter.

Alternative Meditation

It is daytime, and the sweet-smelling air is hot and humid. You are in a lovely courtyard with manicured hedges and bushes. Sitting on a bench beneath a lovely cherry tree, the Sun filters down through its leaves onto your face. To your right you see a large stag leading many deer over a hill. A unicorn runs past, and an eagle flies high overhead.

You get up from the bench and walk down a cobbled path towards a set of tall buildings. One is a temple, another a court of law, and the rest comprise a large university. You ascend the steps of the temple and look in through a set of double doors which have opened at your approach. In the temple, you see many priests around a great stone Altar, making offerings of sweet incense. You descend the stairs and go to the courthouse. As you approach, the doors open, and inside the building you see a judge seated high above a courtroom of lawyers. You listen to the debates and hear the arguments of law. You leave the courthouse and return to the courtyard. As you view the university's many structures, you see professors and students going in and out of the buildings.

You return to the cherry tree and again sit beneath it. Before you quit this visualization, make an offering of your own Light to the Powers of Jupiter.

Aspirant

The Jovial Candle has been consecrated and holds within it the force of Jupiter. With this power, the Temple of Jupiter has been created. So mote it be.

CLOSING

Go to the East and face the center of the room.

Aspirant

I now release any spirits that may have been attracted to this ceremony. Go in peace to your abodes and habitations and go with the blessings of Jupiter.

Purify and consecrate the Temple and your body with the water and incense, as in the Opening. Banish with the banishing Pentagram in all four quarters, as in the Opening. Return to the East.

Aspirant

I now declare this ritual duly completed. So mote it be.

Extinguish the candles.

CONSECRATION OF A CANDLE OF VENUS

To be Performed on the Day of Venus (Friday)

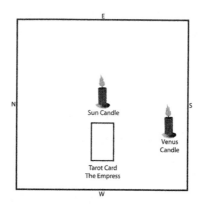

Figure 35: Altar arrangement for Venus

Temple arrangement: Planetary Temple 1st Part (see Introduction), with Air Incense and Fire Candle lit.

Altar cloth: Green.

Candles: Orange Sol Candle (lit), green Venus Candle (unlit).

Tarot Card: *The Empress.*

Incense, Water: In the East, with incense lit (rose or other Venusian incense).

Music: Suitable ambient or background music.

PREPARATION FOR THE RITE

Sit for a moment at the Altar and contemplate the rite to come. Let the cares and worries of the day dissipate. ✶ Focus on the top of your head and form a mental image of a ray of White Light permeating your body through the top of your head. Visualize this Light descending through the center of your body to your feet. Your body is now filled with Light. ✶ Inhale and exhale this Light through the pores of your body until it is pulsing in and around you. ✶ Imagine the Light extending from your body and filling the room. See the Light creating a barrier separating the room from the outer world. Let nothing exist for you outside of this special time and place.

OPENING

Standing West of the Altar, facing East, say:

<u>**Aspirant**</u>
I banish all worldly influences dwelling within this Temple by the Flaming Star of the Five Elements. I say unto you now, depart!

Go to the East. Make the Banishing Pentagram to the East, then do the same in the South, the West, and the North. Return to the East.

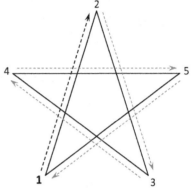

Take up the Cup of Water and sprinkle three times in the East, then do the same in the South, **Banishing Elemental Pentagram**

the West, and the North. Return to the East. Dip your finger in the Cup and touch your forehead, then sprinkle Water toward your feet, and touch your right and left shoulders.

<u>**Aspirant**</u>
I am purified; the Temple is purified; all is purified by the Lustral Waters. *Replace the Cup.*

Take up the incense and wave it three times in the East, then do the same in the South, the West, and the North. Return to the East. Wave the incense toward your forehead, your feet and your right and left shoulders.

Aspirant

I am consecrated; the Temple is consecrated; all is consecrated by Holy Fire. *Replace the Incense.*

Aspirant

(*In East, facing East*) I have purified and consecrated this Temple for the invocation of Venus, and in so doing have created a Temple, that the heavenly forces of Venus may dwell here for a time. So mote it be.

INVOKING THE ELEMENTS

Invoking Air Pentagram

Go to the East and take up the consecrated Elemental Air Incense. Face the East, and with the Incense draw the Invoking Air Pentagram in the air.

Aspirant

Through the power of the Pentagram, I call forth the spirits of Air!

Replace the Incense. Using the index finger, touch the center of the Air Pentagram and draw a line in the air, walking towards the South.

Invoking Fire Pentagram

In the South and facing South, take up the consecrated Elemental Fire Candle. With the Candle draw the Invoking Fire Pentagram.

Aspirant

Through the power of the Pentagram, I call forth the spirits of Fire!

Replace the Candle. Touch the center of the Fire Pentagram and draw a line in the air towards the West.

In the West and facing West, take up the consecrated Elemental Chalice of Water. With the Chalice draw the Invoking Water Pen-Pentagram.

Aspirant

Through the power of the Pentagram, I call forth the spirits of Water!

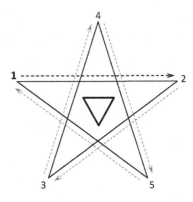

Invoking Water Pentagram

Replace the Chalice. Touch the center of the Water Pentagram and draw a line in the air towards the North.

In the North and facing North, take up the consecrated Elemental Salt. With the Salt draw the Invoking Earth Pentagram.

Aspirant

Through the power of the Pentagram, I call forth the spirits of Earth!

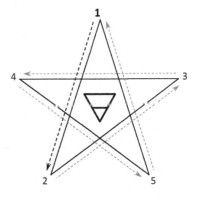

Invoking Earth Pentagram

Replace the Salt. Touch the center of the Earth Pentagram and draw a line in the air towards the East. While standing in the East, turn and face the center of the room.

Aspirant

Hear me, four quarters of the World, for I call out to thee! Grant me the strength to walk the hidden path and discover secret knowledge. Give me your eyes to see and your wisdom to understand, that I may be like you. Grant me your powers that I may call the powers of Venus.

INVOCATION OF SPIRIT

Go to the West of the Altar and face East. In the air before you, draw the two Invoking Spirit Pentagrams:

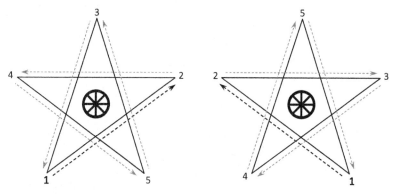

Invoking Passive Spirit Pentagram   Invoking Active Spirit Pentagram

Aspirant

O Thou supreme Life-Spirit, Cause of all Creation, Origin of all, and single Source of every living soul. Of Thee alone is my beginning, and in Thee alone have I no ending. O Thou single source of truth and wisdom, let me ascend to the Higher

Realms on the Chariot of Truth. Bring me over the gulfs and abysses, bear me upward out of gorges and valleys; become for me the source of liberation. Let Thy great brightness cause the path to be lit before me. Let me ascend to the Heavens as if upon a ship of Light, that I may come to know the Planetary Spheres. So mote it be. *Pause for a moment and visualize your aura filled with White Light.*

Optional: Elevating the Temple into the Heavens

Aspirant

All is now in readiness to ascend to the Planetary Powers. I shall quit the material world and enter the higher realms by placing the consecrated Elemental Powers in their zodiacal stations.

Go clockwise to the South, take up the Candle, and go clockwise to the East. Face the East.

Aspirant

In the earthly realm, the East is the station of Elemental Air. However, in the higher realms, the East is the station of Aries, the movable Sign of Fire. (*Place the Candle in the East.*) Through the power of this consecrated emblem of Fire, this quarter is now elevated to the heavens. *Take up the Incense and go clockwise to the West, facing the West.*

Aspirant

In the earthly realm, the West is the station of Elemental Water. However, in the higher realms, the West is the station of Libra, the movable Sign of Air. (*Place the Incense in the West.*) Through the power of this consecrated emblem of Air, this

quarter is now elevated to the heavens. *Take up the Chalice. Go clockwise to the North and face the North.*

Aspirant

In the earthly realm, the North is the station of Elemental Earth. However, in the higher realms, the North is the station of Cancer, the movable Sign of Water. (*Place the Chalice in the North.*) Through the power of this consecrated emblem of Water, this quarter is now elevated to the heavens. *Take up the Salt. Go clockwise to the South and face the South.*

Aspirant

In the earthly realm, the South is the station of Elemental Fire. However, in the higher realms, the South is the station of Capricorn, the movable Sign of Earth. (*Place the Salt in the South.*) Through the power of this consecrated emblem of Earth, this quarter is now elevated to the heavens. *Go to the West of the Altar, and face East.*

FIRST ADVANCEMENT: THE INVOCATION OF VENUS

Aspirant

(*West of Altar, facing East.*) I have opened this Temple to perform a consecration of a Candle of Venus. Unseen Watchers over the sacred Magic, watch over this ceremony of the Light Divine. So mote it be.

Take up the unlit green Venus Candle. Advance to the location of Venus in the Temple (or her symbolic, Hexagrammatic location), facing her.

Aspirant

By the authority of the Six-Rayed Star, the Mystical Seal of Solomon the King and the Symbol of Life, I call forth the Powers of Venus!

With the Candle, draw the Invoking Hexagram of Venus. Draw the symbol of Venus in the center.

Holding the green Candle of Venus, walk clockwise around the room once slowly while saying:

Invoking Venus Hexagram

Aspirant

In the Divine Name YHVH Tzabaoth (Yod Heh Vav Heh Tzah-bah-oth), and in the name of the great Archangel ANIEL, I call to Venus, the radiant giver of love and the ruler of the forces of generation. You who are divinely robed in Light and possessed of perfect beauty, I call you forth. Flawless harmony and symmetry are your perfumes, for you are the lady of the house of jubilation, and the one who fills the sanctuary with joy. You are the queen of merriment, the goddess of fertility, and your power is now present in the working of this rite.

Return to the Venus Hexagram, touch the Candle to the symbol of Venus in the center, and move clockwise back to the Altar. Place the Candle in its proper position on the Altar, still facing Venus.

Aspirant

You are the giver of gladness, bathing all beings in the light of your loving eyes. You are the song and sweet laughter, one who bestows love and ecstasy. The languid house of the heavenly stars is your abode, and it is love and peace that open your doors. You bring forth joy and harmony and beauty in life. Your smile fills the air with sparkling light, and the fragrance of flowering blossoms. Through the inspirational glory of your presence, I consecrate this Candle of Venus.

Make a circle around the Venus Candle, draw in the circle the Invoking Hexagram of Venus, and place the sigil of Venus in the center. Visualize the GREEN Hexagram sink into the Candle.

Take the Venus Candle to the East, and face East. Make the GREEN symbol of Venus in the air to the East, with the Candle.

Symbol of Venus

Aspirant

I stand before the rising of Venus. The Venusian Powers dawn within my mind, and I breathe in the mysteries of the Magic of the Venus. (*Visualize the symbol of Venus rising out of darkness while its rays fill your body with its bright green color.*) I establish the Power of Venus in the East. *Go to the South and face the South. Make the green symbol of Venus.*

Aspirant

Venus reaches her zenith and shines brightly in the heavens. I project the Venusian Powers through the Magic of the Light. (*Visualize the green light of Venus raying out of your body in brilliant streams of light.*) **I establish the Power of Venus in the South.** *Go to the West and face the West. Make the green symbol of Venus.*

Aspirant
Venus is in her setting and now sheds an inner Light. I take the Venusian Powers within me, and they dwell within my soul. (*Visualize the green symbol of Venus glowing in your heart.*) **I establish the Power of Venus in the West.** *Go to the North and face the North. Make the green symbol of Venus.*

Aspirant
Venus is at her nadir, now dwelling in the hidden realms. I will explore the worlds of mystery in the Venusian Light. (*Visualize the symbol of Venus on a green door in front of you; see the door begin to open.*) **I establish the Power of Venus in the North.** *Return to the West of the Altar and sit, facing the East.*

Light the Venus Candle from the Sol Candle. Visualize the Venus Candle glowing in a vibrant GREEN light. Place the Venus Candle in its proper position on the Altar.

SECOND ADVANCEMENT:
MEDITATION ON *THE EMPRESS*

Turn the color of your aura to GREEN. Take up the Tarot card *The Empress* and study its image while saying:

Aspirant
Daughter of the Mighty Ones, the wisdom of understanding, and the union of the powers of force and form. You who are the universal mother, the all-loving one. You are the nurturer

and the creation of earthly life. All of nature in its splendorous glory was born from your womb, for your domain is over all growing things. You are Venus, the goddess of all things beautiful. You are Demeter, the goddess of abundance and giver of earthly gifts. Object of Desire is your name, the love of the beloved. Beauty, art, pleasure, and love are yours to give. Earthly Paradise are you, and the fruitful mother of thousands. You are fertility in all endeavors, the flowing fountain of all beauty and delight.

Close your eyes and visualize yourself in the imagery of the card. Note any thoughts or sensations that arise. Before you quit this visualization, make an offering of your own Light to the Powers of Venus.

Alternative Meditation

It is nighttime, just before dawn, and the air is slightly chilly and moist. You are sitting in an apple orchard, beneath a large apple tree whose branches are heavy-laden with its luscious red fruit. Clear gems of dew sparkle on the soft green grasses and the leaves of the trees. As you sit beneath the tree, you notice close to your right a baby rabbit munching on some sweet clover. You hear the sweet song of the nightingale off in the distance.

You walk down a grassy pathway until you come to a magnificent lodge surrounded by gardens of white roses. Dark blue and streaked with gold, lapis lazuli fountains spray gentle mists of clear water over the rose bushes, and small ponds of white water lilies line the walkway to the entrance. The air is scented with the perfume of the delicate flowers.

As you approach the lodge, the doors swing wide and you look into an inviting, candle-lit bed chamber beautifully prepared for a pair of lovers who are soon to come. The large, four-poster bed is covered in soft velvet, sky-blue with earthen brown trim. Goose feathered pillows fluffed up fat and supple lean against the walnut headboard. On a small table by the bed are many enchanting and sweet desserts, bordered with goblets of warmed brandy wine. A scented bath is prepared in a white porcelain tub, lined in a soft green fabric. Soft and harmonious music fills the room with sweet sound.

You gently close the door behind you as you leave and return to the apple orchard. Before you quit this visualization, make an offering of your own Light to the Powers of Venus.

Aspirant

The Venusian Candle has been consecrated and holds within it the force of Venus. With this power, the Temple of Venus has been created. So mote it be.

CLOSING

Go to the East and face the center of the room.

Aspirant

I now release any spirits that may have been attracted to this ceremony. Go in peace to your abodes and habitations and go with the blessings of Venus.

Purify and consecrate the Temple and your body with the water and incense, as in the Opening. Banish with the banishing Pentagram in all four quarters, as in the Opening. Return to the East.

Aspirant

I now declare this ritual duly completed. So mote it be.

Extinguish the candles.

CONSECRATION OF A CANDLE OF SATURN
To be Performed on the Day of Saturn (Saturday)

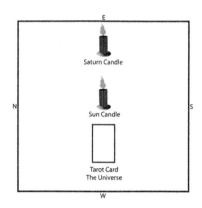

Figure 36: Altar arrangement for Saturn

Temple arrangement: Planetary Temple 1st Part (see Introduction), with Air Incense and Fire Candle lit.

Altar cloth: Blue-violet.

Candles: Orange Sol Candle (lit), blue-violet Saturn Candle (unlit).

Tarot Card: *The World/Universe.*

Incense, Water: In the East, with incense lit (myrrh or other Saturnian incense).

Music: Suitable ambient or background music.

PREPARATION FOR THE RITE

Sit for a moment at the Altar and contemplate the rite to come. Let the cares and worries of the day dissipate. ✷ Focus on the top of your head and form a mental image of a ray of White Light permeating your body through the top of your head. Visualize this Light descending through the center of your body to your feet. Your body is now filled with Light. ✷ Inhale and exhale this Light through the pores of your body until it is pulsing in and around you. ✷ Imagine the Light extending from your body and filling the room. See the Light creating a barrier separating the room from the outer world. Let nothing exist for you outside of this special time and place.

OPENING

Standing West of the Altar, facing East, say:

Aspirant
I banish all worldly influences dwelling within this Temple by the Flaming Star of the Five Elements. I say unto you now, depart!

Go to the East. Make the Banishing Pentagram to the East, then do the same in the South, the West, and the North. Return to the East.

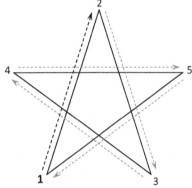

Take up the Cup of Water and sprinkle three times in the East, then do the same in the South,

Banishing Elemental Pentagram

the West, and the North. Return to the East. Dip your finger in the Cup and touch your forehead, then sprinkle Water toward your feet, and touch your right and left shoulders.

Aspirant
I am purified; the Temple is purified; all is purified by the Lustral Waters. *Replace the Cup.*

Take up the incense and wave it three times in the East, then do the same in the South, the West, and the North. Return to the East. Wave the incense toward your forehead, your feet and your right and left shoulders.

<u>Aspirant</u>

I am consecrated; the Temple is consecrated; all is consecrated by Holy Fire. *Replace the Incense.*

<u>Aspirant</u>

(In East, facing East) **I have purified and consecrated this Temple for the invocation of Saturn, and in so doing have created a Temple, that the heavenly forces of Saturn may dwell here for a time. So mote it be.**

INVOKING THE ELEMENTS

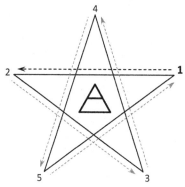

Invoking Air Pentagram

Go to the East and take up the consecrated Elemental Air Incense. Face the East, and with the Incense draw the Invoking Air Pentagram in the air.

<u>Aspirant</u>
Through the power of the Pentagram, I call forth the spirits of Air!

Replace the Incense. Using the index finger, touch the center of the Air Pentagram and draw a line in the air, walking towards the South.

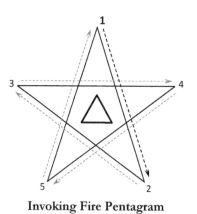

Invoking Fire Pentagram

In the South and facing South, take up the consecrated Elemental Fire Candle. With the Candle draw the Invoking Fire Pentagram.

Aspirant
Through the power of the Pentagram, I call forth the spirits of Fire!

Replace the Candle. Touch the center of the Fire Pentagram and draw a line in the air towards the West.

In the West and facing West, take up the consecrated Elemental Chalice of Water. With the Chalice draw the Invoking Water Pen-Pentagram.

Aspirant
Through the power of the Pentagram, I call forth the spirits of Water!

Invoking Water Pentagram

Replace the Chalice. Touch the center of the Water Pentagram and draw a line in the air towards the North.

In the North and facing North, take up the consecrated Elemental Salt. With the Salt draw the Invoking Earth Pentagram.

Aspirant
Through the power of the Pentagram, I call forth the spirits of Earth!

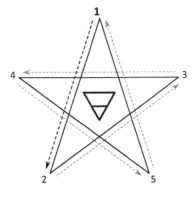

Invoking Earth Pentagram

Replace the Salt. Touch the center of the Earth Pentagram and draw a line in the air towards the East. While standing in the East, turn and face the center of the room.

Aspirant

Hear me, four quarters of the World, for I call out to thee! Grant me the strength to walk the hidden path and discover secret knowledge. Give me your eyes to see and your wisdom to understand, that I may be like you. Grant me your powers that I may call the powers of Saturn.

INVOCATION OF SPIRIT

Go to the West of the Altar and face East. In the air before you, draw the two Invoking Spirit Pentagrams:

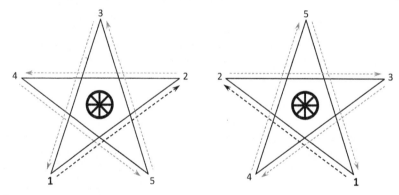

Invoking Passive Spirit Pentagram   Invoking Active Spirit Pentagram

Aspirant

O Thou supreme Life-Spirit, Cause of all Creation, Origin of all, and single Source of every living soul. Of Thee alone is my beginning, and in Thee alone have I no ending. O Thou single source of truth and wisdom, let me ascend to the Higher

Realms on the Chariot of Truth. Bring me over the gulfs and abysses, bear me upward out of gorges and valleys; become for me the source of liberation. Let Thy great brightness cause the path to be lit before me. Let me ascend to the Heavens as if upon a ship of Light, that I may come to know the Planetary Spheres. So mote it be. *Pause for a moment and visualize your aura filled with White Light.*

Optional: Elevating the Temple into the Heavens

Aspirant

All is now in readiness to ascend to the Planetary Powers. I shall quit the material world and enter the higher realms by placing the consecrated Elemental Powers in their zodiacal stations.

Go clockwise to the South, take up the Candle, and go clockwise to the East. Face the East.

Aspirant

In the earthly realm, the East is the station of Elemental Air. However, in the higher realms, the East is the station of Aries, the movable Sign of Fire. (*Place the Candle in the East.*) Through the power of this consecrated emblem of Fire, this quarter is now elevated to the heavens. *Take up the Incense and go clockwise to the West, facing the West.*

Aspirant

In the earthly realm, the West is the station of Elemental Water. However, in the higher realms, the West is the station of Libra, the movable Sign of Air. (*Place the Incense in the West.*) Through the power of this consecrated emblem of Air, this

quarter is now elevated to the heavens. *Take up the Chalice. Go clockwise to the North and face the North.*

Aspirant

In the earthly realm, the North is the station of Elemental Earth. However, in the higher realms, the North is the station of Cancer, the movable Sign of Water. (*Place the Chalice in the North.*) Through the power of this consecrated emblem of Water, this quarter is now elevated to the heavens. *Take up the Salt. Go clockwise to the South and face the South.*

Aspirant

In the earthly realm, the South is the station of Elemental Fire. However, in the higher realms, the South is the station of Capricorn, the movable Sign of Earth. (*Place the Salt in the South.*) Through the power of this consecrated emblem of Earth, this quarter is now elevated to the heavens. *Go to the West of the Altar, and face East.*

FIRST ADVANCEMENT: THE INVOCATION OF SATURN

Aspirant

(*West of Altar, facing East.*) I have opened this Temple to perform a consecration of a Candle of Saturn. Unseen Watchers over the sacred Magic, watch over this ceremony of the Light Divine. So mote it be.

Take up the unlit blue-violet Saturn Candle. Advance to the location of Saturn in the Temple (or his symbolic, Hexagrammatic location), facing him.

Aspirant

By the authority of the Six-Rayed Star, the Mystical Seal of Solomon the King and the Symbol of Life, I call forth the Powers of Saturn!

With the Candle, draw the Invoking Hexagram of Saturn. Draw the symbol of Saturn in the center.

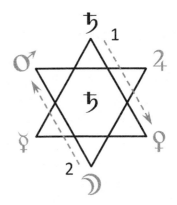

Holding the blue-violet Candle of Saturn, walk clockwise around the room once slowly while saying:

Aspirant

In the Divine Name YHVH   Invoking Saturn Hexagram

ELOHIM (Yod Heh Vav Heh El-oh-heem) and in the name of the great Archangel, KASSIEL, I call to Saturn. You are he who is mystery, the divine understanding, and the protector of the dead. You are the ancient and wise one. Sower and the Reaper are you, and you bear the scepter of elder night. Through time and necessity do you rule. You are all that has been, that which is, and that which will be, and your power is now present in the working of this rite.

Return to the Saturn Hexagram, touch the Candle to the symbol of Saturn in the center, and move clockwise back to the Altar. Place the Candle in its proper position on the Altar, still facing Saturn.

Aspirant

You are the concealed one, the most ancient one. The mother-father of the Heavens. Through mystery and the secret

seeds of life do you move. You bear the scepter of elder night, and your domain is the vast flowing ocean of time. Those who create and form know you, and to them time is no enemy, nor eternity a stranger. The silent one who works unseen in the darkness, are you. Through your enduring fidelity, you bring the labors on earth to their full harvest. Through the veiled glory of your presence, I consecrate this Candle of Saturn.

Make a circle around the Saturn Candle, draw in the circle the Invoking Hexagram of Saturn, and place the sigil of Saturn in the center. Visualize the BLUE-VIOLET Hexagram sink into the Candle.

Take the Saturn Candle to the East, and face East. Make the BLUE-VIOLET symbol of Saturn in the air to the East, with the Candle.

$$\hbar$$

Symbol of Saturn

Aspirant

I stand before the rising of Saturn. The Saturnine Powers dawn within my mind, and I breathe in the mysteries of the Magic of the Saturn. (*Visualize the symbol of Saturn rising out of darkness while its rays fill your body with its bright blue-violet color*). I establish the Power of Saturn in the East. *Go to the South and face the South. Make the blue-violet symbol of Saturn.*

Aspirant

Saturn reaches his zenith and shines brightly in the heavens. I project the Saturnine Powers through the Magic of the Light. (*Visualize the indigo light of Saturn raying out of your body in brilliant streams of light.*) I establish the Power of Saturn in the South. *Go to the West and face the West. Make the blue-violet symbol of Saturn.*

Aspirant

Saturn is in his setting and now sheds an inner Light. I take the Saturnine Powers within me, and they dwell within my soul. (*Visualize the indigo symbol of Saturn glowing in your heart.*) I establish the Power of Saturn in the West. *Go to the North and face the North. Make the blue-violet symbol of Saturn.*

Aspirant

Saturn is at his nadir, now dwelling in the hidden realms. I will explore the worlds of mystery in the Saturnine Light. (*Visualize the symbol of Saturn on an indigo door in front of you; see the door begin to open.*) I establish the Power of Saturn in the North. *Return to the West of the Altar and sit, facing the East.*

Light the Saturn Candle from the Sol Candle. Visualize the Saturn Candle glowing in a vibrant BLUE-VIOLET light. Place the Saturn Candle in its proper position on the Altar.

SECOND ADVANCEMENT:
MEDITATION ON *THE UNIVERSE*

Turn the color of your aura to BLUE-VIOLET. Take up the Tarot card *The Universe* and study its image while saying:

Aspirant

Great One of the Night of Time, Foundation of the Cosmic Elements and the Material World. You who give form to the Elements. You who are the doorway to life and to death. You who are the Gate to the higher realms. You are Gaia, mother of the land, sea and sky. You are Demeter and Ceres, Goddesses of fields and fertility. You are Danu, mother of all

living things. You are Isis, Queen of the Earth. Through you comes the ending of the cycle of life, a pause before the next cycle begins. You are completeness, representing cosmic consciousness and the potential of perfect union with the One Power of the universe. The four Kerubim are the fourfold structure of the physical world, which frame the sacred center of Spirit, the place where the Divine is manifest. This is the zenith of development, of eternity and completion, the harmony between spirit and body.

Close your eyes and visualize yourself in the imagery of the card. Note any thoughts or sensations that arise. Before you quit this visualization, make an offering of your own Light to the Powers of Saturn.

Alternative Meditation

It is daytime, but cloudy and dark. The air is cold and dry. You are sitting on the chilled ground beneath a secluded weeping willow tree which stands at the opening of a dark cave. In the distance is the grey shore of a body of water. You are alone: no other is in sight. Above, in the branches of the willow tree, you hear a screech; looking up, you see a large black crow flapping its wings. You feel movement beneath your legs and discover that a mole is digging in the earth below. A mouse scurries past you, running from a snake in slithering pursuit.

You stand and look into the cave. Its mouth reveals a passage that descends deep into the earth, into a mysterious, black darkness. But deep within, you see a soft blue-violet glow emanating from within the living rock, preparing future treasures through the long labor of pressure and time.

You turn from the cave and walk through gloomy and dimly-lit woods of aged and withered trees and eventually come to a sacred burial ground. A crooked lead fence surrounds the graveyard. Many and varied are the old stone markers and crypts which are scattered throughout the rocky ground of the cemetery. You hear the cold, dry wind howling and swirling between them. You take a moment to look at the ancient headstones: some are round, some square, and some are tall statues. You run your hands over them and feel their cold, stone textures. You begin to imagine ghosts of the dead walking around the cemetery. They may or may not come and speak with you.

You return to the willow tree and again are seated on the ground. Before you quit this visualization, make an offering of your own Light to the Powers of Saturn.

Aspirant
The Saturnine Candle has been consecrated and holds within it the force of Saturn. With this power, the Temple of Saturn has been created. So mote it be.

CLOSING

Go to the East and face the center of the room.

Aspirant
I now release any spirits that may have been attracted to this ceremony. Go in peace to your abodes and habitations and go with the blessings of Saturn.

Purify and consecrate the Temple and your body with the water and incense, as in the Opening. Banish with the banishing Pentagram in all four quarters, as in the Opening. Return to the East.

Aspirant
I now declare this ritual duly completed. So mote it be.

Extinguish the candles.

CREATING A MAGICAL UNIVERSE:
A RITUAL OF THE PLANETS

To be Performed on the Day of Sol (Sunday)

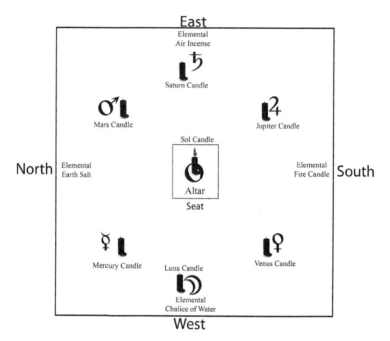

**Figure 37: Temple arrangement (1st Part),
Planetary culmination ritual**

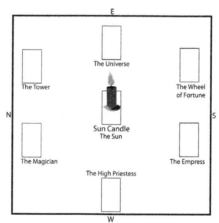

**Figure 38: Altar arrangement (1st Part),
Planetary culmination ritual**

Temple arrangement: Planetary Temple 1st Part (see Introduction), with Air Incense and Fire Candle lit.

Altar cloth: Orange.

Altar arrangement: As in diagram above, with lighter nearby.

Placement of Elemental emblems:

Elemental Fire Candle: East (symbolizes Aries, Ascendant)

Elemental Earth Salt: South (Capricorn, Midheaven)

Elemental Air Incense: West (Libra, Descendant)

Elemental Water Chalice: North (Cancer, Nadir)

Planetary Candles (consecrated): Unlit and arranged on small plates or platforms in the Hexagrammatic Planetary positions (see diagram above).

Incense, Water: In the East, incense lit (frankincense/Solar incense).

Music: Suitable ambient or background music.

PREPARATION FOR THE RITE

Sit for a moment at the Altar and contemplate the rite to come. Let the cares and worries of the day dissipate. ✶ Focus on the top of your head and form a mental image of a ray of White Light permeating your body through the top of your head. Visualize this Light descending through the center of your body to your feet. Your body is now filled with Light. ✶ Inhale and exhale this Light through the pores of your body until it is pulsing in and around you. ✶ Imagine the Light extending from your body and filling the room. See the Light creating a barrier separating the room from the outer world. Let nothing exist for you outside of this special time and place.

Opening

Standing West of the Altar, facing East, say:

Aspirant

I banish all worldly influences dwelling within this Temple by the Flaming Star of the Five Elements. I say unto you now, depart!

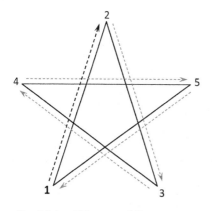

Banishing Elemental Pentagram

Go to the East. Make the Banishing Pentagram to the East, then do the same in the South, the West, and the North. Return to the East.

Take up the Cup of Water and sprinkle three times in the East, then do the same in the South, the West, and the North. Return to the East. Dip your finger in the Cup and touch your forehead, then sprinkle Water toward your feet, and touch your right and left shoulders.

Aspirant

I am purified; the Temple is purified; all is purified by the Lustral Waters. *Replace the Cup.*

Take up the incense and wave it three times in the East, then do the same in the South, the West, and the North. Return to the East. Wave the incense toward your forehead, your feet and your right and left shoulders.

Aspirant

I am consecrated; the Temple is consecrated; all is consecrated by Holy Fire. *Replace the Incense.*

Aspirant

(*In East, facing East*) **I have purified and consecrated this Temple for the invocation of the Planetary spheres, and in so doing have created a Temple, that the heavenly forces of the Planets may dwell here for a time. So mote it be.**

INVOKING THE ELEMENTS

Go to the East and take up the consecrated Elemental Air Incense. Face the East, and with the Incense draw the Invoking Air Pentagram in the air.

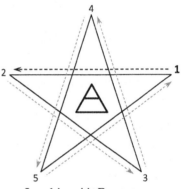

Invoking Air Pentagram

Aspirant

Through the power of the Pentagram, I call forth the spirits of Air!

Replace the Incense. Using the index finger, touch the center of the Air Pentagram and draw a line in the air, walking towards the South.

In the South and facing South, take up the consecrated Elemental Fire Candle. With the Candle draw the Invoking Fire Pentagram.

Invoking Fire Pentagram

Aspirant

Through the power of the Pentagram, I call forth the spirits of Fire!

Replace the Candle. Touch the center of the Fire Pentagram and draw a line in the air towards the West.

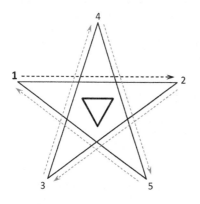

Invoking Water Pentagram

In the West and facing West, take up the consecrated Elemental Chalice of Water. With the Chalice draw the Invoking Water Pentagram.

Aspirant

Through the power of the Pentagram, I call forth the spirits of Water!

Replace the Chalice. Touch the center of the Water Pentagram and draw a line in the air towards the North.

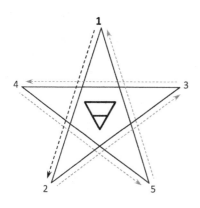

Invoking Earth Pentagram

In the North and facing North, take up the consecrated Elemental Salt. With the Salt draw the Invoking Earth Pentagram.

Aspirant

Through the power of the Pentagram, I call forth the spirits of Earth!

Replace the Salt. Touch the center of the Earth Pentagram and draw a line in the air towards the East. While standing in the East, turn and face the center of the room.

<u>Aspirant</u>

Hear me, four quarters of the World, for I call out to thee! Grant me the strength to walk the hidden path and discover secret knowledge. Give me your eyes to see and your wisdom to understand, that I may be like you. Grant me your powers that I may call the powers of the Planets of the ancients.

INVOCATION OF SPIRIT

Go to the West of the Altar and face East. In the air before you, draw the two Invoking Spirit Pentagrams:

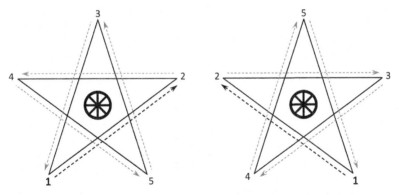

Invoking Passive Spirit Pentagram   Invoking Active Spirit Pentagram

<u>Aspirant</u>

O Thou supreme Life-Spirit, Cause of all Creation, Origin of all, and single Source of every living soul. Of Thee alone is my beginning, and in Thee alone have I no ending. O Thou single source of truth and wisdom, let me ascend to the Higher

Realms on the Chariot of Truth. Bring me over the gulfs and abysses, bear me upward out of gorges and valleys; become for me the source of liberation. Let Thy great brightness cause the path to be lit before me. Let me ascend to the Heavens as if upon a ship of Light, that I may come to know the Planetary Spheres. So mote it be. *Pause for a moment and visualize your aura filled with White Light.*

Optional: Elevating the Temple into the Heavens

<u>Aspirant</u>

All is now in readiness to ascend to the Planetary Powers. I shall quit the material world and enter the higher realms by placing the consecrated Elemental Powers in their zodiacal stations.

Go clockwise to the South, take up the Candle, and go clockwise to the East. Face the East.

<u>Aspirant</u>

In the earthly realm, the East is the station of Elemental Air. However, in the higher realms, the East is the station of Aries, the movable Sign of Fire. (*Place the Candle in the East.*) Through the power of this consecrated emblem of Fire, this quarter is now elevated to the heavens. *Take up the Incense and go clockwise to the West, facing the West.*

<u>Aspirant</u>

In the earthly realm, the West is the station of Elemental Water. However, in the higher realms, the West is the station of Libra, the movable Sign of Air. (*Place the Incense in the West.*) Through the power of this consecrated emblem of Air, this

quarter is now elevated to the heavens. *Take up the Chalice. Go clockwise to the North and face the North.*

Aspirant

In the earthly realm, the North is the station of Elemental Earth. However, in the higher realms, the North is the station of Cancer, the movable Sign of Water. (*Place the Chalice in the North.*) **Through the power of this consecrated emblem of Water, this quarter is now elevated to the heavens.** *Take up the Salt. Go clockwise to the South and face the South.*

Aspirant

In the earthly realm, the South is the station of Elemental Fire. However, in the higher realms, the South is the station of Capricorn, the movable Sign of Earth. (*Place the Salt in the South.*) **Through the power of this consecrated emblem of Earth, this quarter is now elevated to the heavens.** *Go to the West of the Altar, and face East.*

FIRST ADVANCEMENT: CREATION OF A MAGICAL UNIVERSE

Stand to the West of the Altar, facing East. Remain for a brief moment in silence. The bright white light from the spirit invocation begins to recede and eventually disappears. Visualize being surrounded by complete darkness, a void wherein nothing exists.

Aspirant

Nothing exists. There is no light, no sound, only emptiness and silence, a vast stillness in an infinite void. *Stand for a brief moment and contemplate the dark silence.*

Aspirant

Suddenly, in the depths of the void, there arises a shining light. At first, the smallest of points, single and alone, growing larger and larger, illuminating the darkness of the void.

Draw six Solar Hexagrams in the air over the Altar:

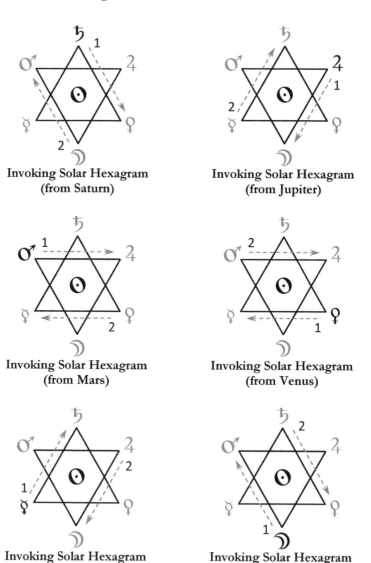

Invoking Solar Hexagram
(from Saturn)

Invoking Solar Hexagram
(from Jupiter)

Invoking Solar Hexagram
(from Mars)

Invoking Solar Hexagram
(from Venus)

Invoking Solar Hexagram
(from Mercury)

Invoking Solar Hexagram
(from Luna)

Aspirant

And the void was filled with light, scintillating and warm, illuminating the darkness with brilliant inspiration. In the Divine Name YHVH Eloah V'Daath (Yod Heh Vav Heh El-oh-ah Veh-Da-ath), and in the name of the great Archangel Michael, I call forth the light of the Sun. *Light the orange Sol Candle on the Altar.*

Aspirant

The flame of mystical creation is now awakened, and the darkness has been made light.

Take up the Sol Candle and go clockwise to the East, facing the blue-violet Saturn Candle.

Aspirant

And the Divine Light glowed brightly, and illumination reigned supreme; but there was no form, neither the cohesion of the Light nor the beginnings of structure. The purpose of the Sun was to create life in the void, but life cannot develop without form.

Place the Sol Candle next to the Saturn Candle, and draw the Hexagram of Saturn towards the East.

Light the Saturn Candle from the Sol Candle, and hold the Saturn Candle aloft.

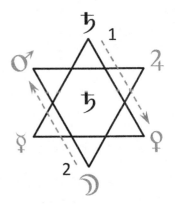

Invoking Saturn Hexagram

Aspirant

Through the power of Saturn the

divine imagination was born, whose thoughts gave shape to the void. The patient and laborious process of the crystallization of the universe was begun, and time was created. In the divine name YHVH ELOHIM (Yod Heh Vav Heh El-oh-heem), and in the name of the great Archangel KASSIEL, I call forth the light of Saturn.

Replace the Saturn Candle. Take the Sol Candle and walk directly to the Southeast, facing the Jupiter Candle.

Aspirant

The light of the universe was crystallizing, forming itself, but the laws of formation had not yet been created. Order amidst the chaos was necessary, an organization and preservation, the structuring of the Divine light into interacting elements. The purpose of the Sun was to create life in the void, but life cannot develop without interrelation.

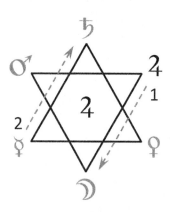

Invoking Jupiter Hexagram

Place the Sol Candle next to the Jupiter Candle, and draw the Hexagram of Jupiter towards the Southeast.

Light the Jupiter Candle from the Sol Candle, and hold it aloft.

Aspirant

Through the power of Jupiter divine laws were born, whose thoughts gave beneficent order to the void. Kindness, virtue, love were embedded into the pattern of the universe. In the divine name EL and in the name of the great Archangel SACHIEL (Sah-khee-el), I call forth the light of Jupiter.

Replace the Jupiter Candle. Take the Sol Candle and walk directly to the Northeast, facing the Mars Candle.

Aspirant

The light of the universe had created harmonies and laws, but laws must be defended and Divine Will must prevail. Discipline and dynamism, the energy to project life outward and implement the Divine Plan was necessary. The purpose of the Sun was to create life in the void, but life cannot develop without and motivation and drive.

Place the Sol Candle next to the Mars Candle, and draw the Hexagram of Mars towards the Northeast.

Light the Mars Candle from the Sol Candle, and hold it aloft.

Invoking Mars Hexagram

Aspirant

Through the power of Mars, Divine Justice was born, whose thoughts gave potency and force to the void. Power, determination and strength were embedded into the pattern of the universe. In the Divine Name ELOHIM GIBOR, and in the name of the great Archangel ZAMAEL, I call forth the light of Mars.

Replace the Mars Candle. Take the Sol Candle and walk directly to the West of the Altar, facing East.

Aspirant

The Sun had created the heavens and the patterns of life. The light of the universe had illuminated the darkness and had placed therein Divine imaginings and formation, love and laws, power and justice. Yet the work of the Sun was not complete. To be fully realized, life had to be reflected in physical form, to be made manifest, and so humans were born under the light of the Sun. Yet humanity, in whom was embedded the divine pattern of the universe, was to be given a certain purpose, and that was to search for, know, and realize its Divine origins.

Take the Sol Candle and walk directly to the Southwest, facing the Venus Candle.

Aspirant

The Sun now manifested life on earth through Nature's countless forms, and it was there that humanity was born. Humans were given emotion and desire in order that they may know their divine origins. The purpose of the Sun was to manifest life on earth, but human life cannot develop without creativity, aspiration and love.

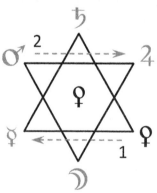

Invoking Venus Hexagram

Place the Sol Candle next to the Venus Candle, and draw the Hexagram of Venus towards the Southwest.

Light the Venus Candle from the Sol Candle, and hold it aloft.

Aspirant

Through the power of Venus

human love and desire were born, whose imagination gave tangible form to the divine light. Creative inspiration and a yearning for happiness were embedded into the pattern of the human mind. In the Divine Name YHVH TZABAOTH (Yod Heh Vav Heh Tzah-ba-oth) and in the name of the great Archangel ANAEL, I call forth the light of Venus.

Replace the Venus Candle. Take the Sol Candle and walk straight to the Northwest, facing the Mercury Candle.

Aspirant

Human love and desire had brought about companionship and pleasure to the people of the world, but this was not enough for humans to be complete. Humans possess Mind, and their minds had to be stimulated and educated in order to know their Divine origins. The purpose of the Sun was to manifest life on earth, but human life cannot develop without intelligence, curiosity and a thirst for knowledge.

Place the Sol Candle next to the Mercury Candle, and draw the Hexagram of Mercury towards the Northwest.

Light the Mercury Candle from the Sol Candle, and hold it aloft.

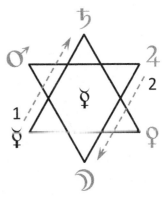

Invoking Mercury Hexagram

Aspirant

Through the power of Mercury, speech, learning, and a desire to know the mysteries were born, whose expressions gave rational form to the Divine light. Intelligence and communication were embedded into the pattern of the human mind. In the Divine Name ELOHIM TZABAOTH (El-oh-heem Tzah-bah-oth), and in the name of the great Archangel RAPHAEL, I call forth the light of Mercury.

Replace the Mercury Candle. Take the Sol Candle and walk directly to the West, facing the Moon Candle.

Aspirant

Humans now possessed creativity and intellect, but this was not enough to stimulate the desire to know their Divine origins. The Sun therefore placed a reflection of itself deep within the human psyche, behind the mind. And there the Sun placed a love of honest science, a delight in novelty, and a steadfast desire for freedom. The purpose of the Sun was to manifest life on earth, but human life cannot evolve without free movement and change.

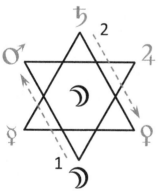

Invoking Luna Hexagram

Place the Sol Candle next to the Luna Candle, and draw the Hexagram of Luna towards the West.

Light the Luna Candle from the Sol Candle, and hold it aloft.

Aspirant

Through the power of the Moon, a reflection of the Sun was born in the human mind, whose expression gave a yearning of the intellect to know and manifest the Divine light. The love of freedom and a desire to comprehend Divine origins were embedded into the pattern of the human mind. In the Divine Name SHADDAI EL CHAI

(Shah-dye El Khye), and in the name of the great Archangel GABRIEL, I call forth the light of the Moon.

Replace the Luna Candle. Take the Sol Candle and walk directly to the Altar, placing the Sol Candle on *The Sun* card.

Aspirant

The higher is reflected in the lower, and the lower reaches to the heights. Through the power of the Sun I have created a magical universe within this Temple, wherein the human may come to know the Divine, and the Divine may manifest in the human.

SECOND ADVANCEMENT: ASCENDING THE LADDER OF LIGHTS
FORMING THE SIX-RAYED STAR IN THE TEMPLE

Aspirant

(*West of Altar, facing East.*) **The Sun in the center of the Planets is the mediator of all powers, earthly and celestial, and in the Sun of the mortal body, the divine and the human are united in one soul. The force of the Sun is outpouring, but its essence draws us inward: for the Sun draws all bodies to itself, causing them to seek the center. In this seeking, we must sacrifice the particulars of our mortal selves, revealing within ourselves the divine light shining.**

I will now begin the ascending journey by awakening the powers of the Sun within me, for the Sun in the Self illuminates the Divine light within: the light that shines in the darkness, though the darkness comprehends it not.

Take up the Sol Candle and strongly visualize the aura turning to ORANGE.

Aspirant

Powers of the Sun, you who are the Shining Crown of the Day, hear me now. I am one who ascends the Ladder of Lights. Swing wide your gates and allow me to enter your realm. *Visualize the ORANGE symbol of the Sun glowing in your heart.*

Aspirant

In my quest for the light I sacrifice all arrogance, conceit, self-importance and unjust superiority over any living creature. As an embodiment of the Sun, I shall strive to acquire the qualities of good judgment, honor, faithfulness and kindness expressed towards all.

Replace the Sol Candle on the Altar, and walk straight to the Luna Candle in the West. Take up the Luna Candle and, facing West, strongly visualize the aura turning to BLUE.

Aspirant

Powers of the Moon, you who are the Shining Crown of the Night, hear me now. I am one who ascends the Ladder of Lights. Swing wide your gates and allow me to enter your realm. *Visualize the BLUE symbol of the Moon glowing in your heart.*

Aspirant

In my quest for the light I sacrifice my wandering energies of increase and decrease. As a steadfast embodiment of Luna I shall strive to acquire the qualities of tenderness, peacefulness and a love of freedom from care.

Take the Luna Candle directly to the Altar and place it on *The High Priestess* card. Walk directly to the Mercury Candle, take it up, and strongly visualize the aura turning to YELLOW.

Aspirant

Powers of Mercury, you who are the Swift Ones, hear me now. I am one who ascends the Ladder of Lights. Swing wide your gates and allow me to enter your realm. *Visualize the YELLOW symbol of Mercury glowing in your heart.*

Aspirant

In my quest for the light I sacrifice all malevolent and spiteful conspiracies or collusions. As an embodiment of Mercury I shall strive, as a student of the Mysteries, to acquire the qualities of a true seeker of occult knowledge, desiring to explore all forms of learning.

Take the Mercury Candle to the West of the Altar and place it on *The Magician* card. Walk directly to the Venus Candle, take it up, and strongly visualize the aura turning to GREEN.

Aspirant

Powers of Venus, you who are the Beauteous Ones, hear me now. I am one who ascends the Ladder of Lights. Swing wide your gates and allow me to enter your realm. *Visualize the GREEN symbol of Venus glowing in your heart.*

Aspirant

In my quest for the light I sacrifice the illusion of longing, for the undue desire of the material is a root of unhappiness. As an embodiment of Venus I shall strive to acquire the qualities of love and mirth, and I shall delight in the arts.

Take the Venus Candle to the West of the Altar and place it on *The Empress* card. Go to the East of the Altar, pause to face East, and then walk directly to the Mars Candle. Take up the Candle and strongly visualize the aura turning to RED.

Aspirant

Powers of Mars, you who are the Valiant Ones, hear me now. I am one who ascends the Ladder of Lights. Swing wide your gates and allow me to enter your realm. *Visualize the RED symbol of Mars glowing in your heart.*

Aspirant

In my quest for the light I sacrifice all cruelty and harshness, and also I sacrifice all careless and rash actions. As an embodiment of Mars I shall strive to acquire the qualities of courage, determination and discipline.

Take the Mars Candle to the East of the Altar, and place it on *The Tower* card. Walk directly to the Jupiter Candle, take it up, and strongly visualize the aura turning to VIOLET.

Aspirant

Powers of Jupiter, you who are the Beneficent Ones, hear me now. I am one who ascends the Ladder of Lights. Swing wide your gates and allow me to enter your realm. *Visualize the VIOLET symbol of Jupiter glowing in your heart.*

Aspirant

In my quest for the light I sacrifice all selfish impulses for wealth and worldly goods, and the practice of hypocrisy. As an embodiment of Jupiter I shall strive to acquire the qualities of wisdom, generosity, and humbleness.

Take the Jupiter Candle to the East of the Altar and place it on *The Wheel* card. Walk straight to the Saturn Candle, take it up while facing East, and strongly visualize the aura turning BLUE-VIOLET.

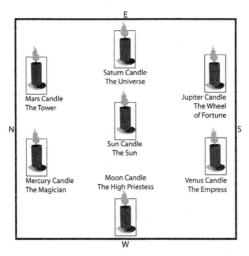

Figure 39: Planetary Altar with all Candles and Tarot cards

Aspirant

Powers of Saturn, you who are the Austere Ones, hear me now. I am one who ascends the Ladder of Lights. Swing wide your gates and allow me to enter your realm. *Visualize the BLUE-VIOLET symbol of Saturn glowing in your heart.*

Aspirant

In my quest for the light I sacrifice all forms of deceit and dishonesty. As an embodiment of Saturn I shall strive to acquire the qualities of imagination, patience and diligent labor.

Take the Saturn Candle to the East of the Altar and place it on *The Universe* card. Move clockwise to the Western side of the Altar, and face East.

<u>Aspirant</u>

A magical universe have I formed from the Planetary lights. I have descended through the spheres and risen to the heights. In my journey I have acquired the virtues of the travelers and through those virtues I have manifested their powers in this Temple. I sing praises to the Wandering Lights of the universe.

I sing praise to the Sower and the Reaper. Silent One who works unseen in the darkness, I praise you. Through your gift of enduring fidelity, I shall bring my labors on earth to their full harvest.

I sing praise to Truth and Fairness, and I call to the Divine Liberality. Oh Divine One of Benevolent Rule, I praise you. Through your gift of a generous heart, charitable acts shall I embrace.

I sing praise to the Mighty Guardian who enchains the forces of darkness, the great power who motivates loyalty and confirms the steadfast heart. Through your gift of strong resolve, I will be a powerful adversary of any malevolent force.

I sing praise to the Mediator of the Planetary Powers, who is reborn again and again from the darkest of nights into the gentle light of the dawn. Oh Divine One of the sky, master of eternity, who fills the heavens with rays of golden fire, I praise you. Through your gift of life and joy renewed, I shall emit your light to the outer world.

I sing praise to the Lady of Beauty and Grace, who fills my sanctuary with joy and sweet laughter. Oh Divine One of loving eyes, bring peace and elegance into my life. Through your gift of the inspiration, creations of great beauty and delight shall be mine to give.

I sing praise to the Traveler between the Worlds, the great scribe, the keeper of the signs, the sigils, and the words of power. Oh Divine One, great in the magical art, bring to me skill and knowledge. Through your gift of magical learning, I shall know the hidden ways of life and the mysteries shall be mine to behold.

I sing the praises of the Giver of Dreams and the Maker of Enchantments. Oh Divine One who is the gracious opener of hidden doors, guide my steps into the Mysteries. Through your gift of happy vision, the threshold to the unseen realms has been opened to me.

I give thanks and praise to all Planetary powers. May your gifts be mind to hold and share and may they ever abide in this sacred Temple of the mysteries. So mote it be.

Sit and meditate on any one of the Planets, or feel the energies invoked.

CLOSING

Go to the East and face the center of the room.

Aspirant
I now release any spirits that may have been attracted to this ceremony. Go in peace to your abodes and habitations and go with the blessings of the Wanderers.

Purify and consecrate the Temple and your body with the water and incense, as in the Opening. Banish with the banishing Pentagram in all four quarters, as in the Opening. Return to the East.

Aspirant

I now declare this ritual duly completed. So mote it be.

Extinguish the candles.

PART 3: THE ZODIACAL RITES

Introduction

Now that you have worked with the Elements and the Planets, you are ready to advance to the Zodiacal Signs. Let's start by distinguishing modern notions of signs, from the traditional ones (including in traditional magic).

In traditional astrology, the signs are not primarily the rich, well-defined personality types which moderns take them to be. One good reason for this is that traditional astrology is not primarily psychological. But apart from that, the signs in themselves have a number of classifications which do not obviously fit well together, especially as personality types. Some of these derive from geocentric astronomy, others from the constellations, as well as other sources. For example, the watery signs are known as the "mute" signs, because the animals depicted in their constellations (crabs, scorpions, fish) do not make sounds. In the northern hemisphere, the signs from Capricorn through Gemini are known as the "crooked" signs, because when they rise in the east, they have shallow angles, like someone walking bent over with a cane. Now, all of these characteristics have meanings in traditional astrology, including (sometimes) personality characteristics, but the relevance of these properties depends on the context. So when a traditional astrologer or magician thinks, "Taurus," the first thought is not "A *person* whose *mind* is concerned with creature comforts," *et cetera*. Instead, Taurus is immediately considered a feminine, earthy, fixed sign, and so on. Likewise, it may be relevant to a horary question about a lost object, that Taurus indicates stables and pastures, but not in other contexts.

Another reason to think that the signs are not quite as rich as in modern astrology, is that they are more abstract. This is partly due to their lacking clear, unifying features (see above), but also because they are higher up in the heavens: so, purely in themselves they are less "tangible" than the world of our experience. Technically speaking, the signs cannot even be "earthy" or "fiery," because traditionally the Elements are here in our world of sensation, not in the heavens. Rather, the "elemental" or even gendered relationships between signs are depicted through geometric shapes like triangles and hexagons which only translate to sensible and concrete Elemental and gendered relationships in our world. So, the "fiery" signs Aries, Leo, and Sagittarius, have a triangular relationship to each other, and thus they are called the "triplicity" of fire. Likewise, since signs alternate in their gender (Taurus, Cancer, Virgo, and so on, are feminine), drawing a line from one to the other according to the same gender will create a hexagon. But the heavens are not on fire, and the signs do not have genitals, but they may indicate such things in our world of experience.

For these reasons, you might think that the signs should have been put first in this book. But we are putting them last, because we are imagining the inspired movement of the soul, whose exposure and experience and wisdom gets *richer* as it moves *upwards*. You might also consider that while the zodiacal signs (or at least the constellations of the same name) are images of certain animals, these animals are for the most part envisioned as *living beings*,[1] and the principle of life is more active and rich than mere Elements taken by themselves. In the simple, Platonic-style universe we described in the Introduction to this book, everything from the astrological entities on down was organized by a life-principle, the World Soul. So although the signs are higher and in some sense more abstract, they are closer to a grand, organizing principle of eternal Life. Indeed, the motion of the Sun through the signs is intimately related to the annual and seasonal cycle of Life.

In these rituals, we will experience the signs through three important categories: (1) as the houses or domiciles of the planets, as (2) triplicities and quadruplicities, and (3) as ruled by certain angelic and Divine names. Thus, you will be recapturing and integrating the astrological perspectives you've already been exposed to, and looking forward to further spiritual work and beings. And because this book is more concerned with the individual human being's soul, we will indeed focus on how the signs' categories relate to the soul and values.

As for (1), you have already been exposed to the Planets in earlier rituals. So, you will invoke Martial energy for Aries and Scorpio, and Saturnian energy for Aquarius and Capricorn: this employs the usual Invoking Planetary Hexagrams.

As for (2), you are already familiar with the triplicities and quadruplicities, but here you will use slightly different Invoking Pentagrams. Each of the Signs will use an Invoking Pentagram of its Element, but in the middle you will draw the symbol for the Sign itself, as well as intoning (3) Divine Names for the Sign. These names are of several types, but there are two special types

---

[1] Obviously, Libra (the Balance) does not depict a living being.

pertaining to each individual Sign. The first Divine Name is a permutation of the more exalted, fourfold Name of God in the Hebrew Bible,[2] which we abbreviate as YHVH. Its true pronunciation is unknown and considered too sacred to speak anyway, so the Hebrew word *Adonai* ("my lord") is often substituted instead.[3]

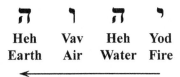

Heh	Vav	Heh	Yod
Earth	Air	Water	Fire

Figure 40: Elemental attributions for the *Tetragrammaton*

Read right to left (as Hebrew is read), each of the letters Yod, Heh, Vav, Heh, is attributed in a certain way to an Element: Yod is a creative and commanding masculine principle, associated with Fire; the first Heh a creative and loving feminine principle, associated with Water; their combination is taken to comprise the Vav, a reconciling principle associated with Air. The final Heh represents the Earthy principle of concrete manifestation. In Western Orders like the Golden Dawn, these letters are put in different combinations so as to yield a unique permutation for each Sign, which will will use here (but we will not review the method for constructing them.)

The second Name is that of the traditional Archangel of each Sign, again as taught in Western groups such as the Golden Dawn.

---

[2] This name is known in magical circles as the *Tetragrammaton*, from the Greek for "four letters."

[3] By interspersing the vowels from *Adonai* (ah-oh-ah) through the fourfold Name, one yields roughly the name "Jehovah" or "Jahovah."

A Brief Synopsis of the Zodiacal Rituals

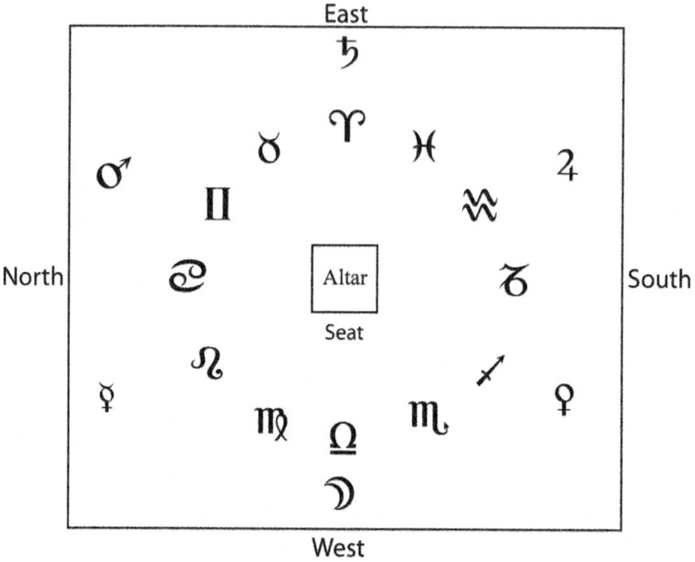

Figure 41: Symbolic Temple arrangement for Zodiacal rituals

As with the Planetary rituals, we offer two possibilities for the Temple arrangement. If you know how to find the actual locations of the Signs and Planets, then go to those parts of the Temple or face those directions at the appropriate times. For example, if you are performing a Scorpio ritual, go to or face the locations of Scorpio itself and Mars himself: in your location and at the time of your ritual, Scorpio might be towards the Northeast, and Mars in the West. (But as we suggested in the section on elections, it should normally be in the East or South, on the Ascendant or Midheaven.)

But if you do not feel confident about finding these locations with a computer program or other means, then use the symbolic arrangement in the figure above: the Signs are arranged starting from Aries in the East, and the Planets are in the usual Hexagrammatic places. In the Scorpio-Mars example above, you would face Scorpio's symbolic position near the Southwest, and Mars in the Northeast.

Remember, if you find it hard to carry this book around during a ritual, then photocopy the relevant pages and use those instead.

Ritual Items:

- Consecrated Elemental emblem for the Sign's triplicity, on the Altar.
- Altar cloth of the appropriate color of the Sign (or its triplicity).
- Consecrated Planetary Candle for the ruler of the Sign, on the Altar.
- Tarot card attributed to the Sign, on the Altar.
- Water and incense (of the Elemental scent, lit)[4] in the East.

Preparation and Opening

The Preparation for the Rite, and its Opening, are the same as in the previous rites.

First Advancement: Invoking the Triplicity

First, invoke the Element of the Sign using the Elemental Pentagram in the appropriate quarter. As before, this brings the Elemental energy into manifestation.

Second Advancement: Invoking the Lord of the Sign

Next, advance to the location of the lord of the Sign relative to the Temple, or to its symbolic, Hexagrammatic position. Using the unlit Planetary Candle, invoke the Planetary lord using its Invoking Hexagram; then turn your aura to the Planetary color, so as to align yourself with that energy. Then light the Candle.

Third Advancement: Invoking the Sign

Third, advance to the location of the Sign relative to the Temple, or to its symbolic position as described above. Invoke the Sign using the appropriate Invoking Pentagram, and recite a speech drawn from the mythology of its constellation. (You will note that the myths often match key ideas in the Tarot cards.) Touch the symbol of the Sign in the Pentagram, and visualize its colored light[5] flowing into your aura.

---

4 See Appendix 3 for a list of typical scents associated with the Elements.
5 The Golden Dawn attributes a different color to each Sign, based on the color wheel. Aries is red, Leo yellow, and Sagittarius blue, while the signs in between have an intermediary color. For example, Taurus is red-orange, Gemini orange, Cancer orange-yellow, and so on. See Appendix 1 and the rituals themselves, for a list of the zodiacal colors.

Fourth Advancement : Meditation

Finally, perform a contemplative meditation on the Tarot card attributed to the Sign. Visualize yourself within the card, and note any thoughts or impressions that arise. If you like, record yourself reading the Tarot meditation beforehand, and listen to it as you visualize.

As before, we have designed alternative meditations which envision an encounter with the Archangel of the Sign. After visualizing the symbol of the Sign, walk mentally through it like a door: you will enter upon a landscape indicative of the Sign, with an image of the Archangel based on the physical forms traditionally attributed to the Signs.

Closing

The Closing is the same as in the previous rituals.

Invoking the Triplicities: A Ritual of the Signs

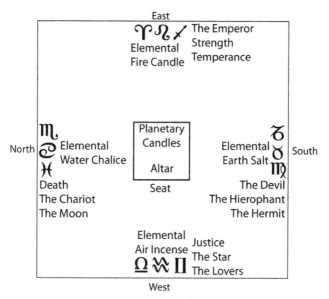

Figure 42: Invoking the Triplicities Temple

The culmination ritual for the Signs draws on the triplicities. Rather than invoking each Sign separately, they are experienced in their triplicity groupings, with each Sign representing one of the modes of the quadruplicities.

The consecrated Elemental emblems are distributed with the Signs into the macrocosmic quarters, and the consecrated Planetary Candles are on the Altar to represent the lords of the Signs.

Preparation and Opening

The Preparation for the Rite and the Opening are the same as in the previous rituals.

Invocation of Spirit

Invoke Spirit, as the Elemental nature closest to the celestial realm of the Signs.

Four Advancements: The Triplicities

For each triplicity, advance to its macrocosmic quarter and invoke it using the corresponding Pentagram. Circumambulate ("walk around") the Temple while reciting a speech about that triplicity, in order to draw its energy into the ritual. Upon returning to the Pentagram, invoke each Sign through its zodiacal symbol, while reciting the Divine Names and requesting a blessing related to each Sign. Turn your aura the appropriate color of the Sign, in order to attune yourself to that energy and blessing.

Fifth Advancement: The Blessed Meal of the Signs

In this last part, the consecrated Elemental emblems are brought from the quarters to the Altar, and placed according to their microcosmic quarters. Recite the Prayer of Osiris over the Elements (or any similar prayer of a dying and resurrecting God, or one involving separation and reunification), and then partake of each one, so as to physically take in the zodiacal powers.

Closing

The Closing is the same as in the previous rituals.

INVOCATION OF THE POWERS OF ARIES

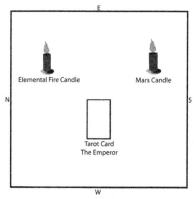

Figure 43: Altar arrangement for Aries

Temple arrangement: Basic zodiacal Temple.

Altar cloth: Red.

Altar implements: Fire Candle (unlit), Mars Candle (unlit), with a lighter nearby.

Tarot Card: *The Emperor*, on Altar.

Incense, Water: In the East, with incense lit.

Music: Suitable ambient or background music.

PREPARATION FOR THE RITE

Sit for a moment at the Altar and contemplate the rite to come. Let the cares and worries of the day dissipate. ✛ Focus on the top of your head and form a mental image of a ray of White Light permeating your body through the top of your head. Visualize this Light descending through the center of your body to your feet. Your body is now filled with Light. ✛ Inhale and exhale this Light through the pores of your body until it is pulsing in and around you. ✛ Imagine the Light extending from your body and filling the room. See the Light creating a barrier separating the room from the outer world. Let nothing exist for you outside of this special time and place.

OPENING

Standing West of the Altar, facing East, say:

Aspirant
I banish all worldly influences dwelling within this Temple by the Flaming Star of the Five Elements. I say unto you now, depart!

Go to the East. Make the Banishing Pentagram to the East, then do the same in the South, the West, and the North. Return to the East.

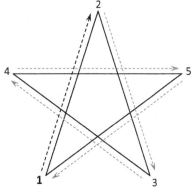

Take up the Cup of Water and sprinkle three times in the East, then do the same in the South,

Banishing Elemental Pentagram

the West, and the North. Return to the East. Dip your finger in the Cup and touch your forehead, then sprinkle Water toward your feet, and touch your right and left shoulders.

Aspirant
I am purified; the Temple is purified; all is purified by the Lustral Waters. *Replace the Cup.*

Take up the incense and wave it three times in the East, then do the same in the South, the West, and the North. Return to the East. Wave the incense toward your forehead, your feet and your right and left shoulders.

<u>Aspirant</u>

I am consecrated; the Temple is consecrated; all is consecrated by Holy Fire. *Replace the Incense.*

<u>Aspirant</u>

(In East, facing East) I have purified and consecrated this Temple for the invocation of Aries, and in so doing have created a Temple, that the heavenly forces of the Ram may dwell here for a time. Unseen Watchers over the sacred Magic, watch over this ceremony of the Light Divine. So mote it be.

First Advancement: Invoking Elemental Fire

Take the Fire Candle to the South and draw the red Invoking Fire Pentagram towards the South.

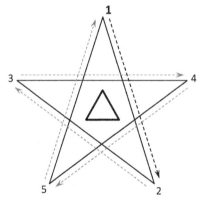

Invoking Fire Pentagram

<u>Aspirant</u>

Hear me, those who dwell in the Southern Quarter of the Universe, for I call out to thee! Through the Divine Name ELOHIM, I have called you forth under the auspices of Fire, that I may bring to power and presence the zodiacal Sign of Aries. Grant me the strength to walk the hidden path and discover secret knowledge. Give me your eyes to see and your wisdom to understand, that I may perceive hidden things. Grant me the powers of Fire, that I may bring forth Aries in this sacred place.

Pause for a moment and fill the aura with RED Light. Walk clockwise West of the Altar, replace the Fire Candle, and light it.

SECOND ADVANCEMENT: INVOCATION OF MARS

At the Altar, take up the Mars Candle and face the location of Mars.

Aspirant
I shall quit the material and seek the spiritual!

Go to the location of Mars. With the Candle, trace the Invoking Hexagram of Mars, and the symbol of Mars in it.

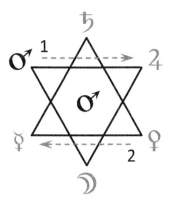

Invoking Mars Hexagram

Aspirant
Powerful Mars, who fills the Universe with your Martial essence, through your Divine Name ELOHIM GIBOR, I invoke you. Grant unto me the presence of your Great Archangel KAMAEL, that he may lead me in my search for the powers of Aries. KAMAEL, come forth and call to presence the light of Mars, that he may illuminate the inner realms of my being, and I may be awakened to the presence of Aries. I make this petition to you, that through the Divine Presence, I may rend the Veils of Darkness from my mortal vision and comprehend the secrets of the Sign of the Ram.

Pause for a moment and fill the aura with RED Light. Walk clockwise West of the Altar, replace the Mars Candle, and light it.

THIRD ADVANCEMENT: INVOCATION OF ARIES

<u>Aspirant</u>

(*Facing Aries*) **To the forces of Aries that I now prepare to invoke, I have awakened this Temple with the powers of Fire. I have invoked Mars, who is your lord. Come forward and be present with me in this sacred rite. You who are the powers of a fiery impulse and the thrust necessary for a new life, I call you forth. New beginnings, the direct release of energy, and self-assertion shall reign in this Temple. Open your realm to me, that I may know you and awaken your powers within my soul.**

Go the location of Aries, and face it.

<u>Aspirant</u>

In the Divine Name YHVH (Yod Heh Vav Heh) and in the name of MALKHIDAEL the great Archangel, I invoke the power of Aries. *Trace the Invoking Aries Pentagram, and draw its symbol in the center.*

Invoking Aries Pentagram

Visualize the RED Pentagram of Aries glowing in the air.

<u>Aspirant</u>
The Greek hero Jason was the son of the King of Iolkos. Pelias, his uncle, murdered his father and stole the throne.

To keep him safe, Jason's mother hid him away on the Mountain of Pelion. When Jason turned 20 years of age, he returned to Iolkos to reclaim his birthright. But Pelias challenged him first to retrieve a Golden Fleece, to prove himself worthy to rule. The Fleece was from a golden ram sacrificed by the son of Helios, the Sun God, and hung in a sacred grove guarded by a fierce dragon.

Touch the symbol of Aries with your index finger. Visualize the RED Light of Aries flowing down your arm into your heart. Hold this visualization while saying:

<u>Aspirant</u>

Determined to reclaim his throne, Jason set out to find the Golden Fleece. Upon arriving at his destination, he asked the son of Helios to give him the sacred skin of the ram. Reluctantly, the king agreed, but only if Jason could overcome certain further challenges. Those challenges were to yoke fire-breathing bulls, plough and sow a field with a dragon's teeth, and then overpower the warriors who would arise from the ploughed field. With the help of Medea, a powerful sorceress, Jason succeeded in the task and returned home with the Golden Fleece, where he reclaimed his father's throne.

FOURTH ADVANCEMENT: MEDITATION ON *THE EMPEROR*

Return to the West of the Altar and take up the Tarot card *The Emperor*. Sit and face Aries, turn your aura to RED, and study the card while saying:

<u>Aspirant</u>

Son of the Morning, Chief among the Mighty, I call to you, for yours are the powers of great creative energy and the right of rule. You are the warrior king who laid down his sword and took up the scepter. Absolute authority is yours to wield, and your strength is the stability you bring to the realm. You are Zeus, who slew the evil of his father Kronos and became the ruler of Olympus. Your authority and stability bring great comfort, self-worth and power. You are the Masculine Principle, the Animus and the Patriarch. You are power, authority, and the symbol of experience. The All-Father is your name, for you give structure and stability. But you are also enthusiasm, energy, and aggression. In your most positive aspects are you the intelligent and great monarch of an orderly, lawful, and thriving Empire.

Close your eyes and visualize yourself in the imagery of the card. Note any thoughts or sensations that arise. Before you quit this visualization, make an offering of your own Light to the Powers of Aries.

Alternative meditation: the Archangel Malkhidael

Visualize the symbol of Aries in front of you. Once this symbol is firmly established, go through the symbol like a door.

It is daytime in the spring, and you are standing on newly-ploughed ground. The marks of the plow in the soil are clearly visible. In the distance you see a herd of cattle and some sheep grazing on a low hillside. You silently call to the Archangel Malkhidael.

Malkhidael appears before you in the image of a man somewhat short in stature, dressed in a red robe. He has a dark complexion, a strong but lean build, with a long neck and broad shoulders. His face is long and angular, with a black beard, hair and eyebrows. His nature is quick-witted, bold and courageous. Ask Malkhidael about the nature of Aries and how it can aid in your spiritual growth. Note any thoughts or sensations that arise. At the conclusion of this meditation, Malkhidael gives you the symbol of Aries on an iron medallion which you place around your neck. Before you quit this visualization, make an offering of your own Light to the Powers of Aries.

Aspirant

I have acquired the qualities of Aries and they now reside within me. So mote it be.

CLOSING

Go to the East and face the center of the room.

Aspirant

I now release any spirits that may have been attracted to this ceremony. Go in peace to your abodes and habitations and go with the powers of Aries.

Purify and consecrate the Temple and your body with the water and incense, as in the Opening. Banish with the banishing Pentagram in all four quarters, as in the Opening. Return to the East.

Aspirant

I now declare this ritual duly completed. So mote it be.

Extinguish the candles.

INVOCATION OF THE POWERS OF TAURUS

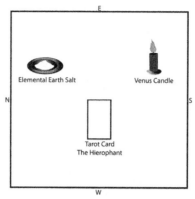

Figure 44: Altar arrangement for Taurus

Temple arrangement: Basic zodiacal Temple.

Altar cloth: Red-orange, or green (Earthy triplicity).

Altar implements: Earth Salt, Venus Candle (unlit), with a lighter nearby.

Tarot Card: *The Hierophant*, on Altar.

Incense, Water: In the East, with incense lit.

Music: Suitable ambient or background music.

PREPARATION FOR THE RITE

Sit for a moment at the Altar and contemplate the rite to come. Let the cares and worries of the day dissipate. ☿ Focus on the top of your head and form a mental image of a ray of White Light permeating your body through the top of your head. Visualize this Light descending through the center of your body to your feet. Your body is now filled with Light. ☿ Inhale and exhale this Light through the pores of your body until it is pulsing in and around you. ☿ Imagine the Light extending from your body and filling the room. See the Light creating a barrier separating the room from the outer world. Let nothing exist for you outside of this special time and place.

OPENING

Standing West of the Altar, facing East, say:

<u>**Aspirant**</u>
I banish all worldly influences dwelling within this Temple by the Flaming Star of the Five Elements. I say unto you now, depart!

Go to the East. Make the Banishing Pentagram to the East, then do the same in the South, the West, and the North. Return to the East.

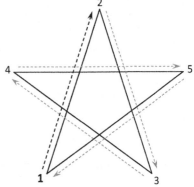

Take up the Cup of Water and sprinkle three times in the East, then do the same in the South,

Banishing Elemental Pentagram

the West, and the North. Return to the East. Dip your finger in the Cup and touch your forehead, then sprinkle Water toward your feet, and touch your right and left shoulders.

<u>**Aspirant**</u>
I am purified; the Temple is purified; all is purified by the Lustral Waters. *Replace the Cup.*

Take up the incense and wave it three times in the East, then do the same in the South, the West, and the North. Return to the East. Wave the incense toward your forehead, your feet and your right and left shoulders.

<u>Aspirant</u>

I am consecrated; the Temple is consecrated; all is consecrated by Holy Fire. *Replace the Incense.*

<u>Aspirant</u>

(*In East, facing East*) I have purified and consecrated this Temple for the invocation of Taurus, and in so doing have created a Temple, that the heavenly forces of the Bull may dwell here for a time. Unseen Watchers over the sacred Magic, watch over this ceremony of the Light Divine. So mote it be.

FIRST ADVANCEMENT: INVOKING ELEMENTAL EARTH

Take the Earth Salt to the North and draw the green Invoking Earth Pentagram towards the North.

Invoking Earth Pentagram

<u>Aspirant</u>

Hear me, those who dwell in the Northern Quarter of the Universe, for I call out to thee! Through the Divine Name ADONAI, I have called you forth under the auspices of Earth, that I may bring to power and presence the zodiacal Sign of Taurus. Grant me the strength to walk the hidden path and discover secret knowledge. Give me your eyes to see and your wisdom to understand, that I may perceive hidden things. Grant me the powers of Earth, that I may bring forth Taurus in this sacred place.

Pause for a moment and fill the aura with GREEN Light. Walk clockwise to the West of the Altar and replace the Earth Salt.

SECOND ADVANCEMENT: INVOCATION OF VENUS

At the Altar, take up the Venus Candle and face the location of Venus.

Aspirant
I shall quit the material and seek the spiritual!

Go to the location of Venus. With the Candle, trace the Invoking Hexagram of Venus, and the symbol of Venus in it.

Aspirant
Creative Venus, who fills the Universe with your beautiful essence, through your Divine Name YHVH TZABAOTH (Yod Heh Vav Heh Tzah-bah-oth), I invoke you. Grant unto me the presence of your Great Archangel ANAEL, that she may lead me in my search for the powers of Taurus. ANAEL, come forth and call to

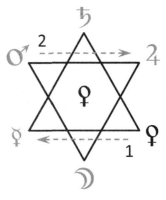

Invoking Venus Hexagram

presence the light of Venus, that she may illuminate the inner realms of my being and I may be awakened to the presence of Taurus. I make this petition to you, that through the Divine Presence, I may rend the Veils of Darkness from my mortal vision and comprehend the secrets of the Sign of the Bull.

Pause for a moment and fill the aura with GREEN Light. Walk clockwise West of the Altar, replace the Venus Candle, and light it.

THIRD ADVANCEMENT: INVOCATION OF TAURUS

Aspirant

(*Facing Taurus*) **To the forces of Taurus that I now prepare to invoke, I have awakened this Temple with the powers of Earth. I have invoked Venus, who is your lord. Come forward and be present with me in this sacred rite. You who are the power of the diligence and focus, I call you forth. Productiveness, material pleasure, and heightened perception, shall reign in this Temple. Open your realm to me, that I may know you and awaken your powers within my soul.**

Go the location of Taurus, and face it.

Aspirant

In the Divine Name YHHV (Yod Heh Heh Vav) and in the name of ASMODEL the great Archangel, I invoke the power of Taurus. *Trace the Invoking Taurus Pentagram, and draw its symbol in the center.*

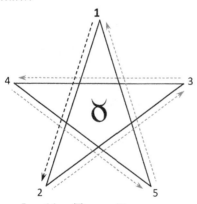

Invoking Taurus Pentagram

Visualize the RED-ORANGE Pentagram of Taurus glowing in the air.

Aspirant

Zeus, the father of the Gods, fell in love with Europa, a beautiful Phoenician princess. As she was never out of

the presence of her father's guards, Zeus transformed himself into a beautiful white bull with golden horns, and he drew near the princess while she was gathering flowers in her garden. Europa, mesmerized by the beauty of the white bull who breathed from his mouth a saffron crocus, made him her own. One day, Europa climbed onto his back and he jumped into the ocean, swimming away with her to the island of Crete. They were welcomed by the king of Crete, who was known as the Ruler of the Stars.

Touch the symbol of Taurus with your index finger. Visualize the RED-ORANGE Light of Taurus flowing down your arm into your heart. Hold this visualization while saying:

<u>Aspirant</u>
After reaching Crete, Zeus revealed himself to Europa and professed his love for her, and she bore him three sons: one who became the king of Crete and later was to judge the Underworld; a second who presided over Hera's Orchard, and a third whom Zeus allowed to live for three generations and who also became a judge in the Afterlife. The King of Crete, the Ruler of the Stars, became the consort of Europa and stepfather to her sons, and he spoke with Zeus every nine years, also receiving the laws of the land from him.

FOURTH ADVANCEMENT: MEDITATION ON *THE HIEROPHANT*

Return to the West of the Altar and take up the Tarot card *The Hierophant*. Sit and face Taurus, turn your aura to RED-ORANGE, and study the card while saying:

Aspirant

Magus of the Eternal Gods, the Wisdom and Fountain of Mercy, I call to you. You who link that which is above to that which is below, be present with me in the working of this rite. Great expounder of the mysteries, your lesson is not understood by the intellect alone, but also is understood through feelings and perception, for you are the link between sensory experience and inner illumination. Ruler over the earthly realm, worldly concerns are yours to bear, for your duty it is to preserve knowledge and divine wisdom. You are the teacher in the quest for the meaning of life, the guide for the spirit seeking a connection between the physical and spiritual worlds, which leads to self-understanding and knowledge.

Close your eyes and visualize yourself in the imagery of the card. Note any thoughts or sensations that arise. Before you quit this visualization, make an offering of your own Light to the Powers of Taurus.

Alternative meditation: the Archangel Asmodel

Visualize the symbol of Taurus in front of you. Once this symbol is firmly established, go through the symbol like a door.

It is nighttime in the spring, and you are standing in a pasture near a stable of horses. Close by the pasture are some small trees that line a newly-planted wheat field. You silently call to the Archangel Asmodel.

Asmodel appears before you in the image of a woman, short in stature, dressed in a red-orange robe. She has a pale complexion, with a strong, full and well-set build. Her face is lovely, surrounded by curly, thick, black hair. She has a broad forehead, big eyes and a full mouth. Her nature is cautious and reserved. Ask Asmodel about the nature of Taurus and how it can aid in your spiritual growth. Note any thoughts or sensations that arise. At the conclusion of this meditation, Asmodel gives you the symbol of Taurus on a copper medallion which you place around your neck. Before you quit this visualization, make an offering of your own Light to the Powers of Taurus.

Aspirant
I have acquired the qualities of Taurus and they now reside within me. So mote it be.

CLOSING

Go to the East and face the center of the room.

Aspirant
I now release any spirits that may have been attracted to this ceremony. Go in peace to your abodes and habitations and go with the powers of Taurus.

Purify and consecrate the Temple and your body with the water and incense, as in the Opening. Banish with the banishing Pentagram in all four quarters, as in the Opening. Return to the East.

Aspirant
I now declare this ritual duly completed. So mote it be.

Extinguish the candles.

Invocation of the Powers of Gemini

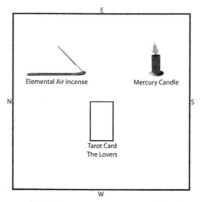

Figure 45: Altar arrangement for Gemini

Temple arrangement: Basic zodiacal Temple.
Altar cloth: Orange, or yellow (Airy triplicity).
Altar implements: Air incense, Mercury Candle (unlit), with a lighter nearby.
Tarot Card: *The Lovers*, on Altar.
Incense, Water: In the East, with incense lit.
Music: Suitable ambient or background music.

Preparation for the Rite

Sit for a moment at the Altar and contemplate the rite to come. Let the cares and worries of the day dissipate. ✠ Focus on the top of your head and form a mental image of a ray of White Light permeating your body through the top of your head. Visualize this Light descending through the center of your body to your feet. Your body is now filled with Light. ✠ Inhale and exhale this Light through the pores of your body until it is pulsing in and around you. ✠ Imagine the Light extending from your body and filling the room. See the Light creating a barrier separating the room from the outer world. Let nothing exist for you outside of this special time and place.

OPENING

Standing West of the Altar, facing East, say:

Aspirant

I banish all worldly influences dwelling within this Temple by the Flaming Star of the Five Elements. I say unto you now, depart!

Go to the East. Make the Banishing Pentagram to the East, then do the same in the South, the West, and the North. Return to the East.

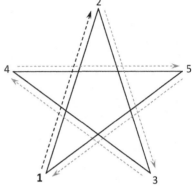

Take up the Cup of Water and sprinkle three times in the East, then do the same in the South,

Banishing Elemental Pentagram

the West, and the North. Return to the East. Dip your finger in the Cup and touch your forehead, then sprinkle Water toward your feet, and touch your right and left shoulders.

Aspirant

I am purified; the Temple is purified; all is purified by the Lustral Waters. *Replace the Cup.*

Take up the incense and wave it three times in the East, then do the same in the South, the West, and the North. Return to the East. Wave the incense toward your forehead, your feet and your right and left shoulders.

Aspirant

I am consecrated; the Temple is consecrated; all is consecrated by Holy Fire. *Replace the Incense.*

Aspirant

(In East, facing East) I have purified and consecrated this Temple for the invocation of Gemini, and in so doing have created a Temple, that the heavenly forces of the Twins may dwell here for a time. Unseen Watchers over the sacred Magic, watch over this ceremony of the Light Divine. So mote it be.

FIRST ADVANCEMENT: INVOKING ELEMENTAL AIR

Take the Air Incense to the East and draw the yellow Invoking Air Pentagram towards the East.

Invoking Air Pentagram

Aspirant

Hear me, those who dwell in the Eastern Quarter of the Universe, for I call out to thee! Through the Divine Name YHVH (Yod Heh Vav Heh), I have called you forth under the auspices of Air, that I may bring to power and presence the zodiacal Sign of Gemini. Grant me the strength to walk the hidden path and discover secret knowledge. Give me your eyes to see and your wisdom to understand, that I may perceive hidden things. Grant me the powers of Air, that I may bring forth Gemini in this sacred place.

Pause for a moment and fill the aura with YELLOW Light. Walk clockwise to the West of the Altar, replace the Air Incense, and light it.

SECOND ADVANCEMENT: INVOCATION OF MERCURY

At the Altar, take up the Mercury Candle and face Mercury's location.

Aspirant
I shall quit the material and seek the spiritual!
Go to the location of Mercury. With the Candle, trace the Invoking Hexagram of Mercury, and the symbol of Mercury in it.

Aspirant
Free-spirited Mercury, who fills the Universe with your dual essence, through your Divine Name ELOHIM TZABAOTH (El-oh-heem Tzah-bah-oth), I invoke you. Grant unto me the presence of your Great Archangel RAPHAEL, that he may lead me in my search for the powers of Gemini. RAPHAEL, come forth

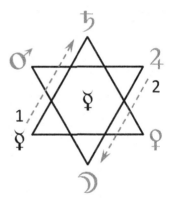

Invoking Mercury Hexagram

and call to presence the light of Mercury, that he may illuminate the inner realms of my being, and I may be awakened to the presence of Gemini. I make this petition to you, that through the Divine Presence, I may rend the Veils of Darkness from my mortal vision and comprehend the secrets of the Sign of the Twins.

Pause for a moment and fill the aura with YELLOW Light. Walk clockwise West of the Altar, replace the Mercury Candle, and light it.

THIRD ADVANCEMENT: INVOCATION OF GEMINI

<u>Aspirant</u>

(*Facing Gemini*) **To the forces of Gemini that I now prepare to invoke, I have awakened this Temple with the powers of Air. I have invoked Mercury, who is your lord. Come forward and be present with me in this sacred rite. You who are the power of the seeker and intense curiosity, I call you forth. Adaptability, communication, and expressive speech shall reign in this Temple. Open your realm to me, that I may know you and awaken your powers within my soul.**

Go the location of Gemini, and face it.

<u>Aspirant</u>

In the Divine Name YVHH (Yod Vav Heh Heh) and in the name of AMBRIEL the great Archangel, I invoke the powers of Gemini.

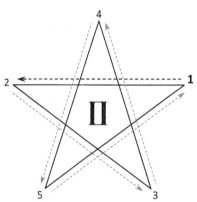

Invoking Gemini Pentagram

Trace the Invoking Gemini Pentagram, and draw its symbol in the center.

Visualize the ORANGE Pentagram of Gemini glowing in the air.

<u>Aspirant</u>

The twins Castor and Pollux

were born of Queen Leda, although they had different fathers, one human and one divine. For Leda was made pregnant by Zeus in the form of a swan, and by her husband, King Tyndarus of Sparta. Pollux, the son of Zeus, was immortal and renowned for his strength. Castor, the son of Tyndarus, was mortal and famous for his skill with horses. Both brothers voyaged in search of the Golden Fleece as Argonauts, and then fought in the Trojan War to bring their sister, Helen, home to her husband.

Touch the symbol of Gemini with your index finger. Visualize the ORANGE Light of Gemini flowing down your arm into your heart. Hold this visualization while saying:

Aspirant

The twins were young, handsome, and adventurous. They took part in many adventures together and were well known for their energy and curiosity. They were united by the warmest affection, and inseparable in all their enterprises. After the Argonaut expedition, Castor and Pollux fought a war with Idas and Lynceus, where the mortal Castor was slain. Pollux, inconsolable over the loss of his brother, prayed to Zeus to allow Castor to share his immortality. Zeus, acknowledging the heroism of both brothers, consented and reunited the pair in the heavens as the constellation Gemini.

FOURTH ADVANCEMENT: MEDITATION ON *THE LOVERS*

Return to the West of the Altar and take up the Tarot card *The Lovers*. Sit and face Gemini, turn your aura to ORANGE, and study the card while saying:

Aspirant

Children of the Voice Divine, Oracles of the Mighty Gods, I call to you. It is your path that connects the human to the Divine, the conscious and the unconscious, mirror reflections of each other which unite again as one. Your power is the inspiration to fuse the lower with the higher, to reach the celestial heights through the union of complementary selves, for in you is the harmony of opposites. The connection and binding of one heart to another is your gift for you are devotion, the melding of one with another, the universal principle of true relationship. Through you comes the realization that two or more parts uniting together create something greater than the two parts individually. For you are synergy, the spiritual and the physical, the container and the contained, the one and the many, the observer and the observed, the human and the divine.

Close your eyes and visualize yourself in the imagery of the card. Note any thoughts or sensations that arise. Before you quit this visualization, make an offering of your own Light to the Powers of Gemini.

Alternative meditation: the Archangel Ambriel

Visualize the symbol of Gemini in front of you. Once this symbol is firmly established, go through the symbol like a door.

It is daytime in the late spring, and you are standing high in the mountains looking over a valley below. You silently call to the Archangel Ambriel.

Ambriel appears before you in an image of a man, tall and straight in stature, dressed in an orange robe. He has a dark complexion, and his arms and legs are very long, with small hands and feet. His face is surrounded by dark brown hair. His piercing eyes are hazel and alert. His nature is open and pleasant. Ask Ambriel about the nature of Gemini and how it can aid in your spiritual growth. Note any thoughts or sensations that arise. At the conclusion of this meditation, Ambriel gives you the symbol of Gemini on a quicksilver medallion which you place around your neck. Before you quit this visualization, make an offering of your own Light to the Powers of Gemini.

<u>Aspirant</u>
I have acquired the qualities of Gemini and they now reside within me. So mote it be.

CLOSING

Go to the East and face the center of the room.

<u>Aspirant</u>
I now release any spirits that may have been attracted to this ceremony. Go in peace to your abodes and habitations and go with the powers of Gemini.

Purify and consecrate the Temple and your body with the water and incense, as in the Opening. Banish with the banishing Pentagram in all four quarters, as in the Opening. Return to the East.

<u>Aspirant</u>
I now declare this ritual duly completed. So mote it be.

Extinguish the candles.

Invocation of the Powers of Cancer

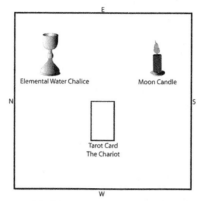

Figure 46: Altar arrangement for Cancer

Temple arrangement: Basic zodiacal Temple.

Altar cloth: Orange-yellow, or blue (Watery triplicity).

Altar implements: Chalice of wine/juice (with a few the drops of consecrated Water), Moon Candle (unlit), with a lighter nearby.

Tarot Card: *The Chariot*, on Altar.

Incense, Water: In the East, with incense lit.

Music: Suitable ambient or background music.

Preparation for the Rite

Sit for a moment at the Altar and contemplate the rite to come. Let
the cares and worries of the day dissipate. ☩ Focus on the top of your
head and form a mental image of a ray of White Light permeating your
body through the top of your head. Visualize this Light descending
through the center of your body to your feet. Your body is now filled
with Light. ☩ Inhale and exhale this Light through the pores of your
body until it is pulsing in and around you. ☩ Imagine the Light extending
from your body and filling the room. See the Light creating a barrier separating the room from the outer world. Let nothing exist for you outside
of this special time and place.

OPENING

Standing West of the Altar, facing East, say:

Aspirant
I banish all worldly influences dwelling within this Temple by the Flaming Star of the Five Elements. I say unto you now, depart!

Go to the East. Make the Banishing Pentagram to the East, then do the same in the South, the West, and the North. Return to the East.

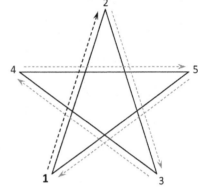

Take up the Cup of Water and sprinkle three times in the East, then do the same in the South,

Banishing Elemental Pentagram

the West, and the North. Return to the East. Dip your finger in the Cup and touch your forehead, then sprinkle Water toward your feet, and touch your right and left shoulders.

Aspirant
I am purified; the Temple is purified; all is purified by the Lustral Waters. *Replace the Cup.*

Take up the incense and wave it three times in the East, then do the same in the South, the West, and the North. Return to the East. Wave the incense toward your forehead, your feet and your right and left shoulders.

<u>Aspirant</u>

I am consecrated; the Temple is consecrated; all is consecrated by Holy Fire. *Replace the Incense.*

<u>Aspirant</u>

(*In East, facing East*) I have purified and consecrated this Temple for the invocation of Cancer, and in so doing have created a Temple, that the heavenly forces of the Crab may dwell here for a time. Unseen Watchers over the sacred Magic, watch over this ceremony of the Light Divine. So mote it be.

First Advancement: Invoking Elemental Water

Take the Water Chalice to the West and draw the blue Invoking Water Pentagram towards the West.

Invoking Water Pentagram

<u>Aspirant</u>

Hear me, those who dwell in the Western Quarter of the Universe, for I call out to thee! Through the Divine Name EL, I have called you forth under the auspices of Water, that I may bring to power and presence the zodiacal Sign of Cancer. Grant me the strength to walk the hidden path and discover secret knowledge. Give me your eyes to see and your wisdom to understand, that I may perceive hidden things. Grant me the powers of Water, that I may bring forth Cancer in this sacred place.

Pause for a moment and fill the aura with BLUE Light. Walk clockwise to the West of the Altar and replace the Water Chalice.

SECOND ADVANCEMENT: INVOCATION OF LUNA

At the Altar, take up the Luna Candle and face the location of Luna.

Aspirant
I shall quit the material and seek the spiritual!

Go to the location of Luna. With the Candle, trace the Invoking Hexagram of Luna, and the symbol of Luna in it.

Aspirant
Mysterious Moon, who fills the Universe with your reflective essence, through your Divine Name SHADDAI EL CHAI (Shahdye El Khye), I invoke you. Grant unto me the presence of your Great Archangel GABRIEL, that she may lead me in my search for

Invoking Luna Hexagram

the powers of Cancer. GABRIEL, come forth and call to presence the light of the Moon, that she may illuminate the inner realms of my being, and I may be awakened to the presence of Cancer. I make this petition to you, that through the Divine Presence, I may rend the Veils of Darkness from my mortal vision and comprehend the secrets of the Sign of the Crab.

Pause for a moment and fill the aura with BLUE Light. Walk clockwise West of the Altar, replace the Luna Candle, and light it.

THIRD ADVANCEMENT: INVOCATION OF CANCER

<u>Aspirant</u>

(*Facing Cancer*) **To the forces of Cancer that I now prepare to invoke, I have awakened this Temple with the powers of Water. I have invoked the Moon, who is your lord. Come forward and be present with me in this sacred rite. You who are the power of growth and security, I call you forth. Emotional support, sensitivity, and a sense of belonging shall reign in this Temple. Open your realm to me, that I may know you and awaken your powers within my soul.**

Go the location of Cancer, and face it.

<u>Aspirant</u>

In the Divine Name HVHY (Heh Vav Heh Yod) and in the name of MURIEL the great Archangel, I invoke the powers of Cancer.

Invoking Cancer Pentagram

Trace the Invoking Cancer Pentagram, and draw its symbol in the center.

Visualize the ORANGE-YELLOW Pentagram of Cancer glowing in the air.

<u>Aspirant</u>

In his second trial, Hercules was sent to kill the Hydra, a monstrous, nine-headed serpent

who had been terrorizing the countryside. The Hydra's bite possessed poisonous venom, and one of its many heads was immortal and indestructible. To accomplish his task, Hercules lured the creature from its lair by attacking it with flaming arrows. Upon emerging, Hercules seized the Hydra but it wound one of its coils around his foot, and the hero could not break free. Hercules attacked the many heads of the Hydra, but each severed head was replaced by two more.

Touch the symbol of Cancer with your index finger. Visualize the ORANGE-YELLOW Light of Cancer flowing down your arm into your heart. Hold this visualization while saying:

Aspirant
Watching the battle between Hercules and the Hydra, the Goddess Hera sent Karkinos, the giant Crab, to aid the serpent and distract the hero, putting him at a disadvantage. While Hercules was held fast by the Hydra, Karkinos grabbed his foot with its claws. The valiant hero crushed the Crab under his foot. The battle raged on, and Hercules was victorious, for he removed all of the heads of the Hydra and the serpent was slain. Although the Crab had lost his battle, Hera, grateful for its heroic effort, placed the Crab's image in the night sky as a reward for its service.

FOURTH ADVANCEMENT: MEDITATION ON *THE CHARIOT*

Return to the West of the Altar and take up the Tarot card *The Chariot*. Sit and face Cancer, turn your aura to ORANGE-YELLOW, and study the card while saying:

Aspirant

Child of the Powers of Water, Lord of the Triumph of Light, I call to you. You, who are a symbol of conquest and victory, be present with me in the working of this rite. War and struggle and a hard-won victory give control over enemies, obstacles, nature or beasts. Through strength and willpower, you overcome all obstacles and challenges, even against many foes, and this struggle ultimately makes you stronger. The combined powers are yours to control, ever ready to move forward while keeping balance both within and without. From one plane to the next do you move, from water to land, from conscious to unconscious, from earthly to spiritual and yet back again. Loyalty and faith are your gifts, along with a steadfast belief that will lead to victory no matter what the odds.

Close your eyes and visualize yourself in the imagery of the card. Note any thoughts or sensations that arise. Before you quit this visualization, make an offering of your own Light to the Powers of Cancer.

Alternative meditation: the Archangel Muriel

Visualize the symbol of Cancer in front of you. Once this symbol is firmly established, go through the symbol like a door.

It is nighttime in the summer, and you are standing near a river, beside which is a deep well. You silently call to the Archangel Muriel.

Muriel appears before you in the image of a woman, short in stature with large breasts, dressed in an orange-yellow robe. She has a pale complexion, with a round face, rather small eyes, and thin brown hair. Her nature is somber and subdued. Ask Muriel about the nature of Cancer and how it can aid in your spiritual growth. Note any thoughts or sensations that arise. At the conclusion of this meditation, Muriel gives you the symbol of Cancer on a silver medallion which you place around your neck. Before you quit this visualization, make an offering of your own Light to the Powers of Cancer.

Aspirant

I have acquired the qualities of Cancer and they now reside within me. So mote it be.

CLOSING

Go to the East and face the center of the room.

Aspirant

I now release any spirits that may have been attracted to this ceremony. Go in peace to your abodes and habitations and go with the powers of Cancer.

Purify and consecrate the Temple and your body with the water and incense, as in the Opening. Banish with the banishing Pentagram in all four quarters, as in the Opening. Return to the East.

Aspirant

I now declare this ritual duly completed. So mote it be.

Extinguish the candles.

INVOCATION OF THE POWERS OF LEO

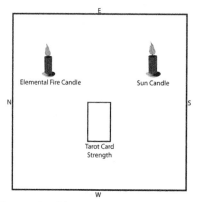

Figure 47: Altar arrangement for Leo

Temple arrangement: Basic zodiacal Temple.

Altar cloth: Yellow, or red (Fiery triplicity).

Altar implements: Fire Candle (unlit), Sun Candle (unlit), with a lighter nearby.

Tarot Card: *Strength*, on Altar.

Incense, Water: In the East, with incense lit.

Music: Suitable ambient or background music.

PREPARATION FOR THE RITE

Sit for a moment at the Altar and contemplate the rite to come. Let the cares and worries of the day dissipate. ✛ Focus on the top of your head and form a mental image of a ray of White Light permeating your body through the top of your head. Visualize this Light descending through the center of your body to your feet. Your body is now filled with Light. ✛ Inhale and exhale this Light through the pores of your body until it is pulsing in and around you. ✛ Imagine the Light extending from your body and filling the room. See the Light creating a barrier separating the room from the outer world. Let nothing exist for you outside of this special time and place.

OPENING

Standing West of the Altar, facing East, say:

Aspirant
I banish all worldly influences dwelling within this Temple by the Flaming Star of the Five Elements. I say unto you now, depart!

Go to the East. Make the Banishing Pentagram to the East, then do the same in the South, the West, and the North. Return to the East.

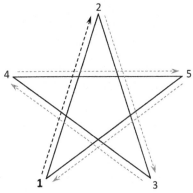

Take up the Cup of Water and sprinkle three times in the East, then do the same in the South,

Banishing Elemental Pentagram

the West, and the North. Return to the East. Dip your finger in the Cup and touch your forehead, then sprinkle Water toward your feet, and touch your right and left shoulders.

Aspirant
I am purified; the Temple is purified; all is purified by the Lustral Waters. *Replace the Cup.*

Take up the incense and wave it three times in the East, then do the same in the South, the West, and the North. Return to the East. Wave the incense toward your forehead, your feet and your right and left shoulders.

Aspirant
I am consecrated; the Temple is consecrated; all is consecrated by Holy Fire. *Replace the Incense.*

<u>Aspirant</u>

(*In East, facing East*) **I have purified and consecrated this Temple for the invocation of Leo, and in so doing have created a Temple, that the heavenly forces of the Lion may dwell here for a time. Unseen Watchers over the sacred Magic, watch over this ceremony of the Light Divine. So mote it be.**

First Advancement: Invoking Elemental Fire

Take the Fire Candle to the South and draw the red Invoking Fire Pentagram towards the South.

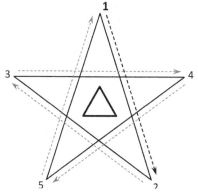

Invoking Fire Pentagram

<u>Aspirant</u>
Hear me, those who dwell in the Southern Quarter of the Universe, for I call out to thee! Through the Divine Name ELOHIM, I have called you forth under the auspices of Fire, that I may bring to power and presence the zodiacal Sign of Leo. Grant me the strength to walk the hidden path and discover secret knowledge. Give me your eyes to see and your wisdom to understand, that I may perceive hidden things. Grant me the powers of Fire, that I may bring forth Leo in this sacred place.

Pause for a moment and fill the aura with RED Light. Walk clockwise West of the Altar, replace the Fire Candle, and light it.

SECOND ADVANCEMENT: INVOCATION OF SOL

Aspirant

(*Taking Sol Candle, and facing Sol.*) **I shall quit the material and seek the spiritual!** *Go to Sol, and use the Candle to trace his Invoking Hexagrams and symbol.*

**Invoking Solar Hexagram
(from Saturn)**

**Invoking Solar Hexagram
(from Jupiter)**

**Invoking Solar Hexagram
(from Mars)**

**Invoking Solar Hexagram
(from Venus)**

**Invoking Solar Hexagram
(from Mercury)**

**Invoking Solar Hexagram
(from Luna)**

Aspirant

Illuminating Sun, who fills the Universe with your solar essence, through your Divine Name YHVH ELOAH V'DAATH (Yod Heh Vav Heh El-oh-ah Veh-Dah-ath), I invoke you. Grant unto me the presence of your Great Archangel MICHAEL, that he may lead me in my search for the powers of Leo. MICHAEL, come forth and call to presence the light of the Sun, that he may illuminate the inner realms of my being, and I may be awakened to the presence of Leo. I make this petition to you, that through the Divine Presence I may rend the Veils of Darkness from my mortal vision and comprehend the secrets of the Sign of the Lion.

Pause for a moment and fill the aura with ORANGE Light. Walk clockwise West of the Altar, replace the Sol Candle, and light it.

THIRD ADVANCEMENT: INVOCATION OF LEO

Aspirant

(*Facing Leo*) To the forces of Leo that I now prepare to invoke, I have awakened this Temple with the powers of Fire. I have invoked Sol, who is your lord. Come forward and be present with me in this sacred rite. You who are the powers of self-awareness, self-confidence, and forceful love, I call you forth. Generosity, creativity, and radiance, shall reign in this Temple. Open your realm to me, that I may know you and awaken your powers within my soul.

Go the location of Leo, and face it.

Aspirant

In the Divine Name HVYH (Heh Vav Yod Heh) and in the name of Verkhiel the great Archangel, I invoke the powers of Leo.

Trace the Invoking Leo Pentagram, and draw its symbol in the center.

Invoking Leo Pentagram

Visualize the YELLOW Pentagram of Leo glowing in the air.

Aspirant

In one of his twelve trials, the great Hercules was sent to kill the Namean Lion, a powerful beast whose hide was impenetrable. And the great Hercules did shoot the lion with many arrows, but to no avail. It was imperative that the task be completed, so the strong one conquered the lion with his bare hands.

Touch the symbol of Leo with your index finger. Visualize the YELLOW Light of Leo flowing down your arm into your heart. Hold this visualization while saying:

Aspirant

In order to prove his victory, Hercules took the pelt of the lion to the king of Tyrins, but the king, fearing the power of Hercules, hid in a wine jar. Having seen the cowardice of the king, the great and strong hero Hercules kept the skin of the Namean Lion for his own armor. Know this now: the Lion, who is the Sun, creates a solar hero. Hera, the wife of Zeus

and Goddess of women and marriage, was the godmother of the lion. To give the lion a place of honor, Hera placed him among the stars, that he would reside and shine in the heavens forever.

Fourth Advancement: Meditation on *Strength*

Return to the West of the Altar and take up the Tarot card *Strength*. Sit and face Leo, turn your aura to YELLOW, and study the card while saying:

<u>Aspirant</u>
Daughter of the Flaming Sword, Leader of the Lion, you are the glory of strength. I call to you and take your strength within me. The lion, which is brute strength, is held in check by the woman, whose calm serenity tames the wild beast. She has mastered the chaos of living in the world. Hercules, the solar hero for his twelve labors, was the son of Zeus, and he accomplished his works through his discipline and strength. Gilgamesh, the King of Ur, though his many trials with his comrade Enkidu, became a great king through the mastery of discipline. This was a lesson hard learned, for when he used brute force, Enkidu was slain and his friend was lost to him forever. I will tread the path of strength and shall gain dominion over my baser instincts with the use of a compassionate and controlled intellect.

Close your eyes and visualize yourself in the imagery of the card. Note any thoughts or sensations that arise. Before you quit this visualization, make an offering of your own Light to the Powers of Leo.

Alternative meditation: the Archangel Verkhiel

Visualize the symbol of Leo in front of you. Once this symbol is firmly established, go through the symbol like a door.

It is daytime in the summer, and you are standing in a forest. In a clearing to your left is a large, golden palace. You silently call to the Archangel Verkhiel.

Verkhiel appears before you in the image of a very large man, with broad shoulders and a narrow waist and hips, dressed in a yellow robe. He has ruddy cheeks, a large, round face, with big eyes and blonde curly hair. His nature is strong and valiant. Ask Verkhiel about the nature of Leo and how it can aid in your spiritual growth. Note any thoughts or sensations that arise. At the conclusion of this meditation Verkhiel gives you the symbol of Leo on a gold medallion which you place around your neck. Before you quit this visualization, make an offering of your own Light to the Powers of Leo.

Aspirant

I have acquired the qualities of Leo and they now reside within me. So mote it be.

CLOSING

Go to the East and face the center of the room.

Aspirant

I now release any spirits that may have been attracted to this ceremony. Go in peace to your abodes and habitations and go with the powers of Leo.

Purify and consecrate the Temple and your body with the water and incense, as in the Opening. Banish with the banishing Pentagram in all four quarters, as in the Opening. Return to the East.

Aspirant
I now declare this ritual duly completed. So mote it be.

Extinguish the candles.

INVOCATION OF THE POWERS OF VIRGO

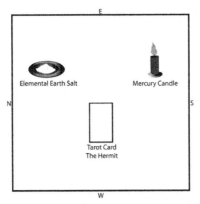

Figure 48: Altar arrangement for Virgo

Temple arrangement: Basic zodiacal Temple.

Altar cloth: Yellow-green, or green (Earthy triplicity).

Altar implements: Earth Salt, Mercury Candle (unlit), with a lighter nearby.

Tarot Card: *The Hermit*, on Altar.

Incense, Water: In the East, with incense lit.

Music: Suitable ambient or background music.

PREPARATION FOR THE RITE

Sit for a moment at the Altar and contemplate the rite to come. Let the cares and worries of the day dissipate. ✛ Focus on the top of your head and form a mental image of a ray of White Light permeating your body through the top of your head. Visualize this Light descending through the center of your body to your feet. Your body is now filled with Light. ✛ Inhale and exhale this Light through the pores of your body until it is pulsing in and around you. ✛ Imagine the Light extending from your body and filling the room. See the Light creating a barrier separating the room from the outer world. Let nothing exist for you outside of this special time and place.

Opening

Standing West of the Altar, facing East, say:

Aspirant

I banish all worldly influences dwelling within this Temple by the Flaming Star of the Five Elements. I say unto you now, depart!

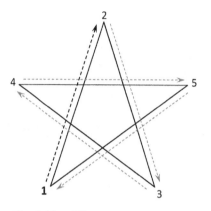

Banishing Elemental Pentagram

Go to the East. Make the Banishing Pentagram to the East, then do the same in the South, the West, and the North. Return to the East.

Take up the Cup of Water and sprinkle three times in the East, then do the same in the South, the West, and the North. Return to the East. Dip your finger in the Cup and touch your forehead, then sprinkle Water toward your feet, and touch your right and left shoulders.

Aspirant

I am purified; the Temple is purified; all is purified by the Lustral Waters. *Replace the Cup.*

Take up the incense and wave it three times in the East, then do the same in the South, the West, and the North. Return to the East. Wave the incense toward your forehead, your feet and your right and left shoulders.

Aspirant

I am consecrated; the Temple is consecrated; all is consecrated by Holy Fire. *Replace the Incense.*

Aspirant

(*In East, facing East*) I have purified and consecrated this Temple for the invocation of Virgo, and in so doing have created a Temple, that the heavenly forces of the Virgin may dwell here for a time. Unseen Watchers over the sacred Magic, watch over this ceremony of the Light Divine. So mote it be.

FIRST ADVANCEMENT: INVOKING ELEMENTAL EARTH

Take the Earth Salt to the North and draw the green Invoking Earth Pentagram towards the North.

Aspirant

Hear me, those who dwell in the Northern Quarter of the Universe, for I call out to thee! Through the Divine Name ADONAI, I have called you forth under the auspices of Earth, that I may bring to power and presence the zodiacal Sign of Virgo. Grant me the strength to walk the hidden path and discover secret knowledge. Give me your eyes to see and your wisdom to understand, that I may perceive hidden things. Grant me the powers of Earth, that I may bring forth Virgo in this sacred place.

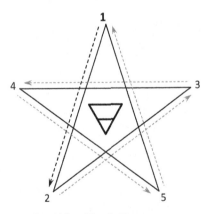

Invoking Earth Pentagram

Pause for a moment and fill the aura with GREEN Light. Walk clockwise to the West of the Altar and replace the Earth Salt.

SECOND ADVANCEMENT: INVOCATION OF MERCURY

At the Altar, take up the Mercury Candle and face the location of Mercury.

Aspirant
I shall quit the material and seek the spiritual!
Go to the location of Mercury. With the Candle, trace the Invoking Hexagram of Mercury, and the symbol of Mercury in it.

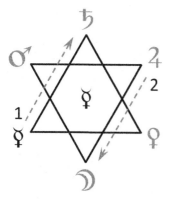

Invoking Mercury Hexagram

Aspirant
Inquisitive Mercury, who fills the Universe with your dual essence, through your Divine Name ELOHIM TZABAOTH (El-oh-heem Tzah-bah-oth), I invoke you. Grant unto me the presence of your Great Archangel RAPHAEL, that he may lead me in my search for the powers of Virgo. RAPHAEL, come forth and call to presence the light of Mercury, that he may illuminate the inner realms of my being, and I may be awakened to the presence of Virgo. I make this petition to you, that through the Divine Presence, I may rend the Veils of Darkness from my mortal vision and comprehend the secrets of the Sign of the Virgin.

Pause for a moment and fill the aura with YELLOW Light. Walk clockwise West of the Altar, replace the Mercury Candle, and light it.

THIRD ADVANCEMENT: INVOCATION OF VIRGO

<u>**Aspirant**</u>
(*Facing Virgo*) **To the forces of Virgo that I now prepare to invoke, I have awakened this Temple with the powers of Earth. I have invoked Mercury, who is your lord. Come forward and be present with me in this sacred rite. You who are the powers of analysis and practical skills, I call you forth. Precision, adaptation, and selection, shall reign in this Temple. Open your realm to me, that I may know you and awaken your powers within my soul.**

Go the location of Virgo, and face it.

<u>**Aspirant**</u>
In the Divine Name HHYV (Heh Heh Yod Vav) and in the name of HAMALIEL the great Archangel, I invoke the power of Virgo.

Trace the Invoking Virgo Pentagram, and draw its symbol in the center.

Visualize the YELLOW-GREEN Pentagram of Virgo glowing in the air.

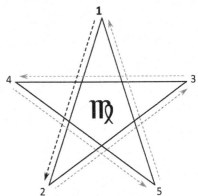

Invoking Virgo Pentagram

<u>Aspirant</u>

During the Golden Age, the Gods lived on the earth and dwelt among human beings. Prometheus, a Titan, stole the Olympic fire and gave it to humans for their use. Outraged, Zeus chained the immortal Prometheus to a rock, where each day an eagle fed on his liver, only to have it grow back to be eaten again and again. In his anger, Zeus then sent Pandora to earth carrying a box filled with evil and pestilence. Pandora unleashed these demons into the world, and only Hope remained behind as a single blessing to comfort humankind in their suffering. The Olympians then left the earth forever.

Touch the symbol of Virgo with your index finger. Visualize the YELLOW-GREEN Light of Virgo flowing down your arm into your heart. Hold this visualization while saying:

<u>Aspirant</u>

But one Goddess remained: Astraea, who was the Daughter of Zeus (the King of the Gods), and Themis (the Goddess of Justice). Astraea is the innocent and pure star-maiden, the Goddess of Virtue, and she had blessed the mortals who dwelled here, for she was a caretaker of humanity. It was she who dwelt the longest amongst the people but eventually, due to the wickedness of humankind, she withdrew to the wilderness and then eventually returned to the heavens. Zeus then placed her amongst the stars where she observes the world from the sky. Astraea will one day come back to earth, bringing with her the return of the Golden Age.

FOURTH ADVANCEMENT: MEDITATION ON *THE HERMIT*

Return to the West of the Altar and take up the Tarot card *The Hermit*. Sit and face Virgo, turn your aura to YELLOW-GREEN, and study the card while saying:

Aspirant

Magus of the Voice of Light, Prophet of the Gods, I call to you. You are the Light-bearer, the one who shows the way to hidden knowledge. From you comes the lesson that purity and self-denial, the desiring of no material thing, are traits that foster spirituality. It is you who stands alone in the wilderness, lantern in hand. You have made the complete journey, both the withdrawal and the return; you have learned the lessons of life and have become the lesson itself. Having attained your spiritual pinnacle, you are now ready to share your knowledge with others. You have used your isolation and the knowledge gained thereby as a tool on the path to reach the heights of awareness. However, your secrets are not for everyone, but only for those who seek them in sincerity and are willing to climb to the heights for the attainment of wisdom.

Close your eyes and visualize yourself in the imagery of the card. Note any thoughts or sensations that arise. Before you quit this visualization, make an offering of your own Light to the Powers of Virgo.

Alternative meditation: the Archangel Hamaliel

Visualize the symbol of Virgo in front of you. Once this symbol is firmly established, go through the symbol like a door.

It is nighttime in the summer, and you are standing in a study with many books. You silently call to the Archangel Hamaliel.

Hamaliel appears before you in the image of a woman, of normal height with a well-formed body, dressed in a yellow-green robe. She has a lovely face with a reddish brown complexion and black hair. Her nature is witty but also studious. Ask Hamaliel about the nature of Virgo and how it can aid in your spiritual growth. Note any thoughts or sensations that arise. At the conclusion of this meditation, Hamaliel gives you the symbol of Virgo on a quicksilver medallion which you place around your neck. Before you quit this visualization, make an offering of your own Light to the Powers of Virgo.

Aspirant
I have acquired the qualities of Virgo and they now reside within me. So mote it be.

CLOSING

Go to the East and face the center of the room.

Aspirant
I now release any spirits that may have been attracted to this ceremony. Go in peace to your abodes and habitations and go with the powers of Virgo.

Purify and consecrate the Temple and your body with the water and incense, as in the Opening. Banish with the banishing Pentagram in all four quarters, as in the Opening. Return to the East.

Aspirant
I now declare this ritual duly completed. So mote it be.

Extinguish the candles.

INVOCATION OF THE POWERS OF LIBRA

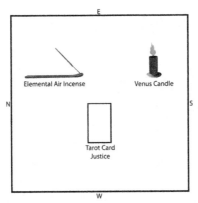

Figure 49: Altar arrangement for Libra

Temple arrangement: Basic zodiacal Temple.

Altar cloth: Green, or yellow (Airy triplicity).

Altar implements: Air incense, Venus Candle (unlit), with a lighter nearby.

Tarot Card: *Justice*, on Altar.

Incense, Water: In the East, with incense lit.

Music: Suitable ambient or background music.

PREPARATION FOR THE RITE

Sit for a moment at the Altar and contemplate the rite to come. Let the cares and worries of the day dissipate. ✠ Focus on the top of your head and form a mental image of a ray of White Light permeating your body through the top of your head. Visualize this Light descending through the center of your body to your feet. Your body is now filled with Light. ✠ Inhale and exhale this Light through the pores of your body until it is pulsing in and around you. ✠ Imagine the Light extending from your body and filling the room. See the Light creating a barrier separating the room from the outer world. Let nothing exist for you outside of this special time and place.

Opening

Standing West of the Altar, facing East, say:

<u>**Aspirant**</u>

I banish all worldly influences dwelling within this Temple by the Flaming Star of the Five Elements. I say unto you now, depart!

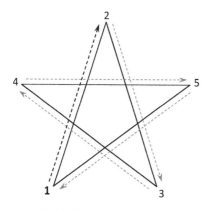

Banishing Elemental Pentagram

Go to the East. Make the Banishing Pentagram to the East, then do the same in the South, the West, and the North. Return to the East.

Take up the Cup of Water and sprinkle three times in the East, then do the same in the South, the West, and the North. Return to the East. Dip your finger in the Cup and touch your forehead, then sprinkle Water toward your feet, and touch your right and left shoulders.

<u>**Aspirant**</u>

I am purified; the Temple is purified; all is purified by the Lustral Waters. *Replace the Cup.*

Take up the incense and wave it three times in the East, then do the same in the South, the West, and the North. Return to the East. Wave the incense toward your forehead, your feet and your right and left shoulders.

<u>Aspirant</u>

I am consecrated; the Temple is consecrated; all is consecrated by Holy Fire. *Replace the Incense.*

<u>Aspirant</u>

(*In East, facing East*) I have purified and consecrated this Temple for the invocation of Libra, and in so doing have created a Temple, that the heavenly forces of the Balance may dwell here for a time. Unseen Watchers over the sacred Magic, watch over this ceremony of the Light Divine. So mote it be.

FIRST ADVANCEMENT: INVOKING ELEMENTAL AIR

Take the Air Incense to the East and draw the yellow Invoking Air Pentagram towards the East.

<u>Aspirant</u>
Hear me, those who dwell in the Eastern Quarter of the Universe, for I call out to thee! Through the Divine Name YHVH (Yod Heh Vav Heh), I have called you forth under the auspices of Air, that I may bring to power and presence the zodiacal

Invoking Air Pentagram

Sign of Libra. Grant me the strength to walk the hidden path and discover secret knowledge. Give me your eyes to see and your wisdom to understand, that I may perceive hidden things. Grant me the powers of Air, that I may bring forth Libra in this sacred place.

Pause for a moment and fill the aura with YELLOW Light. Walk clockwise to the West of the Altar, replace the Air Incense, and light it.

SECOND ADVANCEMENT: INVOCATION OF VENUS

At the Altar, take up the Venus Candle and face the location of Venus.

<u>Aspirant</u>
I shall quit the material and seek the spiritual!

Go to the location of Venus. With the Candle, trace the Invoking Hexagram of Venus, and the symbol of Venus in it.

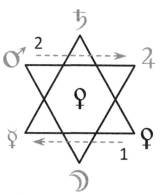

Invoking Venus Hexagram

<u>Aspirant</u>
Beautiful Venus, who fills the Universe with your beautiful essence, through your Divine Name YHVH TZABAOTH (Yod Heh Vav Heh Tzah-bah-oth) I invoke you. Grant unto me the presence of your Great Archangel ANAEL, that she may lead me in my search for the powers of Libra. ANAEL, come forth and call to presence the light of Venus, that she may illuminate the inner realms of my being and I may be awakened to the presence of Libra. I make this petition to you, that through the Divine Presence, I may rend the Veils of Darkness from my mortal vision and comprehend the secrets of the Sign of the Balance.

Pause for a moment and fill the aura with GREEN Light. Walk clockwise West of the Altar, replace the Venus Candle, and light it.

THIRD ADVANCEMENT: INVOCATION OF LIBRA

Aspirant
(*Facing Libra*) **To the forces of Libra that I now prepare to invoke, I have awakened this Temple with the powers of Air. I have invoked Venus, who is your lord. Come forward and be present with me in this sacred rite. You who are the power of balance and harmony, I call you forth. Beauty, equilibrium, and the search for justice, shall reign in this Temple. Open your realm to me, that I may know you and awaken your powers within my soul.**

Go the location of Libra, and face it.

Aspirant
In the Divine Name VHYH (Vav Heh Yod Heh) and in the name of ZURIEL the great Archangel, I invoke the powers of Libra.

Trace the Invoking Libra Pentagram, and draw its symbol in the center

Visualize the GREEN Pentagram of Libra glowing in the air.

Aspirant
Themis was one of the first

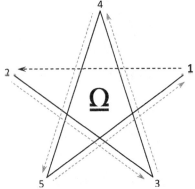

Invoking Libra Pentagram

brides of Zeus, and she bore him six daughters. The first three were Dikē, who was Justice, Eirēnē, who was Peace, and Eunomia, who was the Order of Law. The other three daughters were the Fates. Together these daughters were the establishment of natural law and order. They were the wardens of the skies and the guardians of the gates of heaven. Themis, as the Goddess of Divine Law, was the counselor of Zeus who sat beside her, advising him on the conduct of humanity, reporting on those who breached the primal laws laid down by the Gods. She was assisted in this by her daughter Dikē.

Touch the symbol of Libra with your index finger. Visualize the GREEN Light of Libra flowing down your arm into your heart. Hold this visualization while saying:

Aspirant
Dikē worked for the improvement of humanity, placed on earth to keep justice. When Zeus saw that this task was impossible, he brought her up to the Gods to sit next to him, on the opposite side of her mother. Among the Gods she is the best of all the independent and self-ruling Goddesses. Dikē also goes by the name of Astraea, the Virgin Goddess of the constellation Virgo, for Astraea holds the scales of justice in her hand as the constellation Libra. The two never part, forever linking these two constellations to a single Goddess.

FOURTH ADVANCEMENT: MEDITATION ON *JUSTICE*

Return to the West of the Altar and take up the Tarot card *Justice*. Sit and face Libra, turn your aura to GREEN, and study the card while saying:

Aspirant

Daughter of the Lord of Truth, Holder of the Balances, I call to you. You who are justice, fairness, truth, and the laws of cause and effect, be here present with me in the working of this rite. You are the drive of the will for knowledge, the harmony between reality and instinct, and the use of absolute objectivity. Through you comes the demonstration of harmony and balance, for both are the continual process of correction, the balance and harmony of the inner and outer worlds. Your scales are ever moving, for maintaining this equilibrium is an active process to be continuously maintained. It is Justice who mediates the claims of rights, of morality and of duty, and who creates the system to judge the value these claims. Through your influence, I will search for truth because Justice is truth in action.

Close your eyes and visualize yourself in the imagery of the card. Note any thoughts or sensations that arise. Before you quit this visualization, make an offering of your own Light to the Powers of Libra.

Alternative meditation: the Archangel Zuriel

Visualize the symbol of Libra in front of you. Once this symbol is firmly established, go through the symbol like a door.

It is daytime in the autumn, and you are standing next to a large windmill on the top of a mountain. You silently call to the Archangel Zuriel.

Zuriel appears before you in the image of a man, tall, slim and straight in stature, dressed in a green robe. He has a round and beautiful face, with a lovely pale complexion. His hair is long, smooth and blonde. His nature is liberal and well-tempered. Ask

Zuriel about the nature of Libra and how it can aid in your spiritual growth. Note any thoughts or sensations that arise. At the conclusion of this meditation, Zuriel gives you the symbol of Libra on a copper medallion which you place around your neck. Before you quit this visualization, make an offering of your own Light to the Powers of Libra.

Aspirant
I have acquired the qualities of Libra and they now reside within me. So mote it be.

CLOSING

Go to the East and face the center of the room.

Aspirant
I now release any spirits that may have been attracted to this ceremony. Go in peace to your abodes and habitations and go with the powers of Libra.

Purify and consecrate the Temple and your body with the water and incense, as in the Opening. Banish with the banishing Pentagram in all four quarters, as in the Opening. Return to the East.

Aspirant
I now declare this ritual duly completed. So mote it be.

Extinguish the candles.

INVOCATION OF THE POWERS OF SCORPIO

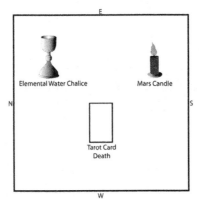

Figure 50: Altar arrangement for Scorpio

Temple arrangement: Basic zodiacal Temple.

Altar cloth: Green-blue, or blue (Watery triplicity).

Altar implements: Chalice of wine/juice (with a few the drops of consecrated Water), Moon Candle (unlit), with a lighter nearby.

Tarot Card: *Death*, on Altar.

Incense, Water: In the East, with incense lit.

Music: Suitable ambient or background music.

PREPARATION FOR THE RITE

Sit for a moment at the Altar and contemplate the rite to come. Let the cares and worries of the day dissipate. ✛ Focus on the top of your head and form a mental image of a ray of White Light permeating your body through the top of your head. Visualize this Light descending through the center of your body to your feet. Your body is now filled with Light. ✛ Inhale and exhale this Light through the pores of your body until it is pulsing in and around you. ✛ Imagine the Light extending from your body and filling the room. See the Light creating a barrier separating the room from the outer world. Let nothing exist for you outside of this special time and place.

OPENING

Standing West of the Altar, facing East, say:

Aspirant

I banish all worldly influences dwelling within this Temple by the Flaming Star of the Five Elements. I say unto you now, depart!

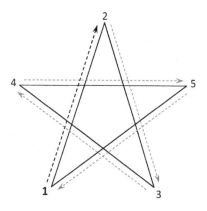

Banishing Elemental Pentagram

Go to the East. Make the Banishing Pentagram to the East, then do the same in the South, the West, and the North. Return to the East.

Take up the Cup of Water and sprinkle three times in the East, then do the same in the South, the West, and the North. Return to the East. Dip your finger in the Cup and touch your forehead, then sprinkle Water toward your feet, and touch your right and left shoulders.

Aspirant

I am purified; the Temple is purified; all is purified by the Lustral Waters. *Replace the Cup.*

Take up the incense and wave it three times in the East, then do the same in the South, the West, and the North. Return to the East. Wave the incense toward your forehead, your feet and your right and left shoulders.

Aspirant

I am consecrated; the Temple is consecrated; all is consecrated by Holy Fire. *Replace the Incense.*

Aspirant

(*In East, facing East*) I have purified and consecrated this Temple for the invocation of Scorpio, and in so doing have created a Temple, that the heavenly forces of the Scorpion may dwell here for a time. Unseen Watchers over the sacred Magic, watch over this ceremony of the Light Divine. So mote it be.

FIRST ADVANCEMENT: INVOKING ELEMENTAL WATER

Take the Water Chalice to the West and draw the blue Invoking Water Pentagram towards the West.

Aspirant

Hear me, those who dwell in the Western Quarter of the Universe, for I call out to thee! Through the Divine Name EL, I have called you forth under the auspices of Water, that I may bring to power and presence the zodiacal Sign of Scorpio. Grant me the strength to walk the hidden

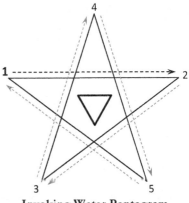

Invoking Water Pentagram

path and discover secret knowledge. Give me your eyes to see and your wisdom to understand, that I may perceive hidden things. Grant me the powers of Water, that I may bring forth Scorpio in this sacred place.

Pause for a moment and fill the aura with BLUE Light. Walk clockwise to the West of the Altar and replace the Water Chalice.

SECOND ADVANCEMENT: INVOCATION OF MARS

At the Altar, take up the Mars Candle and face the location of Mars.

Aspirant
I shall quit the material and seek the spiritual!

Go to the location of Mars. With the Candle, trace the Invoking Hexagram of Mars, and the symbol of Mars in it.

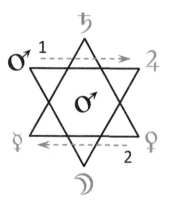

Invoking Mars Hexagram

Aspirant
Valiant Mars, who fills the Universe with your Martial essence, through your Divine Name, ELOHIM GIBOR I invoke you. Grant unto me the presence of your Great Archangel KAMAEL, that he may lead me in my search for the powers of Scorpio. KAMAEL, come forth and call to presence the light of Mars, that he may illuminate the inner realms of my being, and I may be awakened to the presence of Scorpio. I make this petition to you, that through the Divine Presence, I may rend the Veils of Darkness from my mortal vision and comprehend the secrets of the Sign of the Scorpion.

Pause for a moment and fill the aura with RED Light. Walk clock-wise West of the Altar, replace the Mars Candle, and light it.

THIRD ADVANCEMENT: INVOCATION OF SCORPIO

Aspirant

(*Facing Scorpio*) **To the forces of Scorpio that I now prepare to invoke, I have awakened this Temple with the powers of Water. I have invoked Mars, who is your lord. Come forward and be present with me in this sacred rite. You who are the power of the deep change and transformation, I call you forth. Determination, power, and depth of passion shall reign in this Temple. Open your realm to me, that I may know you and awaken your powers within my soul.**

Go the location of Scorpio, and face it.

Aspirant

In the Divine Name VHHY (Vav Heh Heh Yod) and in the name of BARKHIEL the great Archangel, I invoke the powers of Scorpio.

Trace the Invoking Scorpio Pentagram, and draw its symbol in the center.

Visualize the GREEN-BLUE Pentagram of Scorpio glowing in the air.

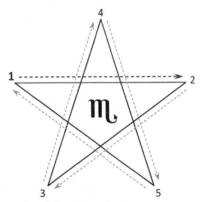

Invoking Scorpio Pentagram

Aspirant

The giant hunter Orion boasted to Artemis, Goddess of the hunt and wild animals, that he would kill every animal on the earth. Although Artemis was a hunter, she also offered protection to all wild creatures. Nevertheless, Artemis took a liking to Orion, because while he was the stronger hunter than she, he had said that she was the better of the two. The brother of Artemis, the God Apollo, was responsible for guarding herds, and Orion's boast angered him. So Apollo persuaded Gaia, the Earth Goddess, to send a giant Scorpion with impenetrable armor to sting Orion to death.

Touch the symbol of Scorpio with your index finger. Visualize the GREEN-BLUE Light of Scorpio flowing down your arm into your heart. Hold this visualization while saying:

Aspirant

Orion faced the Scorpion, whose deadly sting was raised to strike. As they battled, the Scorpion killed the giant hunter. Zeus, Father of the Gods, was watching from the heights, and he raised the Scorpion to the heavens in a tribute. Later, at the request of a sorrowful Artemis, Zeus also put Orion in the heavens, but only to serve as a reminder for mortals to curb their excessive pride. Every winter Orion hunts in the sky, but every summer he sets in the heavens as the constellation of Scorpio rises.

FOURTH ADVANCEMENT: MEDITATION ON *DEATH*

Return to the West of the Altar and take up the Tarot card *Death*. Sit and face Scorpio, turn your aura to GREEN-BLUE, and study the card while saying:

Aspirant

Child of the Great Transformers, Lord of the Gates of Death, I call to you. You are both death and rebirth, the eternal transformation of Nature. The ending of a cycle are you, a loss and a conclusion. But you are also the transition from an old form into a new state of being, a transformation and a regeneration. Sorrow you are at the first, but renewal follows the transition from one form into another. We all must first die in order to be reborn, just as winter heralds the coming spring. It is you who conveys the release necessary for growth and expansion, and through you I stand on the threshold as old concepts and states of being are corrupted and pass away. I step through the doorway to a new form of life.

Close your eyes and visualize yourself in the imagery of the card. Note any thoughts or sensations that arise. Before you quit this visualization, make an offering of your own Light to the Powers of Scorpio.

Alternative meditation: the Archangel Barkhiel

Visualize the symbol of Scorpio in front of you. Once this symbol is firmly established, go through the symbol like a door.

It is nighttime in the autumn, and you are standing in a vineyard. The ground is wet and soft. You silently call to the Archangel Barkhiel.

Barkhiel appears before you in the image of a woman, short and plump in stature, dressed in a green-blue robe. She has a broad and square face with a dark complexion. Her thick hair is dark brown. Her nature is deliberate and sober. Ask Barkhiel about the nature of Scorpio and how it can aid in your spiritual growth. Note any thoughts or sensations that arise. At the conclusion of this meditation, Barkhiel gives you the symbol of Scorpio on an iron medallion which you place around your neck. Before you quit this visualization, make an offering of your own Light to the Powers of Scorpio.

Aspirant

I have acquired the qualities of Scorpio and they now reside within me. So mote it be.

CLOSING

Go to the East and face the center of the room.

Aspirant

I now release any spirits that may have been attracted to this ceremony. Go in peace to your abodes and habitations and go with the powers of Scorpio.

Purify and consecrate the Temple and your body with the water and incense, as in the Opening. Banish with the banishing Pentagram in all four quarters, as in the Opening. Return to the East.

Aspirant

I now declare this ritual duly completed. So mote it be.

Extinguish the candles.

INVOCATION OF THE POWERS OF SAGITTARIUS

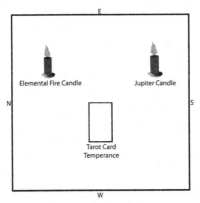

Figure 51: Altar arrangement for Sagittarius

Temple arrangement: Basic zodiacal Temple.

Altar cloth: Blue, or red (Fiery triplicity).

Altar implements: Fire Candle (unlit), Jupiter Candle (unlit), with a lighter nearby.

Tarot Card: *Temperance*, on Altar.

Incense, Water: In the East, with incense lit.

Music: Suitable ambient or background music.

PREPARATION FOR THE RITE

Sit for a moment at the Altar and contemplate the rite to come. Let the cares and worries of the day dissipate. ✠ Focus on the top of your head and form a mental image of a ray of White Light permeating your body through the top of your head. Visualize this Light descending through the center of your body to your feet. Your body is now filled with Light. ✠ Inhale and exhale this Light through the pores of your body until it is pulsing in and around you. ✠ Imagine the Light extending from your body and filling the room. See the Light creating a barrier separating the room from the outer world. Let nothing exist for you outside of this special time and place.

Opening

Standing West of the Altar, facing East, say:

Aspirant

I banish all worldly influences dwelling within this Temple by the Flaming Star of the Five Elements. I say unto you now, depart!

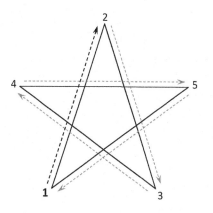

Banishing Elemental Pentagram

Go to the East. Make the Banishing Pentagram to the East, then do the same in the South, the West, and the North. Return to the East.

Take up the Cup of Water and sprinkle three times in the East, then do the same in the South, the West, and the North. Return to the East. Dip your finger in the Cup and touch your forehead, then sprinkle Water toward your feet, and touch your right and left shoulders.

Aspirant

I am purified; the Temple is purified; all is purified by the Lustral Waters. *Replace the Cup.*

Take up the incense and wave it three times in the East, then do the same in the South, the West, and the North. Return to the East. Wave the incense toward your forehead, your feet and your right and left shoulders.

Aspirant

I am consecrated; the Temple is consecrated; all is consecrated by Holy Fire. *Replace the Incense.*

Aspirant

(*In East, facing East*) I have purified and consecrated this Temple for the invocation of Sagittarius, and in so doing have created a Temple, that the heavenly forces of the Archer may dwell here for a time. Unseen Watchers over the sacred Magic, watch over this ceremony of the Light Divine. So mote it be.

FIRST ADVANCEMENT: INVOKING ELEMENTAL FIRE

Take the Fire Candle to the South and draw the red Invoking Fire Pentagram towards the South.

Aspirant

Hear me, those who dwell in the Southern Quarter of the Universe, for I call out to thee! Through the Divine Name ELOHIM, I have called you forth under the auspices of Fire, that I may bring to power and presence the zodiacal Sign of Sagittarius. Grant me the strength to walk the

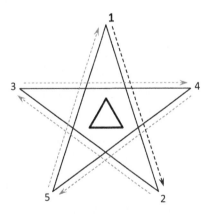

Invoking Fire Pentagram

hidden path and discover secret knowledge. Give me your eyes to see and your wisdom to understand, that I may perceive hidden things. **Grant me the powers of Fire, that I may bring forth Sagittarius in this sacred place.**

Pause for a moment and fill the aura with RED Light. Walk clockwise to the West of the Altar, replace the Fire Candle, and light it.

SECOND ADVANCEMENT: INVOCATION OF JUPITER

At the Altar, take up the Jupiter Candle and face the location of Jupiter.

<u>Aspirant</u>
I shall quit the material and seek the spiritual!

Go to the location of Jupiter. With the Candle, trace the Invoking Hexagram of Jupiter, and the symbol of Jupiter in it.

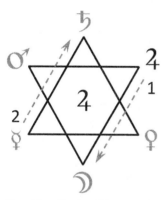

Invoking Jupiter Hexagram

<u>Aspirant</u>
Peaceful Jupiter, who fills the Universe with your Jovial essence, through your Divine Name, EL, I invoke you. Grant unto me the presence of your Great Archangel IOPHIEL (Yoh-fee-el), that he may lead me in my search for the powers of Sagittarius. IOPHIEL, come forth and call to presence the light of Jupiter, that he may illuminate the inner realms of my being and I may be awakened to the presence of Sagittarius. I make this petition to you, that through the Divine Presence, I

may rend the Veils of Darkness from my mortal vision and comprehend the secrets of the Sign of the Archer.

Pause for a moment and fill the aura with VIOLET Light. Walk clockwise West of the Altar, replace the Jupiter Candle, and light it.

THIRD ADVANCEMENT: INVOCATION OF SAGITTARIUS

Aspirant

(*Facing Sagittarius*) **To the forces of Sagittarius that I now prepare to invoke, I have awakened this Temple with the powers of Fire. I have invoked Jupiter, who is your lord. Come forward and be present with me in this sacred rite. You who are the power of the seeker, who pursues all wisdom and knows no fear, and I call you forth. Aspiration, the sense of adventure, of action, and spiritual ideals, shall reign in this Temple. Open your realm to me, that I may know you and awaken your powers within my soul.**

Go the location of Sagittarius, and face it.

Aspirant

In the Divine Name VYHH (Vav Yod Heh Heh) and in the name of ADNAKHIEL the great Archangel, I invoke the powers of Sagittarius.

Trace the Invoking Sagittarius Pentagram, and draw its symbol in the center.

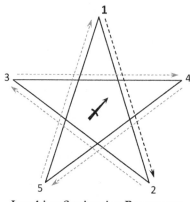

Invoking Sagittarius Pentagram

Visualize the BLUE Pentagram of Sagittarius glowing in the air.

Aspirant

Crotus, a satyr, was the son of the goat-God, Pan, and Eu-phēmē, a nurse to the Muses. Crotus was a child of nature, pure and tame, but also fearless with the brutal instincts necessary to defend himself. The Muses presided over the arts and sciences, which inspired culture as well as civilized behavior and Crotus was raised among them on Mt. Helicon. Satyrs were known as wild, warring, and lustful beasts, but Crotus was different from the others. He was a peaceful soul with great musical talent who grew up to be a skilled hunter, a superb rider, and the inventor of the bow. He delighted in the company of the Muses, and became their devoted protector.

Touch the symbol of Sagittarius with your index finger. Visualize the BLUE Light of Sagittarius flowing down your arm into your heart. Hold this visualization while saying:

Aspirant

Crotus attained great fame for his diligence, for he was very swift in the woods and clever in the musical arts, playing melodies of the human soul that nourished feelings for the Higher. In appreciation, when Crotus died the Muses petitioned Zeus to place him among the stars, in a constellation equal to his extraordinary talents. Zeus wished to display the skills of Crotus so he gave him horse flanks and added arrows, since these would show his strength and swiftness, and

Zeus gave him a Satyr's tail, because the Muses loved Crotus as much as Dionysus loved the satyrs.

FOURTH ADVANCEMENT: MEDITATION ON *TEMPERANCE*

Return to the West of the Altar and take up the Tarot card *Temperance*. Sit and face Sagittarius, turn your aura to BLUE, and study the card while saying:

<u>Aspirant</u>
Daughter of the Reconcilers, the Bringer Forth of Life, I call to you. You, who are the synthesis of opposites, the unification of the external and the internal, the conscious and the unconscious, the human and the divine, be here with me. You stand with one foot on the earth of the material world and the other on the water of the creative mind, and your vessel pours forth a liquid that rises from the lower to the higher. To you belong balance, equity, and repose, for you are a part of the ancient healing through the union of opposites. Through your lesson, I shall balance the spiritual and the material and become temperate, harmonizing extremes and directing my energies toward fulfillment of my spiritual self, maintaining the flow and balanced rhythm of the fires and waters of a spiritual life.

Close your eyes and visualize yourself in the imagery of the card. Note any thoughts or sensations that arise. Before you quit this visualization, make an offering of your own Light to the Powers of Sagittarius.

Alternative meditation: the Archangel Adnakhiel

Visualize the symbol of Sagittarius in front of you. Once this symbol is firmly established, go through the symbol like a door.

It is daytime in the autumn, and you are on a high hill near a herd of large, beautiful war horses. You silently call to the Archangel Adnakhiel.

Adnakhiel appears before you in the image of a man, slightly above-average in height with a strong body, dressed in a blue robe. He has a long and full face with a well-tanned complexion. His chestnut hair is long, flowing to his shoulders. His nature is quick-witted and bold. Ask Adnakhiel about the nature of Sagittarius and how it can aid in your spiritual growth. Note any thoughts or sensations that arise. At the conclusion of this meditation, Adnakhiel gives you the symbol of Sagittarius on a tin medallion which you place around your neck. Before you quit this visualization, make an offering of your own Light to the Powers of Sagittarius.

Aspirant
I have acquired the qualities of Sagittarius and they now reside within me. So mote it be.

CLOSING

Go to the East and face the center of the room.

Aspirant
I now release any spirits that may have been attracted to this ceremony. Go in peace to your abodes and habitations and go with the powers of Sagittarius.

Purify and consecrate the Temple and your body with the water and incense, as in the Opening. Banish with the banishing Pentagram in all four quarters, as in the Opening. Return to the East.

Aspirant
I now declare this ritual duly completed. So mote it be.

Extinguish the candles.

INVOCATION OF THE POWERS OF CAPRICORN

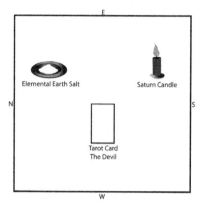

Figure 52: Altar arrangement for Capricorn

Temple arrangement: Basic zodiacal Temple.
Altar cloth: Blue-violet, or green (Earthy triplicity).
Altar implements: Earth Salt, Saturn Candle (unlit), with a lighter near-by.
Tarot Card: *The Devil*, on Altar.
Incense, Water: In the East, with incense lit.
Music: Suitable ambient or background music.

PREPARATION FOR THE RITE

Sit for a moment at the Altar and contemplate the rite to come. Let the cares and worries of the day dissipate. ☥ Focus on the top of your head and form a mental image of a ray of White Light permeating your body through the top of your head. Visualize this Light descending through the center of your body to your feet. Your body is now filled with Light. ☥ Inhale and exhale this Light through the pores of your body until it is pulsing in and around you. ☥ Imagine the Light extending from your body and filling the room. See the Light creating a barrier separating the room from the outer world. Let nothing exist for you outside of this special time and place.

OPENING

Standing West of the Altar, facing East, say:

<u>**Aspirant**</u>
I banish all worldly influences dwelling within this Temple by the Flaming Star of the Five Elements. I say unto you now, depart!

Go to the East. Make the Banishing Pentagram to the East, then do the same in the South, the West, and the North. Return to the East.

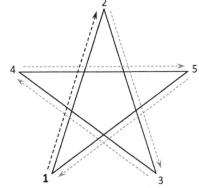

Take up the Cup of Water and sprinkle three times in the East, then do the same in the South,

Banishing Elemental Pentagram

the West, and the North. Return to the East. Dip your finger in the Cup and touch your forehead, then sprinkle Water toward your feet, and touch your right and left shoulders.

<u>**Aspirant**</u>
I am purified; the Temple is purified; all is purified by the Lustral Waters. *Replace the Cup.*

Take up the incense and wave it three times in the East, then do the same in the South, the West, and the North. Return to the East. Wave the incense toward your forehead, your feet and your right and left shoulders.

<u>Aspirant</u>

I am consecrated; the Temple is consecrated; all is consecrated by Holy Fire. *Replace the Incense.*

<u>Aspirant</u>

(*In East, facing East*) I have purified and consecrated this Temple for the invocation of Capricorn, and in so doing have created a Temple, that the heavenly forces of the Sea-goat may dwell here for a time. Unseen Watchers over the sacred Magic, watch over this ceremony of the Light Divine. So mote it be.

First Advancement: Invoking Elemental Earth

Take the Earth Salt to the North and draw the green Invoking Earth Pentagram towards the North.

Invoking Earth Pentagram

<u>Aspirant</u>

Hear me, those who dwell in the Northern Quarter of the Universe, for I call out to thee! Through the Divine Name Adonai, I have called you forth under the auspices of Earth, that I may bring to power and presence the zodiacal Sign of Capricorn. Grant me the strength to walk the hidden path and discover secret knowledge. Give me your eyes to see and your wisdom to understand, that I may perceive hidden things. Grant me the powers of Earth, that I may bring forth Capricorn in this sacred place.

Pause for a moment and fill the aura with GREEN Light. Walk clockwise to the West of the Altar and replace the Earth Salt.

SECOND ADVANCEMENT: INVOCATION OF SATURN

At the Altar, take up the Saturn Candle and face the location of Saturn.

Aspirant
I shall quit the material and seek the spiritual!

Go to the location of Saturn. With the Candle, trace the Invoking Hexagram of Saturn, and the symbol of Saturn in it.

Aspirant
Silent Saturn, who fills the Universe with your brooding essence, through your Divine Name YHVH ELOHIM (Yod Heh Vav Heh El-oh-heem), I invoke you. Grant unto me the presence of your Great Archangel KASSIEL, that she may lead me in my search for the powers of Capricorn. KASSIEL, come

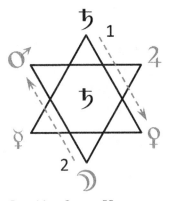

Invoking Saturn Hexagram

forth and call to presence the light of Saturn, that he may illuminate the inner realms of my being and I may be awakened to the presence of Capricorn. I make this petition to you, that through the Divine Presence, I may rend the Veils of Darkness from my mortal vision, and comprehend the secrets of the Sign of the Sea-goat.

Pause for a moment and fill the aura with BLUE-VIOLET Light. Walk clockwise West of the Altar, replace the Saturn Candle, and light it.

THIRD ADVANCEMENT: INVOCATION OF CAPRICORN

<u>Aspirant</u>
(*Facing Capricorn*) **To the forces of Capricorn that I now prepare to invoke, I have awakened this Temple with the powers of Earth. I have invoked Saturn, who is your lord. Come forward and be present with me in this sacred rite. You who are the power of responsibility and practicality, I call you forth. Determination, organization, and accomplishment, shall reign in this Temple. Open your realm to me, that I may know you and awaken your powers within my soul.**

Go the location of Capricorn, and face it.

<u>Aspirant</u>
In the Divine Name HYHV (Heh Yod Heh Vav) and in the name of HANAEL the great Archangel, I invoke the powers of Capricorn.

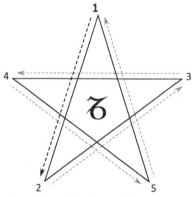
Invoking Capricorn Pentagram

Trace the Invoking Capricorn Pentagram, and draw its symbol in the center.

Visualize the BLUE-VIOLET Pentagram of Capricorn glowing in the air.

<u>Aspirant</u>
When the mother Goddess

Rhea gave birth to Zeus, she feared that her cruel husband Kronos would devour the child, so she secretly took him to a goat nymph, who nursed Zeus with the greatest love and devotion, feeding him on her own rich milk and sweet lavender-scented honey. The goat-God Pan also was nurtured alongside Zeus by the tender goat nymph.

Touch the symbol of Capricorn with your index finger. Visualize the BLUE-VIOLET Light of Capricorn flowing down your arm into your heart. Hold this visualization while saying:

Aspirant

Following an epic battle against the Titans, the Olympian gods sought refuge in Egypt. The monster Typhon, son of the Titan Gaia, sought revenge. Typhon was a fearsome, fire-breathing creature, taller than the mountains and with arms made of dragons' heads. As Typhon attacked, Pan threw himself into the Nile, but in a panic only succeeded in partially transforming his shape; the parts above the water remained a goat, but those under the water transformed into a fish. In the battle, Zeus had been dismembered by Typhon but was saved when Pan let out an ear-splitting cry, confusing the monster long enough for the agile Hermes to collect Zeus' limbs and carefully restore him. In gratitude, Zeus made a place for Pan in the heavens.

FOURTH ADVANCEMENT: MEDITATION ON *THE DEVIL*

Return to the West of the Altar and take up the Tarot card *The Devil*. Sit and face Capricorn, turn your aura to BLUE-VIOLET, and study the card while saying:

Aspirant

Lord of the Gates of Matter, Child of the Forces of Time, I call to you. You who are the ruler of manifested form; you who are the symbol of the both the Higher and the Lower. You are a child of the Elements, for you wings are of Air, your legs are of Earth, your eagle clawed feet are of Water and your torch is of Fire. You are an Adversary, and a tremendous source of strength, an inexhaustible source of energy. Battling you gives me strength, and dominating you is the death of material obsession and an ego-centered consciousness. A Veil you are, an illusion, as perceptions of the world, of reality, are mere blinds to what lies behind it. You are a symbol of the power of blatant materiality in the world. The Greek God Pan, the goat God, is yet another of your names for you are Nature at its wildest, untamed sexuality, and the powerful force of animal desire that pulses through all creation.

Close your eyes and visualize yourself in the imagery of the card. Note any thoughts or sensations that arise. Before you quit this visualization, make an offering of your own Light to the Powers of Capricorn.

Alternative meditation: the Archangel Hanael

Visualize the symbol of Capricorn in front of you. Once this symbol is firmly established, go through the symbol like a door.

It is nighttime in the winter, and you are standing on a barren field with short and thorny bushes. You silently call to the Archangel Hanael.

Hanael appears before you in the image of a woman of average height and a lean body, dressed in a blue-violet robe. Her neck is long, and she has an elongated, slender face with a narrow chin. Her hair is black. Her nature is careful and introverted. Ask Hanael about the nature of Capricorn and how it can aid in your spiritual growth. Note any thoughts or sensations that arise. At the conclusion of this meditation, Hanael gives you the symbol of Capricorn on a lead medallion which you place around your neck. Before you quit this visualization, make an offering of your own Light to the Powers of Capricorn.

Aspirant

I have acquired the qualities of Capricorn and they now reside within me. So mote it be.

CLOSING

Go to the East and face the center of the room.

Aspirant

I now release any spirits that may have been attracted to this ceremony. Go in peace to your abodes and habitations and go with the powers of Capricorn.

Purify and consecrate the Temple and your body with the water and incense, as in the Opening. Banish with the banishing Pentagram in all four quarters, as in the Opening. Return to the East.

Aspirant

I now declare this ritual duly completed. So mote it be.

Extinguish the candles.

INVOCATION OF THE POWERS OF AQUARIUS

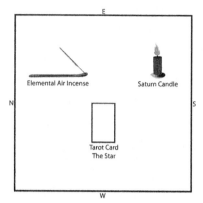

Figure 53: Altar arrangement for Aquarius

Temple arrangement: Basic zodiacal Temple.
Altar cloth: Violet, or yellow (Airy triplicity).
Altar implements: Air incense, Saturn Candle (unlit), with a lighter nearby.
Tarot Card: *The Star*, on Altar.
Incense, Water: In the East, with incense lit.
Music: Suitable ambient or background music.

PREPARATION FOR THE RITE

Sit for a moment at the Altar and contemplate the rite to come. Let the cares and worries of the day dissipate. ⊕ Focus on the top of your head and form a mental image of a ray of White Light permeating your body through the top of your head. Visualize this Light descending through the center of your body to your feet. Your body is now filled with Light. ⊕ Inhale and exhale this Light through the pores of your body until it is pulsing in and around you. ⊕ Imagine the Light extending from your body and filling the room. See the Light creating a barrier separating the room from the outer world. Let nothing exist for you outside of this special time and place.

OPENING

Standing West of the Altar, facing East, say:

Aspirant

I banish all worldly influences dwelling within this Temple by the Flaming Star of the Five Elements. I say unto you now, depart!

Go to the East. Make the Banishing Pentagram to the East, then do the same in the South, the West, and the North. Return to the East.

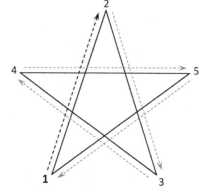

Take up the Cup of Water and sprinkle three times in the East, then do the same in the South,

Banishing Elemental Pentagram

the West, and the North. Return to the East. Dip your finger in the Cup and touch your forehead, then sprinkle Water toward your feet, and touch your right and left shoulders.

Aspirant

I am purified; the Temple is purified; all is purified by the Lustral Waters. *Replace the Cup.*

Take up the incense and wave it three times in the East, then do the same in the South, the West, and the North. Return to the East. Wave the incense toward your forehead, your feet and your right and left shoulders.

Aspirant

I am consecrated; the Temple is consecrated; all is consecrated by Holy Fire. *Replace the Incense.*

Aspirant

(*In East, facing East*) I have purified and consecrated this Temple for the invocation of Aquarius, and in so doing have created a Temple, that the heavenly forces of the Water-bearer may dwell here for a time. Unseen Watchers over the sacred Magic, watch over this ceremony of the Light Divine. So mote it be.

First Advancement: Invoking Elemental Air

Take the Air Incense to the East and draw the yellow Invoking Air Pentagram towards the East.

Invoking Air Pentagram

Aspirant

Hear me, those who dwell in the Eastern Quarter of the Universe, for I call out to thee! Through the Divine Name YHVH (Yod Heh Vav Heh), I have called you forth under the auspices of Air, that I may bring to power and presence the zodiacal Sign of Aquarius. Grant me the strength to walk the hidden path and discover secret knowledge. Give me your eyes to see and your wisdom to understand, that I may perceive hidden things. Grant me the powers of Air, that I may bring forth Aquarius in this sacred place.

Pause for a moment and fill the aura with YELLOW Light. Walk clockwise to the West of the Altar, replace the Air Incense, and light it.

SECOND ADVANCEMENT: INVOCATION OF SATURN

At the Altar, take up the Saturn Candle and face the location of Saturn.

Aspirant

I shall quit the material and seek the spiritual!
Go to the location of Saturn. With the Candle, trace the Invoking Hexagram of Saturn, and the symbol of Saturn in it.

Aspirant

Lofty Saturn, who fills the Universe with your brooding essence, through your Divine Name YHVH ELOHIM I invoke you. Grant unto me the presence of your Great Archangel KASSIEL, that she may lead me in my search for the powers of Aquarius. KASSIEL, come forth and call to presence

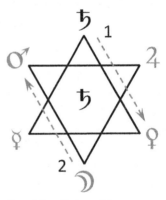

Invoking Saturn Hexagram

the light of Saturn, that he may illuminate the inner realms of my being and I may be awakened to the presence of Aquarius. I make this petition to you, that through the Divine Presence, I may rend the Veils of Darkness from my mortal vision, and comprehend the secrets of the Sign of the Water Bearer.

Pause for a moment and fill the aura with BLUE-VIOLET Light. Walk clockwise West of the Altar, replace the Saturn Candle, and light it.

THIRD ADVANCEMENT: INVOCATION OF AQUARIUS

Aspirant

(*Facing Aquarius*) **To the forces of Aquarius that I now prepare to invoke, I have awakened this Temple with the powers of Air. I have invoked Saturn, who is your lord. Come forward and be present with me in this sacred rite. You who are the power of complex thought and deep explanation, I call you forth. Philosophy, sound counsel, and serene reason, shall reign in this Temple. Open your realm to me, that I may know you and awaken your powers within my soul.**

Go the location of Aquarius, and face it.

Aspirant

In the Divine Name HYVH (Heh Yod Vav Heh) and in the name of KAMBRIEL the great Archangel, I invoke the powers of Aquarius.

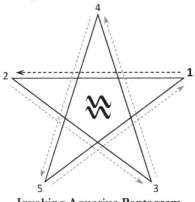

Invoking Aquarius Pentagram

Trace the Invoking Aquarius Pentagram, and draw its symbol in the center.

Visualize the VIOLET Pentagram of Aquarius glowing in the air.

Aspirant

Ganymede, a young prince of

Troy, was an exceptionally handsome young man. When Zeus first saw the beautiful youth, Ganymede was tending his father's sheep on Mount Ida. Because of the young man's beauty, Zeus disguised himself as an eagle and flew to earth, where he swept up Ganymede and carried him to Mount Olympus. There, the youth was to serve as cup-bearer to the Gods. Hera, the wife of Zeus, was furious not only for the strong feelings Zeus felt towards the young man, but also because Ganymede was to occupy the favored position formerly held by her daughter Hēbē, the Goddess of youth.

Touch the symbol of Aquarius with your index finger. Visualize the VIOLET Light of Aquarius flowing down your arm into your heart. Hold this visualization while saying:

<u>Aspirant</u>
However, Zeus was not to be thwarted in his affections, and so Ganymede stayed on Mount Olympus. The youth was very unhappy and never gave up hope that one day he would return to his land and family. As more time passed, Ganymede revolted, refusing to stay in the position of cup-bearer. In his anger, he poured out the wine, ambrosia and water of the Gods, causing inundating rains, producing a massive flood that submerged the entire world. Zeus was very angry and wanted to punish the youth, but in an unexpected show of sympathy he realized he had been unkind to Ganymede, and in compassion made him immortal by placing him in the heavens as the constellation Aquarius.

Fourth Advancement: Meditation on *The Star*

Return to the West of the Altar and take up the Tarot card *The Star*. Sit and face Aquarius, turn your aura to VIOLET, and study the card while saying:

<u>Aspirant</u>
Daughter of the Firmament, Dweller between the Waters, I call to you. You, who are faith, hope and unexpected aid, be present with me in the working of this rite. From you issues forth the gifts of clarity of vision and spiritual insight, but most importantly through you comes the gift of unforeseen help, a healing water to quench spiritual thirst with a guiding light to the future. You are hope and trust in the perceptive understanding of cosmic uniformity, the steadfast intuition that everything abides in balance and harmony. After turmoil and despair, you are the calm following the storm, a breakthrough for a new chance to rise into a higher state of being. Through your calm meditation I may now solve mysteries, discover secrets, and gain new philosophies. Through your aid, I approach the goal of enlightenment.

Close your eyes and visualize yourself in the imagery of the card. Note any thoughts or sensations that arise. Before you quit this visualization, make an offering of your own Light to the Powers of Aquarius.

Alternative meditation: the Archangel Kambriel

Visualize the symbol of Aquarius in front of you. Once this symbol is firmly established, go through the symbol like a door.

It is daytime in the winter, and you are standing on a hill near a little spring of clear water. You silently call to the Archangel Kambriel.

Kambriel appears before you in the image of a man, average in height, with a strong and well-composed body, dressed in a violet robe. He has a long face with a fair and clear complexion, and sandy-colored hair. His nature is pleasant and trusting. Ask Kambriel about the nature of Aquarius and how it can aid in your spiritual growth. Note any thoughts or sensations that arise. At the conclusion of this meditation, Kambriel gives you the symbol of Aquarius on a lead medallion which you place around your neck. Before you quit this visualization, make an offering of your own Light to the Powers of Aquarius.

Aspirant
I have acquired the qualities of Aquarius and they now reside within me. So mote it be.

CLOSING

Go to the East and face the center of the room.

Aspirant
I now release any spirits that may have been attracted to this ceremony. Go in peace to your abodes and habitations and go with the powers of Aquarius.

Purify and consecrate the Temple and your body with the water and incense, as in the Opening. Banish with the banishing Pentagram in all four quarters, as in the Opening. Return to the East.

Aspirant
I now declare this ritual duly completed. So mote it be.

Extinguish the candles.

INVOCATION OF THE POWERS OF PISCES

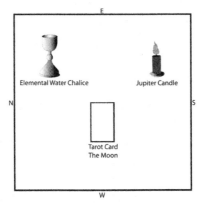

Figure 54: Altar arrangement for Pisces

Temple arrangement: Basic zodiacal Temple.

Altar cloth: Violet-red, or blue (Watery triplicity).

Altar implements: Chalice of wine/juice (with a few the drops of conse-crated Water), Moon Candle (unlit), with a lighter nearby.

Tarot Card: *The Moon*, on Altar.

Incense, Water: In the East, with incense lit.

Music: Suitable ambient or background music.

PREPARATION FOR THE RITE

Sit for a moment at the Altar and contemplate the rite to come. Let the cares and worries of the day dissipate. ✠ Focus on the top of your head and form a mental image of a ray of White Light permeating your body through the top of your head. Visualize this Light descending through the center of your body to your feet. Your body is now filled with Light. ✠ Inhale and exhale this Light through the pores of your body until it is pulsing in and around you. ✠ Imagine the Light extending from your body and filling the room. See the Light creating a barrier sep-arating the room from the outer world. Let nothing exist for you outside of this special time and place.

Opening

Standing West of the Altar, facing East, say:

Aspirant

I banish all worldly influences dwelling within this Temple by the Flaming Star of the Five Elements. I say unto you now, depart!

Go to the East. Make the Banishing Pentagram to the East, then do the same in the South, the West, and the North. Return to the East.

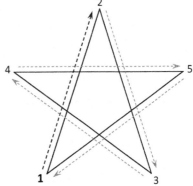

Banishing Elemental Pentagram

Take up the Cup of Water and sprinkle three times in the East, then do the same in the South, the West, and the North. Return to the East. Dip your finger in the Cup and touch your forehead, then sprinkle Water toward your feet, and touch your right and left shoulders.

Aspirant

I am purified; the Temple is purified; all is purified by the Lustral Waters. *Replace the Cup.*

Take up the incense and wave it three times in the East, then do the same in the South, the West, and the North. Return to the East. Wave the incense toward your forehead, your feet and your right and left shoulders.

Aspirant

I am consecrated; the Temple is consecrated; all is consecrated by Holy Fire. *Replace the Incense.*

Aspirant

(*In East, facing East*) I have purified and consecrated this Temple for the invocation of Pisces, and in so doing have created a Temple, that the heavenly forces of the Fishes may dwell here for a time. Unseen Watchers over the sacred Magic, watch over this ceremony of the Light Divine. So mote it be.

FIRST ADVANCEMENT: INVOKING ELEMENTAL WATER

Take the Water Chalice to the West and draw the blue Invoking Water Pentagram towards the West.

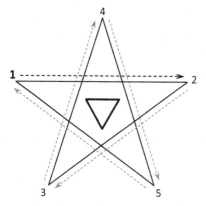

Invoking Water Pentagram

Aspirant

Hear me, those who dwell in the Western Quarter of the Universe, for I call out to thee! Through the Divine Name, EL, I have called you forth under the auspices of Water, that I may bring to power and presence the zodiacal Sign of Pisces. Grant me the strength to walk the hidden path and discover secret knowledge. Give me your eyes to see and your wisdom to understand, that I may perceive hidden things. Grant me the powers of Water, that I may bring forth Pisces in this sacred place.

Pause for a moment and fill the aura with BLUE Light. Walk clockwise to the West of the Altar and replace the Water Chalice.

SECOND ADVANCEMENT: INVOCATION OF JUPITER

At the Altar, take up the Jupiter Candle and face the location of Jupiter.

Aspirant
I shall quit the material and seek the spiritual!

Go to the location of Jupiter. With the Candle, trace the Invoking Hexagram of Jupiter, and the symbol of Jupiter in it.

Aspirant
Plentiful Jupiter, who fills the Universe with your Jovial essence, through your Divine Name, EL, I invoke you. Grant unto me the presence of your Great Archangel IOPHIEL (Yohfee-el), that he may lead me in my search for the powers of Pisces. IOPHIEL, come forth and call to presence the light of Jupi-

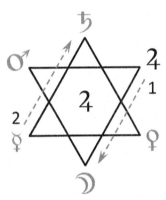

Invoking Jupiter Hexagram

ter, that he may illuminate the inner realms of my being and I may be awakened to the presence of Pisces. I make this petition to you, that through the Divine Presence, I may rend the Veils of Darkness from my mortal vision and comprehend the secrets of the Sign of the Fishes.

Pause for a moment and fill the aura with VIOLET Light. Walk clockwise West of the Altar, replace the Jupiter Candle, and light it.

THIRD ADVANCEMENT: INVOCATION OF PISCES

<u>Aspirant</u>
(*Facing Pisces*) **To the forces of Pisces that I now prepare to invoke, I have awakened this Temple with the powers of Water. I have invoked Jupiter, who is your lord. Come forward and be present with me in this sacred rite. You who are the power of the visionary and mystic, I call you forth. Creativity, the dissolution of boundaries, and a sense of oneness shall reign in this Temple. Open your realm to me that I may know you and awaken your powers within my soul.**

Go the location of Pisces, and face it.

<u>Aspirant</u>
In the Divine Name HHVY (Heh Heh Vav Yod) and in the name of AMNITZIEL the great Archangel, I invoke the powers of Pisces.

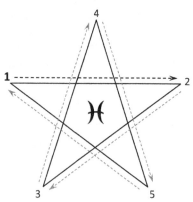

Invoking Pisces Pentagram

Trace the Invoking Pisces Pentagram, and draw its symbol in the center.

Visualize the VIOLET-RED Pentagram of Pisces glowing in the air.

<u>Aspirant</u>
The Olympic Gods had de-

feated the Titans and the Giants in a great war. Mother Earth, the Titan Gaia, coupled with the Underworld Titan Tartarus, and together they created Typhon, a wicked giant with dragon heads for fingers. Fire blazed from the eyes of the dragon heads, and from their mouths came forth a cacophony of sound. Typhon came to Olympus for to avenge the Titans' loss, and many of the Olympic Gods went into hiding for fear of his atrocities.

Touch the symbol of Pisces with your index finger. Visualize the VIOLET-RED Light of Pisces flowing down your arm into your heart. Hold this visualization while saying:

Aspirant

One day, Typhon came upon Aphrodite, the Goddess of Beauty, and her son Eros, the God of Love, on the banks of the Euphrates. To escape from the terrible fate of Typhon, Aphrodite and Eros changed themselves into fish and took cover among the reeds. But when a wind rustled the undergrowth, Aphrodite became fearful and she called to the water nymphs for help. Just then, two large fish came to their aid and led Aphrodite and Eros to safety. To commemorate the day when the Goddess of Beauty and the God of Love were saved from destruction, the savior fish were immortalized among the constellations and hung in the northern sky.

FOURTH ADVANCEMENT: MEDITATION ON *THE MOON*

Return to the West of the Altar and take up the Tarot card *The Moon*. Sit and face Pisces, turn your aura to VIOLET-RED, and study the card while saying:

Aspirant

Ruler of Flux and Reflux, Child of the Sons of the Mighty, I call to you. You who are a symbol of the illusory effect of the power of the material world; you who compels us to look at fears and confront the shadow self, I bring you forth to power and presence. You are one who leads me into the darkest depths of the soul, into the world of the unconscious self, where there are no words or rationality, but instead there simply dwells images and dreams. You are a journey into the darkest of nights, to see what lies behind my own face: for you are a confrontation with the dark side of the self. Despair causes a desperate cry for help. Illusion, hysteria, and fear, root me in place, but your path takes me from the terror of the darkness into the safety of the light. Through you comes voluntary change and transformation.

Close your eyes and visualize yourself in the imagery of the card. Note any thoughts or sensations that arise. Before you quit this visualization, make an offering of your own Light to the Powers of Pisces.

Alternative meditation: the Archangel Amnitziel

Visualize the symbol of Pisces in front of you. Once this symbol is firmly established, go through the symbol like a door.

It is nighttime in the winter, and you are standing near a pond wherein many fish are swimming. You silently call to the Archangel Amnitziel.

Amnitziel appears before you in the image of a woman, short in height with a fleshy body, dressed in a violet-red robe. She has a large and pleasant face, with a pale complexion and light hair. Her nature is somber and cautious. Ask Amnitziel about the nature of Pisces and how it can aid in your spiritual growth. Note any

thoughts or sensations that arise. At the conclusion of this meditation, Amnitziel gives you the symbol of Pisces on a tin medallion
which you place around your neck. Before you quit this visualization, make an offering of your own Light to the Powers of Pisces.

Aspirant
**I have acquired the qualities of Pisces and they now reside
within me. So mote it be.**

CLOSING

Go to the East and face the center of the room.

Aspirant
**I now release any spirits that may have been attracted to this
ceremony. Go in peace to your abodes and habitations and go
with the powers of Pisces.**

Purify and consecrate the Temple and your body with the water
and incense, as in the Opening. Banish with the banishing Pentagram in all four quarters, as in the Opening. Return to the East.

Aspirant
I now declare this ritual duly completed. So mote it be.

Extinguish the candles.

INVOKING THE TRIPLICITIES OF THE ZODIAC

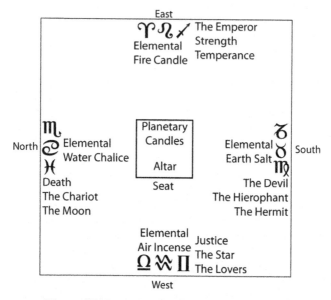

Figure 55: Invoking the Triplicities Temple

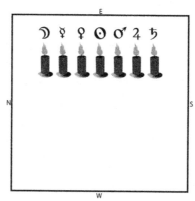

Figure 56: Invoking the Triplicities Altar (Part 1)

Temple arrangement: Basic zodiacal Temple.

Altar cloth: White.

Elemental emblems: In the macrocosmic quarters (see above), the Fire Candle (lit), Water Chalice (wine or juice, with some consecrated Water in it), Air Incense (lit), Earth Salt with Bread.

Planetary Candles: On Altar in ascending order from left to right (see above), all lit.

Tarot Cards: Cards for the Signs of each triplicity, in the macrocosmic quarters (see above).

Incense, Water: In the East, with incense lit.

Music: Suitable ambient or background music.

PREPARATION FOR THE RITE

Sit for a moment at the Altar and contemplate the rite to come. Let the cares and worries of the day dissipate. ✛ Focus on the top of your head and form a mental image of a ray of White Light permeating your body through the top of your head. Visualize this Light descending through the center of your body to your feet. Your body is now filled with Light. ✛ Inhale and exhale this Light through the pores of your body until it is pulsing in and around you. ✛ Imagine the Light extending from your body and filling the room. See the Light creating a barrier separating the room from the outer world. Let nothing exist for you outside of this special time and place.

OPENING

Standing West of the Altar, facing East, say:

<u>Aspirant</u>

I banish all worldly influences dwelling within this Temple by the Flaming Star of the Five Elements. I say unto you now, depart!

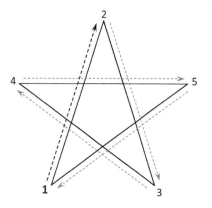

Banishing Elemental Pentagram

Go to the East. Make the Banishing Pentagram to the East, then do the same in the South, the West, and the North. Return to the East.

Take up the Cup of Water and sprinkle three times in the East, then do the same in the South, the West, and the North. Return to the East. Dip your finger in the Cup and touch your forehead, then sprinkle Water toward your feet, and touch your right and left shoulders.

<u>Aspirant</u>

I am purified; the Temple is purified; all is purified by the Lustral Waters. *Replace the Cup.*

Take up the incense and wave it three times in the East, then do the same in the South, the West, and the North. Return to the East. Wave the incense toward your forehead, your feet and your right and left shoulders.

Aspirant

I am consecrated; the Temple is consecrated; all is consecrated by Holy Fire. *Replace the Incense.*

Aspirant

(In East, facing East) I have purified and consecrated this Temple, and in so doing have created a Temple, that the heavenly forces may dwell here for a time. Unseen Watchers over the sacred Magic, watch over this ceremony of the Light Divine. So mote it be.

INVOCATION OF SPIRIT

Go to the West of the Altar and face East. In the air before you, draw the two Invoking Spirit Pentagrams.

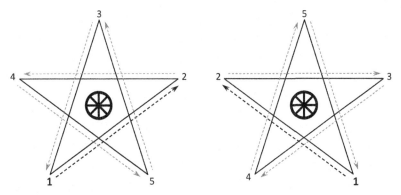

Invoking Passive Spirit Pentagram   Invoking Active Spirit Pentagram

Aspirant

O Thou supreme Life-Spirit, Cause of all Creation, Origin of all, and single Source of every living soul. Of Thee alone is my beginning, and in Thee alone have I no ending. O Thou single source of truth and wisdom, let me ascend to the Higher Realms on the Chariot of Truth. Bring me over the gulfs and abysses, bear me upward out of gorges and valleys; become for me the source of liberation. Let Thy great brightness cause the path to be lit before me. Let me ascend to the Heavens as if upon a ship of Light, that I may come to know the Zodiacal Spheres. So mote it be.

Pause for a moment and visualize your aura filled with White Light.

FIRST ADVANCEMENT: THE FIRE TRIPLICITY

♈   ♌   ♐
Aries   Leo   Sagittarius

Go to the East, take up the Fire Candle, and make the Invoking Fire Pentagram with it towards the East.

Invoking Fire Pentagram

Trace the clockwise Invoking Triangle of Fire (starting at the apex), and visualize the Pentagram in a flaming RED light. Circumambulate the Temple once clockwise, while saying:

Aspirant

I am empowered by Fire. Its masculine energy flows through my being, dry and hot, igniting the flames of courage, dignity and desire. I walk in the realm of the day with celestial Fire as my guide, and I am enflamed with the qualities of leadership, authority and a faithful trust in my essential identity.

Upon returning to the East, face the Pentagram.

<u>Aspirant</u>
I call to the powers of Aries (*make symbol of Aries in Pentagram with Candle*), ruled by Mars, through the Names YHVH (Yod Heh Vav Heh) and MALKHIDAEL, the great Archangel. Be present in the working of this rite, and bestow upon me your gifts of courage and the ability to embrace my true purpose in life. *Visualize the* RED *symbol of Aries glowing in your heart.*

I call upon the powers of Leo (*make symbol of Leo in Pentagram with Candle*), ruled by the Sun, through the Names of HVYH (Heh Vav Yod Heh) and VERKHIEL the great Archangel. Be present in the working of this rite, and bestow upon me your gifts of honest pride for my accomplishments and the proper recognition for those achievements. *Visualize the* YELLOW *symbol of Leo glowing in your heart.*

I call upon the powers of Sagittarius (*make symbol of Sagittarius in Pentagram with Candle*), ruled by Jupiter, through the Names of VYHH (Vav Yod Heh Heh) and ADNAKHIEL the great Archangel. Be present in the working of this rite, and bestow upon me your gifts of a desire and ability to seek what lies beyond the horizon, and to discover the possibilities which answer my greatest questions. *Visualize the* BLUE *symbol of Sagittarius glowing in your heart.*

Place the Fire Candle on the Altar, to the East (but still to the West of the Planetary Candles).

SECOND ADVANCEMENT: THE EARTH TRIPLICITY

♑   ♉   ♍

Capricorn Taurus   Virgo

Go to the South, take up the Earth Salt and Bread, and make the Invoking Earth Pentagram with it towards the South.

Trace the clockwise Invoking Triangle of Earth (starting at the lower apex), and visualize the Pentagram in a flaming GREEN light. Circumambulate the Temple once clockwise, while saying:

Invoking Earth Pentagram

<u>Aspirant</u>

I am made steadfast by Earth. Its feminine energy flows through my being, cold and dry, planting the seeds of determination, an appreciation for beauty, and a practical mind. I walk in the realm of the night with celestial Earth as my guide, and I am implanted with the qualities of practical skill, experience, and respect for the body.

Upon returning to the South, face the Pentagram.

Aspirant

I call to the powers of **Capricorn** (*make symbol of Capricorn in Pentagram with dish*), **ruled by Saturn, through the Names of HYHV (Heh Yod Heh Vav) and** HANAEL **the great Archangel. Be present in the working of this rite and bestow upon me your gifts of steadfast determination and resolve, and an ability to establish traditional and pragmatic leadership.** *Visualize the* BLUE-VIOLET *symbol of Capricorn glowing in your heart.*

I call upon the powers of **Taurus** (*make symbol of Taurus in Pentagram with dish*), **ruled by Venus, through the Names of YHHV (Yod Heh Heh Vav) and** ASMODEL **the great Archangel. Be present in the working of this rite, and bestow upon me your gifts of the understanding that my body is the house of my soul, and an appreciation of beauty and comfort.** *Visualize the* RED-ORANGE *symbol of Taurus glowing in your heart.*

I call upon the powers of **Virgo** (*make symbol of Virgo in Pentagram with dish*), **ruled by Mercury, through the Names of HHYV (Heh Heh Yod Vav) and** HAMALIEL **the great Archangel. Be present in the working of this rite, and bestow upon me your gifts of the cleansing of my mind and body, and the development of my true talents.** *Visualize the* YELLOW-GREEN *symbol of Virgo glowing in your heart.*

Place the Earth Salt and Bread on the Altar, to the South.

THIRD ADVANCEMENT: THE AIR TRIPLICITY

Ω   ♒   Ⅱ

Libra Aquarius Gemini

Go to the West, take up the Air Incense, and make the Invoking Air Pentagram with it towards the West.

Invoking Air Pentagram

Trace the clockwise Invoking Triangle of Air (starting at the apex), and visualize the Pentagram in a flaming YELLOW light. Circumambulate the Temple once clockwise, while saying:

<u>Aspirant</u>
I am inspired by Air. Its masculine energy flows through my being, hot and moist, inspiring me with the qualities of balance, expression, and knowledge. I walk in the realm of the day with celestial Air as my guide, and I breathe in the qualities of intellect, judgment and humanity.

Upon returning to the West, face the Pentagram.

<u>Aspirant</u>
I call to the powers of Libra (*make symbol of Libra in Pentagram with Incense*)**, ruled by Venus, through the Names of VHYH (Vav Heh Yod Heh) and ZURIEL the great Archangel. Be present in the working of this rite, and bestow upon me your gifts of**

harmony and balance in my life, as well as good friendships and justice in worthwhile causes. *Visualize the* GREEN *symbol of Libra glowing in your heart.*

I call upon the powers of Aquarius (*make symbol of Aquarius in Pentagram with Incense*), ruled by Saturn, through the Names of HYVH (Heh Yod Vav Heh) and KAMBRIEL the great Archangel. Be present in the working of this rite, and bestow upon me your gifts of a desire and ability to seek philosophical wisdom, simplicity in my life, and a detachment from material desire. *Visualize the* VIOLET *symbol of Aquarius glowing in your heart.*

I call upon the powers of Gemini (*make symbol of Gemini in Pentagram with Incense*), ruled by Mercury, through the Names of YVHH (Yod Vav Heh Heh) and AMBRIEL the great Archangel. Be present in the working of this rite, and bestow upon me your gifts of a desire and ability to know many things, as in knowledge of the magical arts, a true understanding of the signs and symbols and the words of power. *Visualize the* ORANGE *symbol of Gemini glowing in your heart.*

Place the Air Incense on the Altar, to the West.

FOURTH ADVANCEMENT: THE WATER TRIPLICITY

Cancer Scorpio Pisces

Go to the North, take up the Water Chalice, and make the Invoking Water Pentagram with it towards the North.

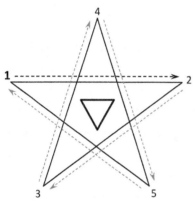

Invoking Water Pentagram

Trace the clockwise Invoking Triangle of Water (starting at the lower apex), and visualize the Pentagram in a flaming BLUE light. Circumambulate the Temple once clockwise, while saying:

Aspirant

I am empathic by Water. Its feminine energy flows through my being, cold and moist, showering me with the qualities of nurturing, secrecy and mysticism. I walk in the realm of the night with celestial Water as my guide, and I am submerged in the qualities of emotion, contemplation and perception.

Upon returning to the North, face the Pentagram.

Aspirant

I call to the powers of Cancer (*make symbol of Cancer in Pentagram with Chalice*), **ruled by the Moon, through the Names of HVHY (Heh Vav Heh Yod) and MURIEL the great Archangel. Be**

present in the working of this rite, and bestow upon me your gifts of nurturing and the ability to value myself and others. *Visualize the* ORANGE-YELLOW *symbol of Cancer glowing in your heart.*

I call upon the powers of Scorpio (*make symbol of Scorpio in Pentagram with Chalice*), ruled by Mars, through the Names of VHHY (Vav Heh Heh Yod) and BARKHIEL the great Archangel. Be present in the working of this rite, and bestow upon me your gifts of understanding the importance of silence and secrecy, an appreciation of death and change, and the ability to release things in life which are passing away. *Visualize the* GREEN-BLUE *symbol of Scorpio glowing in your heart.*

I call upon the powers of Pisces (*make symbol of Pisces in Pentagram with Chalice*), ruled by Jupiter, through the Names of HHVY (Heh Heh Vav Yod) and AMNITZIEL the great Archangel. Be present in the working of this rite, and bestow upon me your gifts of a desire and ability to seek religious and mystical experience, and the longing to experience the spheres beyond the physical realm. *Visualize the* VIOLET-RED *symbol of Pisces glowing in your heart.*

Place the Water Chalice on the Altar, to the North.

FIFTH ADVANCEMENT: THE BLESSED MEAL OF THE SIGNS

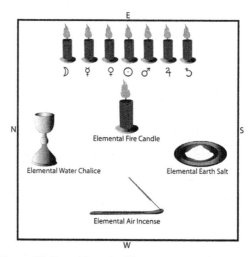

Figure 57: Invoking the Triplicities Altar (Part 2)

Stand at the West of the Altar, and face East.

<u>Aspirant</u>

I give thanks and praise the powers of the celestial Signs who have bestowed their gifts upon me in the working of this rite. I offer to you a gift of my own light. (*Visualize your Aura glowing in a bright, white Light, and extend this light through your breathing to fill the room.*) **I will now partake of a sacred repast, that I may take within my body the powers of the Zodiacal Signs, in my search for the unity of the Divine Light.**

Recite the following invocation, substituting another dying and resurrected God (such as Christ) for Osiris if desired, and "God" for "the Gods" below.

<u>Aspirant</u>

For Osiris, who has been found perfect before the Gods hath said:

These are the Elements of my body, perfected through suffering, glorified through trial.

For the scent of this Incense is as the repressed sigh of my suffering.

And this flame Red Fire is as the energy of mine undaunted will.

The Cup of Wine is the pouring out of the blood of my heart, sacrificed unto regeneration, unto the newer life.

The Bread and Salt are as the foundations of my body, which I destroy in order that they may be renewed.

For I am Osiris Triumphant, even Osiris Onnophris, the Justified One.

I am the one who is clothed in the body of flesh,

Yet in whom is the Spirit of the Great Gods.

I am the Lord of Life, triumphant over death,

Those who partaketh with me shall arise with me.

I am the Manifestor in Matter of those whose abode is in the invisible.

I am purified,

I stand upon the Universe,

I am its reconciler with the Eternal Gods.

I am the Perfector of Matter,

And without me the Universe is not.

I invite you to inhale with me the scent of this sacred incense as a symbol of celestial Air. (*Inhale the scent of the Incense.*) To feel with me the warmth of this flame as a symbol of celestial Fire. (*Feel the warmth of the Candle flame.*) To eat with me this bread and salt as a symbol of celestial Earth. (*Eat some of the Bread and Salt.*)

And finally to drink with me this wine/juice as a symbol of celestial Water.

Drink the Wine, then turn the Chalice upside down in the palm of your hand, and declare:

It is finished!

Take a moment to contemplate, and remain in, the atmosphere of the Working.

CLOSING

Go to the East and face the center of the room.

<u>Aspirant</u>
I now release any spirits that may have been attracted to this ceremony. Go in peace to your abodes and habitations and go with the powers of the celestial Signs.

Purify and consecrate the Temple and your body with the water and incense, as in the Opening. Banish with the banishing Pentagram in all four quarters, as in the Opening. Return to the East.

<u>Aspirant</u>
I now declare this ritual duly completed. So mote it be.

Extinguish the candles.

Appendix 1: Significations of the Elements & Signs

Fiery Signs:

Gender: Masculine

Elemental Qualities: Hot and dry

Direction: East

Sect: Diurnal

Taste: Bitter

Incense: Spicy scents, such as cinnamon

Values and virtues: Leadership, trust in self, sovereignty or royalty

Temperament: Choleric (Angry, ambitious, demanding, tough, clever, generous when obeyed)

Personality: Bold, assertive, leadership, attacking, urgent, self-interested, pushy

	Aries	Leo	Sagittarius
Quadruplicity:	Movable	Fixed	Common
Places:	Stables for small animals, broken or sandy or hilly ground, ceilings	Wilderness and wild beasts, deserts, rocky high places, palaces, parks, near a chimney or hearth	Stables of horses or other large animals, higher lands or grounds, upper rooms, near fire
Animals:	Sheep, rams	Wild animals, lions	Horses
Objects:	Engraved, polished, shiny precious metals, jewelry for the head	Tall trees, bright gems like emeralds and hyacinth; gold, sometimes copper or iron	Gypsum, cheaper fired things like bricks, tiles, earthenware, something made of varied things or dyed of many colors

Body type:	Dry, lean, darker complexion	Large head and eyes, medium height, strong, more yellow, red, curly hair	Ruddy and healthy, strong, taller
Body part:	Head	Heart, midriff	Buttocks and thighs
Personality:	Initiating, demanding, independent, self-interested	Confident, optimistic, authoritative	Idealistic, exploring, trusts self, feeling lucky
Archangel:	Malkhidael	Verkhiel	Adnakhiel
Birthstone:[1]	Bloodstone	Onyx/Sardonyx	Topaz
Color:	Red	Yellow	Blue

Earthy Signs:

Gender: Feminine

Elemental Qualities: Cold and dry

Direction: South

Sect: Nocturnal

Taste: Acidic, vinegary

Incense: Dark earthy scents, patchouli, Dittany of Crete

Values and virtues: Practical skill and experience, respect for the body

Temperament: Melancholic (Moody, careful, austere, not caring about others' opinion, good memory, vengeful)

Personality: Slow, preserving, practical, reliable, limits and rules, physical, boring

	Capricorn	**Taurus**	**Virgo**
Quadruplicity:	Movable	Fixed	Common
Places:	Places of oxen and cows, old wood, sailing	Stables for large animals, pasture, places of sowing,	Studies and libraries, closets, storehouses for

---

[1] There are many different versions of the birthstones. If using them in relation to your own birth chart, consider picking the stone associated with your Ascendant rather than the Sun sign.

	materials, barren scrub, dunghills, low dark rooms, places of low-class people	cellars, low rooms	grain or cheese or butter
Animals:	Goats, insects	Oxen, cattle	Cats, birds
Objects:	Thorny bushes, something cheap or earthenware	Planted fruit trees, objects used in devotions, necklaces	Irrigated crops, small jewelry, coins, fabrics
Body type:	Shorter, dry, lean, thin hair	Short, strong, large and broad features, dark hair	Slender, dark, short limbs
Body part:	Knees	Neck	Belly
Personality:	Responsible, disciplined, respects competence, leadership, tradition	Patient, resists pressure, steadfast, enjoys comfort and security	Practical, analytical, organized, prefers clarity
Archangel:	Hanael	Asmodel	Hamaliel
Birthstone:	Ruby	Sapphire	Carnelian
Color:	Blue-violet	Red-orange	Yellow-green

Airy Signs:

Gender: Masculine

Elemental Qualities: Hot and moist

Direction: West

Sect: Diurnal

Taste: Sweet

Incense: Light, airy scents, such as lavender

Values and virtues: Intellect, judgment, humanity

Temperament: Sanguine (Cheerful, optimistic, open-hearted, friendly, confident, superficial)

Personality: Experimental, rational and verbal, sociable, freedom, flexible, detached, aloof

	Libra	Aquarius	Gemini
Quadruplicity:	Movable	Fixed	Common
Places:	Places near to open air, solitary buildings, mountains, sandy fields, upper rooms	Hilly, uneven places, quarries and places of minerals, roofs and eves, vineyards, near a spring or irrigation	Storehouses, cupboards, containers, walls, high places
Animals:	Hawks and other hunting birds	Creeping animals in water or muck	Light, small animals, flying animals
Objects:	Tall or palm trees, composite objects, things bought based on weight	Tall trees	Tall trees, coins, books
Body type:	Well composed, tall, slim, good-looking, lighter colored features	Short, thick, strong	Tall, dark features but somewhat sanguine, shorter hands and feet
Body part:	Waist and hips	Shins and ankles	Shoulders, arms, hands
Personality:	Desiring justice, balanced interactions, stimulating others	Complex thought, cool and detached, philosophical, explores ideas	Light, curious, exchanging ideas, detached
Archangel:	Zuriel	Kambriel	Ambriel
Birthstone:	Peridot	Garnet	Agate
Color:	Green	Violet	Orange

Watery Signs:

Gender: Feminine

Elemental Qualities: Cold and moist

Direction: North

Sect: Nocturnal

Taste: Salty

Incense: Dreamy, soft, sweetish scents, such as lily or ylang ylang

Values and virtues: Devotion, prayer, empathy

Temperament: Phlegmatic (Sluggish and ambling, deliberate, reserved, content, a dreamer, observant)

Personality: Intimate, imaginative, emotionally connecting, mysterious, few boundaries, hard to detach

	Cancer	Scorpio	Pisces
Quadruplicity:	Movable	Fixed	Common
Places:	Seas, rivers, marshes and washrooms, cisterns, coasts and riverbanks	Places of creeping animals, orchards and vineyards, swamps, stinking pits and standing water	Springs and grounds with much water, fishponds, water mills, buildings near water or wells
Animals:	Crabs, turtles	Crawling, poisonous insects and animals	Fish
Objects:	Medium trees, pearls, something moist	Medium trees, a lustrous stone	Medium trees, watery-looking gems or with mixed colors
Body type:	Short, heavier upper body, round and plump, pale	Heavier, strong, darker complexion, hairy	Short, crooked, fleshy, pale, large face
Body part:	Upper chest, rib cage	Genitals	
Personality:	Nurturing, needy, emotionally supportive	Sensitive, self-protective, vengeful	Empathetic, humane, dramatic, disillusioned
Archangel:	Muriel	Barkhiel	Amnitziel
Birthstone:	Emerald	Beryl	Amethyst
Color:	Orange-yellow	Green-blue	Violet-red

APPENDIX 2: PLANETARY SIGNIFICATIONS & RULERSHIPS

The following planetary significations and rulerships have been largely taken from (1) Persian and Arabic astrological sources,[1] and (2) William Lilly's *Christian Astrology*. To these we have added magically-oriented categories and attributions from the Golden Dawn and other sources. The lists are not meant to be exhaustive, but rather to act as guides.

Significations of Saturn

General qualities: Malefic, diurnal, masculine, cold and dry

Zodiacal rulerships: Capricorn and Aquarius (domicile), Libra (exaltation), Cancer and Leo (detriment), Aries (fall)

Day & night rulerships: Saturday day, Wednesday night

People & professions: Fathers (esp. in nocturnal charts), grandfathers, eunuchs, older brothers, kings (implying age and authority, not glamor), slaves, real estate, and waterside trades, farmers, actors, dyers, smelly or low-class and dirty professions and people, masseurs in baths, sailors, leather-working, professions related to death and dying and inheritance; can imply great wealth or great poverty; magicians; orphans

Activities, events, & experiences: Labor, affliction

Personality & values: Silent and reserved, patient, alone or lonely, sad, deep counsel, gluttonous, stubborn, suspicious, whispering, slow to anger but consumed by it afterwards; fraud; secretive and knowledge of secrets

Spiritual path: Judaism, monotheism; doubting; austerity; paths that focus on labor, self-denial, and guilt

Body type: Dark or swarthy, connected eyebrows, looking down, shaggy, shuffling and stooped, thin, often hairy, small eyes and dry skin

Places & terrain: Prisons, deserts and deserted areas, caves and dark places, stinking and muddy places, sewers, mountains

Animals: Poisonous snakes, creeping animals (rabbits, cats), dirty or abject animals (toads, hogs), eels, tortoises, shellfish, nocturnal animals like bats and owls

---

[1] See Dykes 2010, and Dykes 2011 (*The Search of the Heart*).

Commodities & objects: Antiques and lasting things; cheap and crude objects (clay, leaden, wax), dead things made from living things (fur, leather, wool), heavy and stinking things

Angel: Kassiel

Tarot Card: The Universe/World

Colors: Black or leaden (traditional), blue-violet (Golden Dawn)

Stones & metals: Obsidian, onyx, plain or worthless stones; lead

Scents & herbs: Violet or myrrh incense; poisonous herbs, poppy, moss; willow, cypress, hemp, pine.

Tastes, foods, drink: Unseasoned or plain tastes (but some say harsh or pungent, suggesting bad smells), acorns, the meat of gourds and squash

Significations of Jupiter

General qualities: Benefic, diurnal, masculine, hot and moist

Zodiacal rulerships: Sagittarius and Pisces (domicile), Cancer (exaltation), Gemini and Virgo (detriment), Capricorn (fall)

Day & night rulerships: Thursday day, Monday night

People & professions: Judges, religious hermits, jewelers, professions dealing in wealth and assets, law, peacemaking, public figures or people who cultivate a public image,

Activities, events, & experiences:

Personality & values: Patience, trust, happiness and truth, noble ideals, wisdom and philosophy; the priesthood; generosity and modesty; joy and fun, much sexual intercourse; partnership; charity; false modesty and hypocrisy (when the public image is in conflict with actual values and actions), love of money, careless and ignorant

Spiritual path: Polytheism; Christianity

Body type: Tall and upright, a deep belly, ruddy and healthy complexion, large forehead and eyes, strong legs

Places & terrain: Grand and beautiful places, religious buildings, neat and clean places, public places of oratory or justice

Animals: Clean fattened animals for eating and working, dogs and cats, stags, oxen and elephants, tigers, eagles

Commodities & objects: Ornaments used by either gender; clean and moist things

Angel: Sachiel

Tarot Card: The Wheel of Fortune

Colors: White or ashen or green (traditional), violet (Golden Dawn)

Stones & metals: Sapphire, amethyst, lapis lazuli, emerald (traditional), marble; tin

Scents & herbs: Clean herbs of good odor; cedar, cloves, mace and nutmeg, saffron; cherry and mulberry and olive trees

Tastes, foods, drink: Sweet tastes, figs and pears and berries, apples, sweet cucumbers; wheat and barley and glutinous grains

Significations of Mars

General qualities: Malefic, nocturnal, masculine, hot and dry

Zodiacal rulerships: Aries and Scorpio (domicile), Capricorn (exaltation), Libra and Taurus (detriment), Cancer (fall)

Day & night rulerships: Tuesday day, Saturday night

People & professions: Brothers; general, soldier, robber, craftsman, archer, butcher; all professions involving iron, fire, blood, danger, heat, and loud machinery; medicine (esp. surgical procedures), veterinarians and shepherds; fugitives

Activities, events, & experiences: Foreign travel, war and conflicts, abortion and miscarriage, everything which happens abruptly or with disturbance, drinking parties, theft, divorce

Personality & values: Unjust, oppressive, angry, selfish, shamelessness, powerful lust, provocative, practical jokes and being boisterous, powerful and masculine; perseverance, seeking victory and glory, resentful of authority figures, pride, courage and boldness, moving fast, cursing and lack of self-control when speaking, deception

Spiritual path: Warlike faiths; hesitant or a Devil's advocate in faith; changing faith or an enemy of faith.

Body type: Average height, muscular and dense, reddish in color, a proud, confident look, curly and/or red hair

Places & terrain: Prisons, kitchens, furnaces, places where there is heat (chimneys, volcanoes, ovens), slaughterhouses

Animals: Wild terrestrial and sea animals (bears, lizards, crocodiles, dolphins), poisonous animals, hawks, vultures

Commodities & objects: Weapons, hot things
Angel: Zamael
Tarot Card: The Tower
Colors: Red
Stones & metals: Ruby, garnet, bloodstone, jasper; iron and steel
Scents & herbs: Sharp, spicy scents, red herbs, thorny plants, ginger, garlic
Tastes, foods, drink: Bitter, pungent, and tangy; peppery and sharp tastes, mustard

Significations of the Sun

General qualities: Benefic, diurnal, masculine, hot and dry
Zodiacal rulerships: Leo (domicile), Aries (exaltation), Aquarius (detriment), Libra (fall)
Day & night rulerships: Sunday day, Thursday night
People & professions: Fathers (esp. in a day chart), kings (implying glamor), magnates; leadership and rulership; royal occupations like hunting; prominent positions in the public eye
Activities, events, & experiences: Leadership and management activities (or being connected to such people), victory, fame, official punishments for wrongdoing
Personality & values: Lofty, prudent, respectability, glory, generosity, wisdom, faith, an interested in the sciences and knowledge, clean; but a difficult master to people close to him (easier to associate with him from farther away), overwhelming and controlling
Spiritual path: Death and resurrection religions; Egyptian Solar and Gnostic themes.
Body type: Tall, large, and strong; yellowish or reddish complexion and hair; prominent forehead and eyes; bald or balding.
Places & terrain: Palaces and courts, theaters, magnificent structures
Animals: Lion, white sheep, ram, bull, horse, eagle, peacock, swan
Commodities & objects: Gilded and valuable objects and vessels, esp. golden;
Angel: Michael
Tarot Card: The Sun
Colors: Whiteness (traditional), orange (Golden Dawn)

Stones & metals: Hyacinth, topaz, zircon; gold

Scents & herbs: Resins, amber, musk, marigolds, lignum aloes, peony, cinnamon; oranges and lemons

Tastes, foods, drink: Acidic or sour tastes (perhaps mixed with sweet); pine nuts, foods with varied colors and reddish surfaces, like peaches, apricots, dates.

Significations of Venus

General qualities: Benefic, nocturnal, feminine, cold and moist (medieval) or hot and moist (Ptolemy).

Zodiacal rulerships: Taurus and Libra (domicile), Pisces (exaltation); Scorpio and Aries (detriment), Virgo (fall)

Day & night rulerships: Friday day, Tuesday night

People & professions: Women, wives, mothers; arts and music, decorative professions, wedding preparation, pimps, adulterers

Activities, events, & experiences: Games, dancing, leisure, sexual intercourse

Personality & values: beauty, cleanliness, laughter, joy, esteem, love, trusting, justice, maintaining spiritual practices, sweetness, friendship, eating and drinking, play, charm, flirting, loves shopping; some dishonesty

Spiritual path: Idols and the use of art, paths involving eating and drinking; Islam (probably due to practice of ablution)

Body type: Beautiful, plump, roundness, neat and clean, dimpled

Places & terrain: Houses of prayer, gardens, fountains, bedrooms, places for fun, neat and clean places

Animals: Small plump birds like partridges, quail, hens; small animals like goats, harts, calves

Commodities & objects: Ornaments, beautiful shapes, clothing, ointments, soft things

Angel: Anael

Tarot Card: The Empress

Colors: White (traditional), green (Golden Dawn)

Stones & metals: Emerald, turquoise, malachite; copper or brass

Scents & herbs & plants: Rose, sandalwood; plants with delicious smells and smooth roundish leaves, vines and grapes, tree oils, lilies, daffodils

Tastes, foods, drink: Grease and fat, delicious moist and sweet flavors, intoxicating drinks; oranges, coriander, peaches, plums, apricots, raisins

Significations of Mercury

General qualities: Neutral in benefic/malefic qualities; diurnal when rising before the Sun, nocturnal when rising after the Sun; masculine, inclining to dryness

Zodiacal rulerships: Gemini and Virgo (domicile), Virgo (exaltation); Sagittarius and Pisces (detriment), Pisces (fall)

Day & night rulerships: Wednesday day, Sunday night

People & professions: Younger brothers, slaves and servants; preaching, rhetoric, mathematics and numbers, business deals and measurements, organizing and managing, philosophy, poetry (versifying), literature, scribes, barbers, artisans, alchemists and experimenters

Activities, events, & experiences: oracles and prophesy, speaking, teaching, faith, reading and writing

Personality & values: Rational, analytic, curious and inquiring, organized, valuing learning; cleverness and trickery, ingenuity, seduction; argumentative; cunning and lies; timid, practical

Spiritual path: Hermeticism, Hinduism, rational and analytical paths, philosophy

Body type: Taller, thin, long narrow features, darker complexion

Places & terrain: Shops, markets, schools, public halls

Animals: Ape, fox, squirrel, cunning creatures; parrots, bees.

Commodities & objects: Hand-held objects and instruments, delicate or intricate things, carvings and sculpture, silk and fine embroidery

Angel: Raphael

Tarot Card: The Magician

Colors: Mixed colors or blue (traditional), yellow (Golden Dawn)

Stones & metals: Opal, topaz (traditional), stones with mixed colors like agates; quicksilver

Scents & herbs: Lavender, mastic, complicated scents, plants whose seed comes in husks or pods, anise

Tastes, foods, drink: Acidic or vinegary; leeks or green onions, legumes

Significations of the Moon

General qualities: Benefic, nocturnal, feminine, cool and moist (with a little heat)

Zodiacal rulerships: Cancer (domicile), Taurus (exaltation), Capricorn (detriment), Scorpio (fall)

Day & night rulerships: Monday day, Friday night

People & professions: Queens, mothers, and other older female relatives; the public or masses as a whole, hunters and fishers, water managers and engineers, travelers, launderers; accounting and surveying; messengers, the postal service, transportation; midwives; fugitives

Activities, events, & experiences: Secrets and hidden things (when under the Sun's rays); when waxing, creation and growth and accumulation, but when waning, diminution and destruction and dispersal

Personality & values: Desiring joy and beauty; cheerful, open and not secretive; changeable; not that much into higher sciences; tends to imitate people she is around; caring for the body; not very sexual

Spiritual path: Interested in miracles, sorcery; Hinduism

Body type: Roundish and fleshy, retaining water, a blemish near the eye, short and stout

Places & terrain:

Animals: Aquatic animals, domestic fowl and animals that do work (incl. domesticated cattle), panthers or other larger cats, snails, shellfish

Commodities & objects:

Angel: Gabriel

Tarot Card: The High Priestess

Colors: Grey or yellow (traditional), blue (Golden Dawn)

Stones & metals: Pearls, moonstone, quartz; silver

Scents & herbs: Jasmine, fresh smells like herbs before they are ripe, thick and juicy plants or living in water

Tastes, foods, drink: Salty tastes. Earthy foods like truffles, mushrooms, hashish, grass, leeks, legumes, lettuce, gourds and melons

Appendix 3: Incenses

In ritual, color and scent are employed to manifest a particular force and align the magician with that force. But scents (like colors) do many things to the mind and body of the magician, as well. On a purely practical level, they alter the physiological and psychological makeup of the ritualist, and the effects enhance the ritual working. For instance, a hot and spicy fragrance will energize a person, while a sweet and soft scent will calm the mind.

Scent not only represents the force you are working with but is also a manifestation of that force. Throughout history, incense has been used to sooth the soul, heal the body, pleasure the senses, summon spirits, and appease the gods. Scents have been used for centuries for ritualistic purposes, to reduce stress and emotional trauma, increase energy, inspire moods, or stimulate hormone production. Although the exact origin of incense is unknown, it appears to have been among the earliest spiritual practices and is attested to since early antiquity.

For one thing, scent stimulates the release of hormones. Hormones affect the fight or flight response, as well as digestion and heart rate. Because of this, scents affect us in many ways all at once. Our sense of smell is 10,000 times more sensitive than any other of our senses, and whereas other senses like touch and taste must travel through the body via neurons and the spinal cord before reaching the brain, the sense of smell is relatively immediate, extending directly from cilia and mucus in the nose to receptor neurons and the olfactory bulb, which is part of the brain itself. It is interesting to note that this is the place where our central nervous system is most directly exposed to the environment.[1]

Physiologically, inhaling a fragrance stimulates the part of your brain where taste is analyzed and emotional memories are stored; it also connects to the areas of the brain that deal with heart rate, blood pressure, breathing, stress levels, and hormone balance. Of the five senses, only our sense of smell is linked directly to the emotional center of the brain—the same place where fear, anxiety, depression, anger, and joy reside physiologically.

The scent of a certain fragrance can evoke memories and emotions before we are even consciously aware of it. We tend to react first and think later. Scents can have positive effects on mood, stress reduction, sleep enhancement, self-confidence, and physical and cognitive performance. Thus, scents

---

[1] See for example Ciccarelli and White 2008.

and their specific associations can be used on a greater scale in the future to increase productivity, improve mood or just enhance well-being. It only makes sense, then, to employ them in ritual.

The incenses here are suggestions. Unlike color, whose application to Planets and so on are according to a certain scheme, the attributions of scents are a little harder to pin down. People have their own opinions about scent and how it makes them feel. So although we recommend the perfumes and incenses below, feel free to use others so long as their scents fit the basic concept of the Element, Planet, or Sign you are interested in. (Nevertheless, some scents are less negotiable: rose is not suitable for Mars or Saturn in any event.) When purchasing scents online or in a store, you will often come across blends, and these are fine for ritual use. Decide how the blend makes you feel and then go from there.

The Elements

Earth: Patchouli, Cypress, Vetivert (any earthy incense)

Water: Ylang Ylang, Camphor, Lily (any sweet incense)

Air: Frankincense, Lavender, Benzoin, Peppermint (any pungent and sharp incense)

Fire: Ginger, Cinnamon, Clove, Basil, Nutmeg (any spicy or hot incense)

The Planets

Saturn: Myrrh, Patchouli (earthy and somewhat sharp or bitter scents)

Jupiter: Aloes Wood, Cedar (calm, masculine, and mature scents)

Mars: Cinnamon, Ginger, Dragon's Blood, Tobacco (spicy, strong and masculine scents)

Sun: Frankincense, Vanilla, Orange, Cinnamon, Saffron (hot or warm scents)

Venus: Sandalwood and Rose (beautiful and feminine scents)

Mercury: Copal, Lavender (pungent and mentally stimulating scents)

Moon: Jasmine, Lotus (soft, dreamy scents)

The Signs

Aries: Mix Fire and Mars incenses

Taurus: Mix Earth and Venus incenses

Gemini: Mix Air and Mercury incenses

Cancer: Moon incenses
Leo: Sun incenses
Virgo: Mix Earth and Mercury incenses
Libra: Mix Air and Venus incenses
Scorpio: Mix Water and Mars incenses
Sagittarius: Mix Fire and Jupiter incenses
Capricorn: Mix Earth and Saturn incenses
Aquarius: Mix Air and Saturn incenses
Pisces: Mix Water and Jupiter incenses

APPENDIX 4: INFORMATION ON COLOR

As we have stated several times, the entire makeup of the magician is utilized in ritual. Like scents, colors stimulate several aspects of the human being. Their use is vital in ritual and should never be taken lightly nor ignored.

Color is light and light is energy. Color not only represents the force you are working with, but it is also a manifestation of that force. On a purely psychological level, we visualize color in ritual because it aligns us with the force we are trying to manifest, and this alignment occurs because color affects the human mind. Thus, visualizing the aura, Pentagrams, Hexagrams, and symbols in certain colors, is essential in ritual. Colored candles and symbols allow the magician to physically see the color, which makes visualization much easier. Colored light bulbs or properly-colored and covered recessed lighting saturate the room in the color of the force, giving a more enhanced experience of the ritual.

Although there are cultural differences in the associations of certain colors, for the most part people have intuitive understandings of color and scent. As an example, if you look at a picture with mostly red overtones, you get a feeling of movement and action. If you look at an image done mostly in blues, you sense quiet and calm.

Effects of color

Scientists have found that certain physiological and psychological changes take place in human beings when they are exposed to different colors. This is known as the science of chromodynamics. Colors can stimulate, excite, depress, tranquilize, increase appetite and create a feeling of warmth or coolness. Some are soothing, some are stimulating, some help focus the mind, and some are distracting. Our reaction to color is instantaneous and strong, hence its usefulness in ritual.

Warm colors: reds, oranges, and yellows

Summary. The warm colors cause an increase in the heart rate, respiration, and blood pressure, because they have a stimulating effect on the nervous system. Due to the size of its wavelength, red is understood as the warmest color, and has the strongest effects on the human mind. It increases enthusiasm, encourages action, and is often associated with desire. Orange shares some of the same characteristics, but without as much intensity. It stimulates activity, appetite, and encourages socialization. Yellow encourages communication, activates memory, instills optimism and influences creative thoughts.

Red is symbolic of the heart, strong will and strong emotions. It is a very physical color, and has more personal associations than any other in the spectrum. Being the longest wavelength, red is a very powerful color indeed. It can be understood as the color of energy itself, is recognized as a stimulant, and is inherently exciting. Red draws attention, increases enthusiasm, raises energy levels and encourages action and confidence. It stimulates the adrenal glands, activating the body and the senses, and raises the pulse rate. People surrounded by red find their hearts beating a little faster and often report feeling a bit out of breath. When surrounded by the color red people also get the impression that time is passing faster than it is. The color red relates to the masculine principle, and can activate the "fight or flight" instinct. It is stimulating and lively, but it also can be perceived as demanding and aggressive. In the Golden Dawn system, it is associated with Mars.

Orange, a close relative of red, sparks a sense of fun and flamboyancy, and radiates warmth and energy. In the human psyche, it stimulates physical activity and the appetite, and encourages socialization. Restaurants use it to increase the appetites of their customers. Orange exudes warmth, enthusiasm and excitement. The color is somewhat light-hearted and tends to illustrate youth, fun, and happiness. It is seen as friendly and approachable, less aggressive than red. Orange is also associated with ambition and a new dawn in attitude. It is associated with the Sun.

Yellow is a color of confidence and optimism. The color has been proven to lift spirits and improve self-esteem. It is cheerful and associated with laughter and happiness. A person surrounded by yellow feels optimistic because the brain tends to release more seratonin (a mood-elevating chemical in the brain). It has the power to speed up the metabolism and increase creative thinking. The color yellow stimulates the mental processes and the nervous system. It also activates memory and encourages communication. It is associated with Mercury.

Cool colors: greens, blues, and violets

Summary. The cool colors have the opposite effect of warm colors, and lower the heart rate, respiration, and blood pressure. Because green is often associated with nature, it has a soothing, peaceful, and calming effect on the human mind. It helps to ease nervousness and anxiety, and brings a sense of renewal and self-control. Blue and indigo also calm and sedate the mind, and they have a tendency to lower body temperature and reduce appetite. Violet is a balance between the warm nature of red and the cool nature of blue. It causes the mind to feel calm, yet also uplifts and at the same time inspires through creativity.

Green is soothing and relaxes one mentally as well as physically. It is a cool color that symbolizes nature and the natural world. Green helps alleviate depression, nervousness, and anxiety. It offers a sense of renewal, self-control, harmony and balance. Green strikes the eye in such a way as to require no adjustment whatever, and is therefore restful. Being in the center of the color spectrum, it is the color of balance. Green is thought to relieve stress and help heal. It is the traditional color of peace, harmony, comfortable nurturing, support and well-paced energy. When the world about us contains plenty of green, it indicates the presence of water and little danger of famine, so we are reassured and calmed by the color green on a very primitive level. Green has long been a symbol of fertility and was once the preferred color choice for wedding gowns in the 15th-century. It is associated with Venus.

Seeing the color blue actually causes the body to produce tranquilizing chemicals. It is essentially soothing, affecting us mentally, rather than the physical effects which pertain to red. Strong blues will stimulate clear thought, while lighter, softer blues will calm the mind and aid in concentration. People tend to be more productive in a blue room because they are calm and focused on the task at hand. It is associated with the Moon.

Blue-violet (or indigo) is a deeper blue and symbolizes a mystical borderland of wisdom, self-mastery, and spiritual realization. Blue violet turns the mind inward to personal thoughts, profound insights, and deep understandings. It is associated with Saturn.

Violet has the shortest wavelength. This color embodies the balance of red's stimulation and blue's calm. Violet's effect on the mind is uplifting, but it also calms the mind and nerves. This color stimulates the brain center that is used in problem solving. It creates a sense of spirituality and encourages creativity. It is indicative of spiritual awareness, luxury, authenticity, truth, and quality. It takes awareness to a higher level of thought, even into the realms of spiritual values, because violet encourages deep contemplation and meditation. Being the last visible wavelength, it has associations with time, space and the cosmos. It lends an air of mystery, wisdom, and respect. It is associated with Jupiter.

APPENDIX 5: ALTERNATIVE
PANTHEONS & DIVINE NAMES

In this Appendix we offer a selection of Divine Names or gods and goddesses of other pantheons, for ritualists who prefer them to the Qabalistic Hebrew ones. The lists begin with the Elements, then the Planets. For the Celtic names, we have provided rough pronunciations in italics.

Gods and Goddesses of the Elements

Earth

Greek Goddesses	*Greek Gods*
Gaia: Earth	Hades: Underworld
Demeter: Fertility, Grain, Agriculture	
Persephone: Springs, Queen of the Underworld (wife of Hades)	
Ceres: Agriculture, Grain, Motherly Love	
The Horae: Seasons	
Celtic Goddesses	*Celtic Gods*
Blodeuwedd (*Blod-EYE-weeth*): The Earth in bloom, aspect of the White Goddess of Death and Life	Cernunnos (*KER-nu-noss*): Nature, Fertility
Creiddylad (*Cruyth-IL-ad*): May, Summer Flowers	The Dagda (*DAHG-tha*): Earth, Treaties
Anu: Fertility	Arawn (*AH-raon*): Underworld
Tailtiu (*TAL-chih-uh*): Harvest	
Flidais (*FLEE-daws*): Forest	

Air

Greek Goddesses	*Greek Gods*
Hera: Queen of Heaven	Aether: Upper air
Iris: Rainbow, Divine Messenger	Uranus: Sky
Theia: Sight, Shining light of the clear blue sky	Zeus: King/Ruler of Gods, Mount Olympus, Sky

Celtic Goddesses	Celtic Gods
Arianrhod (*Ah-ree-AN-rod*): Sky	Gwydion (*GWID-ee-yon*): Prince of Powers of Air
	Latobius (*LAH-toh-bee-us*): Sky, Mountains
	Taranis (*TAH-rahn-eez*): Sky, Thunder

Water

Greek Goddesses	Greek Gods
Amphirite: Sea; Consort of Poseidon	Poseidon: Sea, Rivers, Storms, Floods, Drought
Ceto: Ocean	Oceanus (Titan): Earth-encircling river Okeanos, font of all fresh water
Cymopoleia: Giant Storms and Waves; Daughter of Poseidon	Achelous: Rivers
Leucothea: Sea	
Tethys: Rivers, Springs, Steams, Fountains, Clouds	
Celtic Goddesses	Celtic Gods
Don: Deep Sea	Lir (*Ler*): Sea
Acionna: Waters	Llyr (*Khleer*): Sea, Water
	Manannan mac Lir (*MAH-nah-nahn mak leer*): Sea

Fire

Greek Goddesses	Greek Gods
Hestia: Virgin Goddess of Hearth	Hephaestus: Fires, Forge
Celtic Goddesses	Celtic Gods
Belisama (*Bel-i-SAH-mah*): Light, Fire	Goibniu (*GO-beh-new*): Smiths
Brid (*Breet*): Fire	Bel: Fire, Sun

Gods and Goddesses of the Planets

The Moon

Greek Goddesses	Celtic Goddesses
Selene: Moon	Cerridwen (*CARE-id-wen*): Moon, Crone Aspect of Triple Goddess
Artemis: Moon	Morgan (*MOR-gan*): Moon, Fairies
Hecate: Magic, Crossroads, Triple Goddess of Moon	Arianrhod (*Ah-ree-AHN-rod*): Silver Wheel, Full Moon

Mercury

Greek Gods	Celtic Gods
Hermes: Messenger of the Gods	Gwydion (*GWID-eeyon*): Magic, Poetry
	Diancecht (*DEE-an-kech't*): Magic
	Math Mathonwy (*Math Math-ahn-oo-nee*): Magic, Enchantment
	Taliesin (*TAHL-ee-ess-in*): Chief of Bards and Magic

Venus

Greek Goddesses	Celtic Deities
Aphrodite: Beauty	Branwen (*BRAN-wen*): Venus of the Northern Seas
	Maeve (*Mave*): Queen Mab of the Fairies, Goddess of Bealteinne
	Angus mac Og (*Ayngus-mac-Ug*): God of Youth, Love, Beauty

Sun

Greek Gods	Celtic Gods
Helios: Sun, Giver of Light	Bel: Sun, The Brilliant One
Apollo: Sun, Lord of Light	Bran: Sun, The Blessed
Dionysos: Sun, Ecstasy	Grannus (*GRAH-nus*): Sun, The Healer

	Lugh (*Lew*): Sun, The Shining One
	Mabon (*MAY-bon*): Sun, The Divine Child

Mars

Greek Gods	Celtic Deities
Ares: War, Voice of Power	Badb (*Bibe*, Goddess): War; the Battle Raven
Hephaistos: Smiths, Metal-workers, Visible Fire	Morrigu (*MOR-re-gan*): Supreme War Goddess
	Macha (*MOH-ka*, Goddess): War, Great Queen of Phantoms
	Scathach (*SKAH-ha*, Goddess): War; She Who Strikes Fear
	Arawn (*Ah-raon*, God): Revenge, War
	Gwythyr (*GWEE-theer*, God): Victory
	Goibnui (*GOI-nyoo*, God): The Great Smith
	Govannon (*Go-VAN-non*, God): Smiths, Metal-workers

Jupiter

Greek Deities	Celtic Gods
Athene: Goddess of Wisdom	The Dagda (*DAHG-tha*): Lord of Perfect Knowledge, The All-Father, The Great God
Zeus: King of Heaven	Taranis (*TAH-rah-neez*): The Thunderer

Saturn

Greek Deities	Celtic Deities
Hera: The Concealed One, Queen of Heaven	The White Lady: Death, Crone form of the Triple Goddess
Kronos: The Ancient One	Pwyll (*Pwilth*, God): Underworld, Death
Hades: Ruler of Underworld, the Dead	

BIBLIOGRAPHY

Ciccarelli, Saundra and Noland White, *Psychology* (Upper Saddle River, NJ: Prentice Hall Publishing, 2008)

Cicero, Chic and Sandra Tabatha, *The New Golden Dawn Ritual Tarot* (St. Paul, MN: Llewellyn Publications, 1991)

Cicero, Chic and Sandra Tabatha, *Self-Initiation into the Golden Dawn Tradition* (St. Paul, MN: Llewellyn Publications, 1995)

Cicero, Chic and Sandra Tabatha, *The Essential Golden Dawn: An Introduction to High Magic* (St. Paul, MN: Llewellyn Publications, 2003)

Copenhaver, Brian trans. and ed., *Hermetica* (Cambridge: Cambridge University Press, 1992)

Curry, Patrick, *A Confusion of Prophets: Victorian and Edwardian Astrology* (London: Collins & Brown, 1992)

Dennings, Melita and Osborne Phillips, *Planetary Magick* (St. Paul, MN: Llewellyn Publications, 1992)

Dykes, Benjamin, trans. and ed., *Persian Nativities I*: Māshā'allāh & Abū 'Ali (Minneapolis, MN: The Cazimi Press, 2009)

Dykes, Benjamin trans. and ed., *Introductions to Traditional Astrology: Abū Ma'shar & al-Qabīsī* (Minneapolis, MN: The Cazimi Press, 2010)

Dykes, Benjamin, *Traditional Astrology for Today: An Introduction* (Minneapolis, MN: The Cazimi Press, 2011)

Dykes, Benjamin, *The Search of the Heart* (Minneapolis, MN: The Cazimi Press, 2011)

Dykes, Benjamin, *Choices & Inceptions: Traditional Electional Astrology* (Minneapolis, MN: The Cazimi Press, 2012)

Eiseman, Leatrice, *Color: Messages and Meanings* (Cincinnati, OH: Hand Books Press, 2006)

Greenbaum, Dorian Gieseler, *Temperament: Astrology's Forgotten Key* (Bournemouth, England: The Wessex Astrologer, 2005)

Greer, John Michael, *Paths of Wisdom* (St. Paul, MN: Llewellyn Publications, 1996)

Hawkins, Jeff, Sandra Blakeslee, *On Intelligence* (NY: Owl Books, 2004)

Janata, Petr, *Electrophysiological studies of auditory contexts* (Dissertation Abstracts International: Section B: The Sciences of Engineering: University of Oregon, 1997)

Janata, Petr, "The neural architecture of music-evoked autobiographical memories," *Cerebral Cortex* Vol. 19 (2009), pp. 2579-2594.

Lilly, William, *Christian Astrology* vols. 1-2 (Abingdon, MD: Astrology Classics, 2004)

McTaggart, Lynne, *The Intention Experiment: Using your Thoughts to Change your Life and the World* (Free Press, 2008)

Naydler, Jeremy, *Temple of the Cosmos: The Ancient Egyptian Experience of the Sacred* (Rochester, VT: Inner Traditions International, 1996)

Plato, ed. John M. Cooper, *Plato: Complete Works* (Indianapolis: Hackett Publishing Company, 1997)

von Worms, Abraham, Georg Dehn ed., Steven Guth trans., *The Book of Abramelin* (Lake Worth, FL: Ibis Press, 2006)

ABOUT THE AUTHORS

Dr. Benjamin Dykes is a leading medieval astrologer and translator who earned his PhD in philosophy from the University of Illinois. He received his medieval astrology qualification from Robert Zoller and taught philosophy courses at universities in Illinois and Minnesota. In 2007, he published Bonatti's complete *Book of Astronomy*, and since then has translated and published numerous traditional works on nativities, questions, and elections. In 2011 he published *Traditional Astrology for Today* for modern astrologers, and in 2012-13 will release mundane works. He currently offers the *Logos & Light* philosophy lectures on MP3 and speaks to astrological audiences worldwide. See: www.bendykes.com.

Jayne Gibson has been a student of the Western Mystery Tradition for over 20 years, and she is a long-time member of the Hermetic Order of the Golden Dawn. She is a regular contributor to *Hermetic Virtues* magazine, and a writer of occult compositions, whose main focus has been the art of ritual.

CPSIA information can be obtained
at www.ICGtesting.com
Printed in the USA
BVOW06s2013291217
503692BV00004BA/98/P

9 781934 586211